THE INTERNET TRADING COURSE

FINANCIAL TIMES
Prentice Hall

In an increasingly competitive world, we believe it's
quality of thinking that will give you the edge – an idea
that opens new doors, a technique that solves a
problem, or an insight that simply makes sense of it all.
The more you know, the smarter and faster you can go.

That's why we work with the best minds in business
and finance to bring cutting-edge thinking and best
learning practice to a global market.

Under a range of leading imprints, including *Financial
Times Prentice Hall*, we create world-class print
publications and electronic products bringing our
readers knowledge, skills and understanding which
can be applied whether studying or at work.

To find out more about our business publications,
or tell us about the books you'd like to find, you can
visit us at www.business-minds.com

For other Pearson Education publications, visit
www.pearsoned-ema.com

Pearson
Education

FINANCIAL TIMES

THE INTERNET TRADING COURSE

The complete course in online investment

Alpesh B. Patel
and Priyen Patel

FINANCIAL TIMES
Prentice Hall

London New York Toronto Sydney Tokyo Singapore Hong Kong Cape Town
New Delhi Madrid Paris Amsterdam Munich Milan Stockholm

PEARSON EDUCATION LIMITED

Head Office:
Edinburgh Gate
Harlow CM20 2JE
Tel: +44 (0)1279 623623
Fax: +44 (0)1279 431059

London Office:
128 Long Acre
London WC2E 9AN
Tel: +44 (0)20 7447 2000
Fax: +44 (0)20 7240 5771

Website: www.financialminds.com

First published in Great Britain in 2002

The right of Alpesh B. Patel and Priyen Patel to be identified as authors of this work has been asserted by them in accordance with the Copyright, Designs and Patents Act 1988.

ISBN: 0273 65630 9

British Library Cataloguing in Publication Data
A CIP catalogue record for this book can be obtained from the British Library

10 9 8 7 6 5 4 3 2

Designed by Designdeluxe, Bath
Typeset by Northern Phototypesetting Co. Ltd, Bolton
Printed and bound in China PPLC/02

The Publishers' policy is to use paper manufactured from sustainable forests.

Contents

To our mothers – Sakuben and Ramilaben Patel

I am the ruling Queen, the amasser of treasures, full of wisdom, first of those worthy of worship.
In various places, divine powers have sent me. I enter many homes and take numerous forms.

Rig Veda

Women must be honoured and adorned by their fathers, brothers,
husbands and brothers-in-law, who desire their own welfare.
Where women are honoured, there the Gods are pleased. But where
they are not honoured, no sacred rite yields rewards.

Manu Dharma Shastras 3.55–56

About the authors

Priyen Patel

Priyen's interest in trading was sparked as a schoolboy, being raised in the same household as co-author Alpesh. His current interests are in short-term derivatives and spread-betting, CFDs and stock futures trading, with an emphasis on technical analysis.

A recent graduate of Oxford University, like Alpesh he read Philosophy, Politics and Economics at St.Anne's College. Unlike his co-author, Priyen won prizes and did far better in his degree.

Alpesh B. Patel

LLB; MA (Oxon); AKC;
Visiting Fellow Corpus Christi College,
Oxford (2001–2); Barrister-at-Law

Trading

Described by Channel 4 as the UK's best known internet trader, Alpesh started programming computers in BASIC at the age of 10 and buying stocks 18 years ago at the age of 12 (although he seems normal nowadays), moving on from privatization stocks to penny shares. He left a legal career to trade full-time.

Today he concentrates on US and UK stocks as well as futures and options trading, making extensive use of the internet for research since he was a Congressional Intern in 1994 and combining this with his own technical analysis systems. On Channel 4's latest *Show Me The Money* series he was number 1 of 45 expert stock pickers.

TV, radio and print

Alpesh writes the *Diary of an Internet Trader* for the weekend *Financial Times*, also appearing on FT.com and weekly for Bloomberg TV in *Bloomberg Money on the Net*.

Books

Alpesh is the author of *Diary of an Internet Trader, Pocket Trading Online, Net Trading, Trading Online* and *The Mind of a Trader* (all published by Pearson Education). His books have been translated into Spanish, German, French, Chinese and Polish. *Trading Online* was the number one best-selling investment book on Amazon UK, and reached number two on the overall bestseller list.

Lectures

Alpesh regularly speaks on online trading, trading psychology and technical analysis around the world and has in the next six months 15 speaking engagements. He has spoken from Guatemala to Spain to Beijing.

Acknowledgements

Once again we owe a great debt to Pearson, knowing they will with relentless effort produce an excellent book. From proofreading and editing, to design, packaging, marketing and sales – we thank all of you involved in making a book that we the authors can be proud of.

Even this morning we received a couple of e-mails from members of the Pearson team which brimmed with enthusiasm – it's a joy to be your partners.

Alpesh B. Patel
Priyen Patel

Introduction

Why you need to read this book

You need an online trading account as much as you need a bank account. Without it you're not making full use of the money you have. But an online trading account is not enough to ensure success.

You need to know what successful online traders and investors know. And the best way you can learn it is through a coursebook – which makes it easier and more fun to learn too.

By the end of the book you will have a professional approach which you can refer to each time you want to trade, and you will know which sites to visit for precisely the type of information you want.

This book contains all the essentials for trading online, from an expert who is used to explaining all the important issues to novices and advanced traders alike.

Poor excuses people make for not trading online

Can't I just use a fund manager rather than trade online?

Why do you need to manage your own money when you can just invest in a fund and have a fund manager do all the work for you? Well, there is ample data to show that giving your money to the so-called professionals does not lead to great returns.

Why do I need to worry about trading online if I am just going to buy and hold for the long term?

The reason so many people trade online is precisely because buy and hold takes so long to give you any returns at all. Just see Figs I.1–I.3.

FIGURE I.1	S&P composite 1906–24

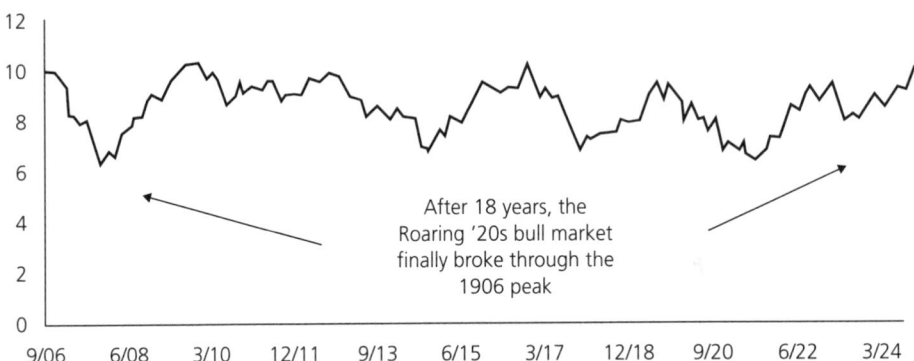

After 18 years, the
Roaring '20s bull market
finally broke through the
1906 peak

FIGURE I.2	S&P composite 1929–54

Stocks take 25 years to
return to 1929 peak

Figures I.4–I.6 make the point that if you are thinking of being a long-term investor, you really need to be very long term because in the short term, portfolio returns are all over the place – only over decades do they rise consistently (portfolio numbers refer to differing levels of risk from 10 the lowest to 90 the greatest).

And how are you going to buy and hold a stock whose share price looks like Fig I.7?

FIGURE I.3 S&P composite 1966–80

This 14-year bear market includes the
crash of 1973–74

Adjusted for inflation, the S&P 500 did not
return to its 1966 peak until 1991

FIGURE I.4 Annual returns over 27 years

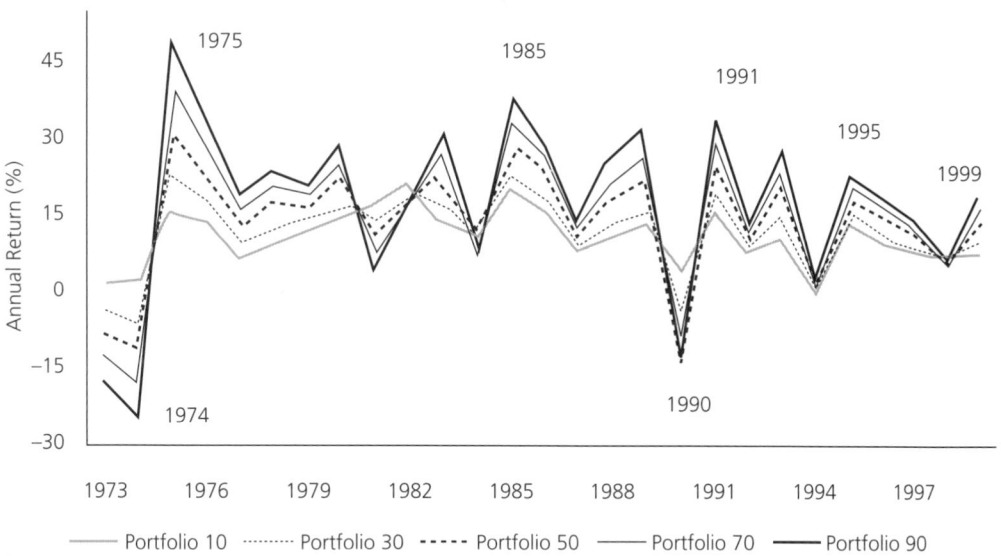

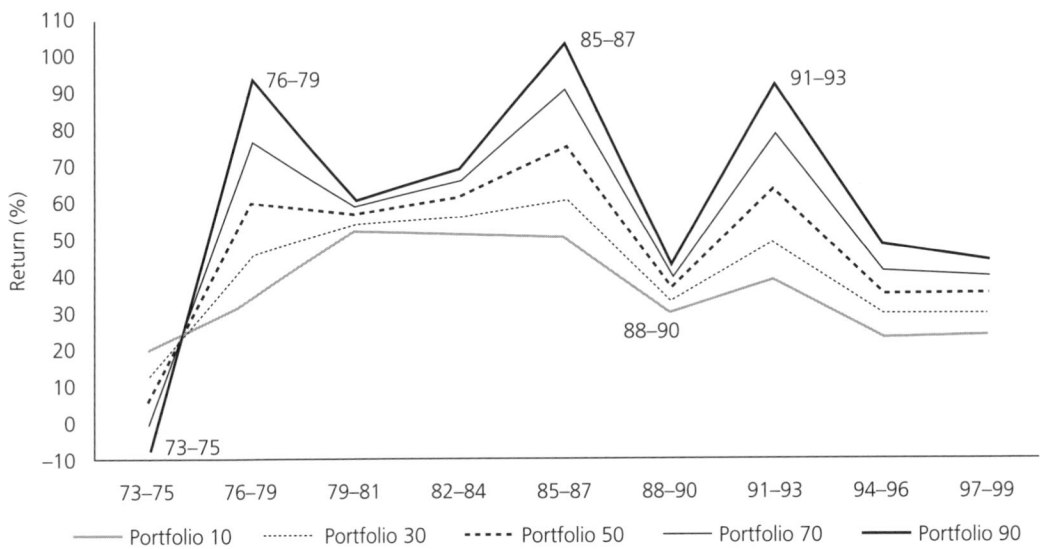

FIGURE I.5 Every 3-year returns over 27 years

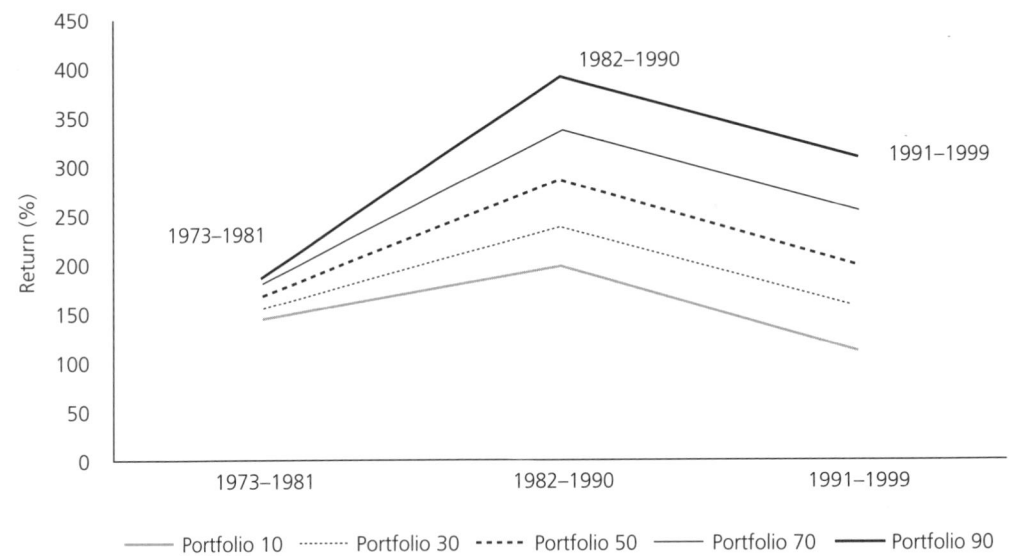

FIGURE I.6 Every 9-year returns over 27 years

FIGURE 1.7
How you can buy and hold this

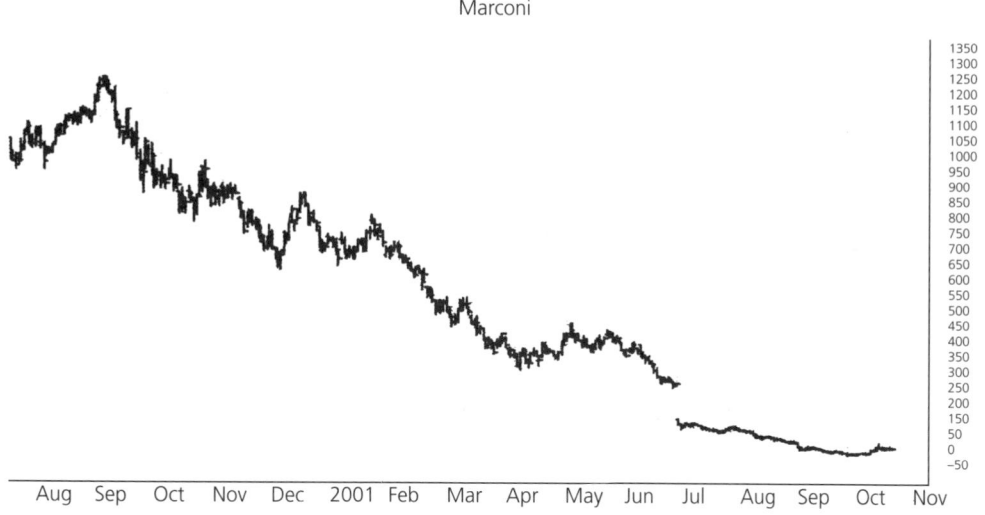

Marconi

FIGURE 1.8
Distribution of daily S&P 500 returns – 1998–2000

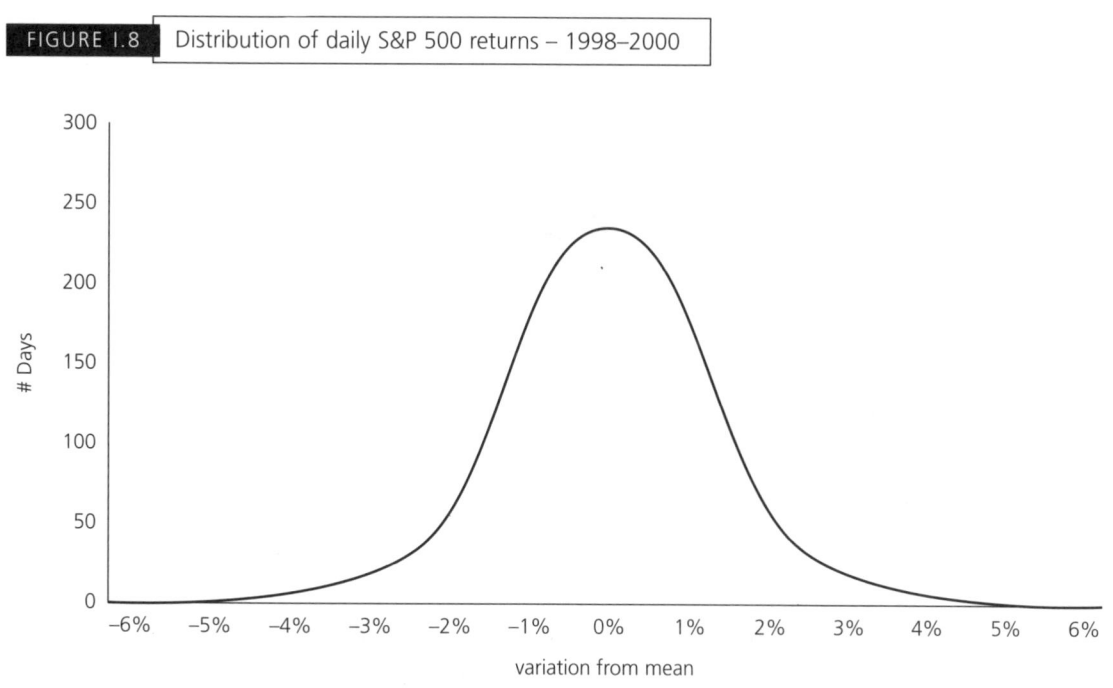

FIGURE I.9

S&P 500 index – distribution of monthly returns 75.5 years, 906 months, 1 Jan 1926 to 30 June 2001

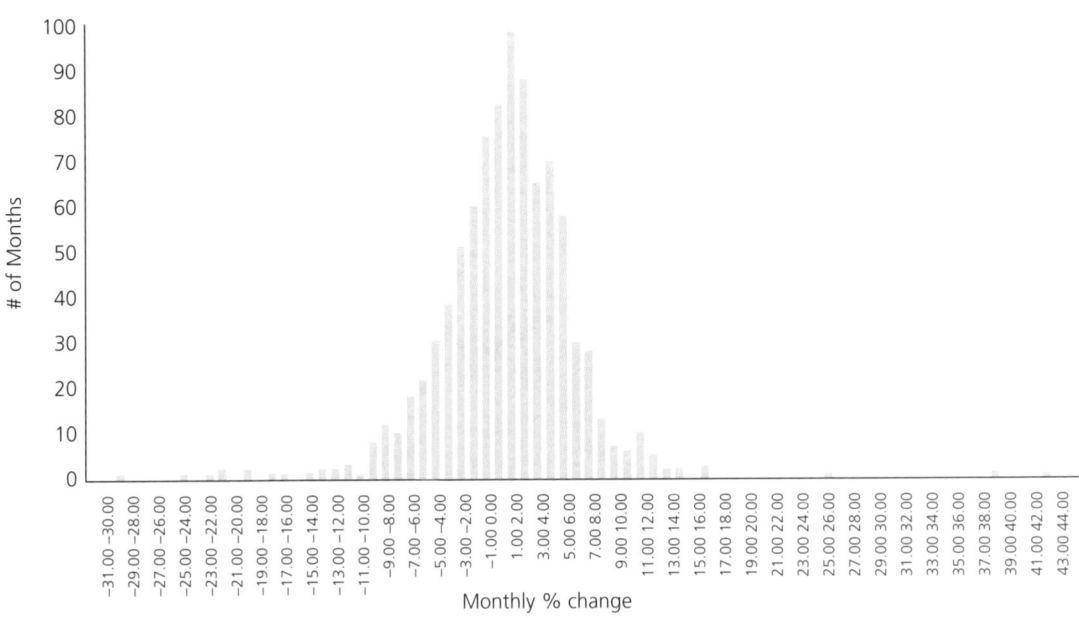

Monthly % change

The other reason we trade online is because we are often trying to pick the big return days, of which there are a few, and avoid the loss-making days, of which there are many, as Figs I.8 and I.9 show.

Surely I don't need to trade online if I am not planning my own research and just looking to follow the analysts?

Well, before you think the easy way to invest is just to follow analyst recommendations, take a look at Fig I.10.

Looking back all the way to 1997, for instance, 16 of the 19 largest US brokerages issued money-losing stock advice, according to investment research firm Investars.com – see Figs I.11–13.

Unfortunately, even when the market keeps falling, you don't get 'sell recommendations'. So in a bear market, you can't rely on them – you're on your own. Therefore you'd better know how to research your trades online.

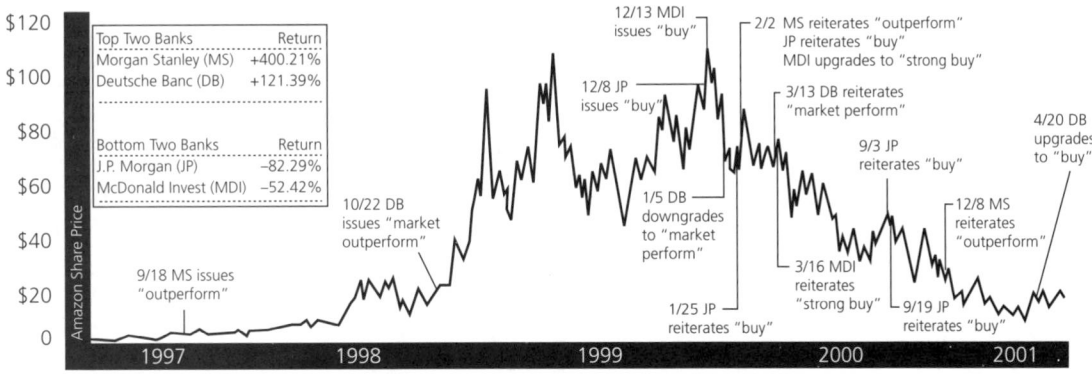

FIGURE I.10 Morgan Stanley's early call helped it nab the best Amazon return

Timing of selected investment bank recommendations for Amazon.com

Top Two Banks	Return
Morgan Stanley (MS)	+400.21%
Deutsche Banc (DB)	+121.39%

Bottom Two Banks	Return
J.P. Morgan (JP)	–82.29%
McDonald Invest (MDI)	–52.42%

9/18 MS issues "outperform"

10/22 DB issues "market outperform"

12/8 JP issues "buy"

12/13 MDI issues "buy"

2/2 MS reiterates "outperform"
JP reiterates "buy"
MDI upgrades to "strong buy"

3/13 DB reiterates "market perform"

4/20 DB upgrades to "buy"

1/5 DB downgrades to "market perform"

9/3 JP reiterates "buy"

12/8 MS reiterates "outperform"

3/16 MDI reiterates "strong buy"

1/25 JP reiterates "buy"

9/19 JP reiterates "buy"

Source: Industry Standard

FIGURE I.11 Only three banks achieve a positive return overall

Hypothetical investment return based on analyst recommendations

All Stocks

Top 5	Investment Bank or Research Firm	Stocks Rated	Return
1	Credit Suisse First Boston	1.558	+6.9%
2	A.G. Edwards	600	+4.4%
3	Salomon Smith Barney	1.348	+0.9%
4	Merrill Lynch	1.491	–1.5%
5	Morgan Stanley	1.184	–2.7%

Bottom 5			
1	Robertson Stephens	633	–48.3%
2	USB Piper Jaffray	617	–22.7%
3	Cain Rauscher	627	–21.5%
4	CBC World Markets	804	–14.7%
5	Deutsche Bank	894	–14.7%

Technology Hardware Stocks

Top 5	Investment Bank or Research Firm	Stocks Rated	Return
1	Merrill Lynch	143	–13.59%
2	Bear Stearns	100	–18.3%
3	A.G.Edwards	55	–18.7%
4	Salomon Smith Barney	149	–18.8%
5	Goldman Sachs	11	–18.3%

Bottom 5			
1	Robertson Stephens	153	–54.9%
2	Cain Rauscher	96	–54.4%
3	Deutsche Banc	90	–51.4%
4	USB Piper Jaffray	82	–50.9%
5	USB PaineWebber	85	–47.1%

Source: Industry Standard

FIGURE I.12 Good times or bad, 'sells' are few ...

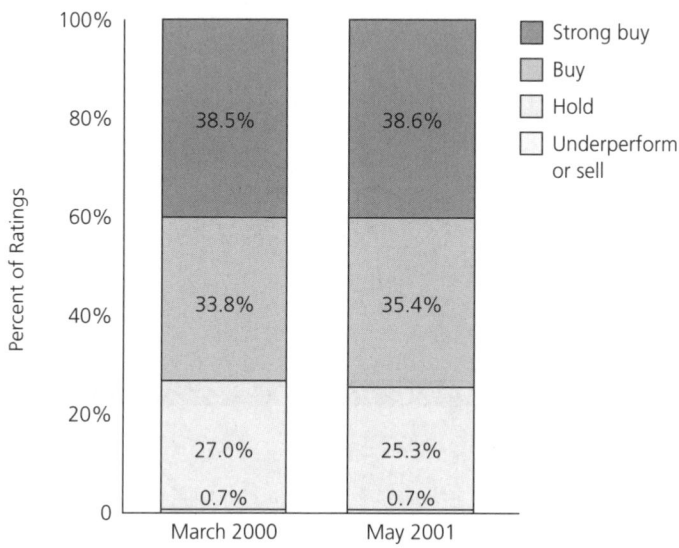

Based on an analysis of total outstanding analyst recommendations on March 24 2000 and May 4 2001
Source: Multex Investor June 2001

FIGURE I.13 ... And positive ratings keep coming

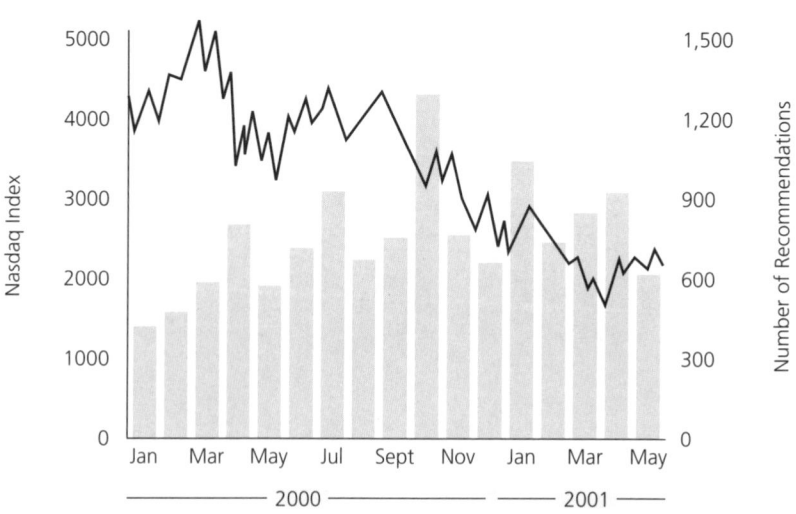

Source: Multex Investor

Why you need to trade online

Perhaps it is because I placed my first trade at the age of 12 to try to earn enough money to avoid a paper round, or perhaps because I could safely be described as an internet geek (freek could be equally applicable) that I am so fanatical about online trading.

It is this fanaticism that makes me wonder why even more people do not want to trade online. I don't mean widows and orphans, but people who already have share brokerage accounts with traditional brokers. Perhaps I can explode some concerns they and even those who do trade online may have.

Consider too the important calculations any sensible investor needs to do before investing. Do you know how to calculate the effect on your portfolio of a 10 per cent market shock? Do you even know why you need to know this? What if I told you the answer is easy to calculate in seconds online but using pen and paper would take months. And do you know what the likely reaction of your portfolio will be six months later? The answer is important because otherwise the next time the market dumps 10 per cent how else do you know to sell or hold on (see Fig I.14)? Not only does this book tell you where to look, it tells you why.

Yet another reason (if you need one) to trade online is to use wonderfully easy tools like these to show you exactly what's moving and where you may want to put your money (Figures I.15, I.16, I.17).

FIGURE I.14 | How world events impact the market

Date	Event	First trading session response to event				Subsequent market behaviour		
		DJIA Close Previous Day	DJIA Close	DJIA Change	DJIA % Change	One Month Change	Six Months Change	One Year Change
1. 1/17/91	US launches bombing attack on Iraq	2,509	2,624	114.6	**4.6%**	11.8%	15.0%	**24.5%**
2. 8/2/90	Iraq invades Kuwait	2,899	2,865	–34.7	**–1.2%**	–8.8%	–3.2%	**5.0%**
3. 3/30/81	President Reagan shot	995	992	–2.6	**–0.3%**	0.6%	–14.3%	**–16.9%**
4. 8/9/74	President Nixon resigns	785	777	–7.6	**–0.97%**	–14.7%	–8.9%	**6.0%**
5. 11/22/63	President Kennedy assassinated	733	711	–21.2	**–2.9%**	6.6%	15.4%	**25.0%**
6. 10/22/62	Cuban Missile Crisis	569	558	–10.5	**–1.9%**	15.6%	27.4%	**34.0%**
7. 9/26/55	President Eisenhower has heart attack	487	456	–31.9	**–6.5%**	0.04%	12.5%	**5.7%**
8. 6/25/50	North Korea invades South Korea	224	214	–10.4	**–4.7%**	–4.5%	7.4%	**15.1%**
9. 12/7/41	Japan attacks Pearl Harbor, Hawaii	117	113	–4.1	**–3.5%**	–0.9%	–6.2%	**2.9%**

Source: dowjones.com Past performance is not a guarantee of future performance.

FIGURE I.15 Investment wonders of the web

Name	Key ?	Latest	Trend	Last update		Change since last close	Change over 1 month
DJ Eu. Technology Stock Idx		209.35	↓	14:10 25/10/01		−8.80 −4.03%	+25.77%
DJ Eu. Financial Stock Idx		204.26	↓	14:10 25/10/01		−4.62 −2.21%	+23.71%
DJ Eu. Basic Materials Stock Idx		159.47	↓	14:11 25/10/01		−1.74 −1.08%	+21.07%
DJ Eu. Consumer Cyclical Stock Idx		136.74	↓	14:13 25/10/01		−1.98 −1.43%	+18.92%
DJ Eu. Industrial Stock Idx		143.46	↓	14:12 25/10/01		−1.49 −1.03%	+14.67%
DJ Eu. Energy Stock Idx		215.99	↓	14:14 25/10/01		−3.82 −1.74%	+14.09%
DJ Eu. Utilities Stock Idx		200.82	↓	14:13 25/10/01		−3.46 −1.69%	+4.91%

FIGURE I.16 Another easy stockpicking tool – do you know how to use it?

Percentage Change in Sector Values over 3 Months

Packaging	+21.8%	Transport	−24.9%
Mining	+4.3%	Insurance	−19.6%
Tobacco	+3.8%	Elec. & Electrical Eqp	−19.5%
Health	+3.5%	Engineering & Mach	−18.5%
Telecom Services	+3.0%	Leis.Entertain & Hot.	−14.5%
Automobiles	+2.7%	IT Hardware	−14.1%
Banks	+2.2%	Aerospace & Defence	−13.6%

FIGURE I.17 We'll point you to great tools like these

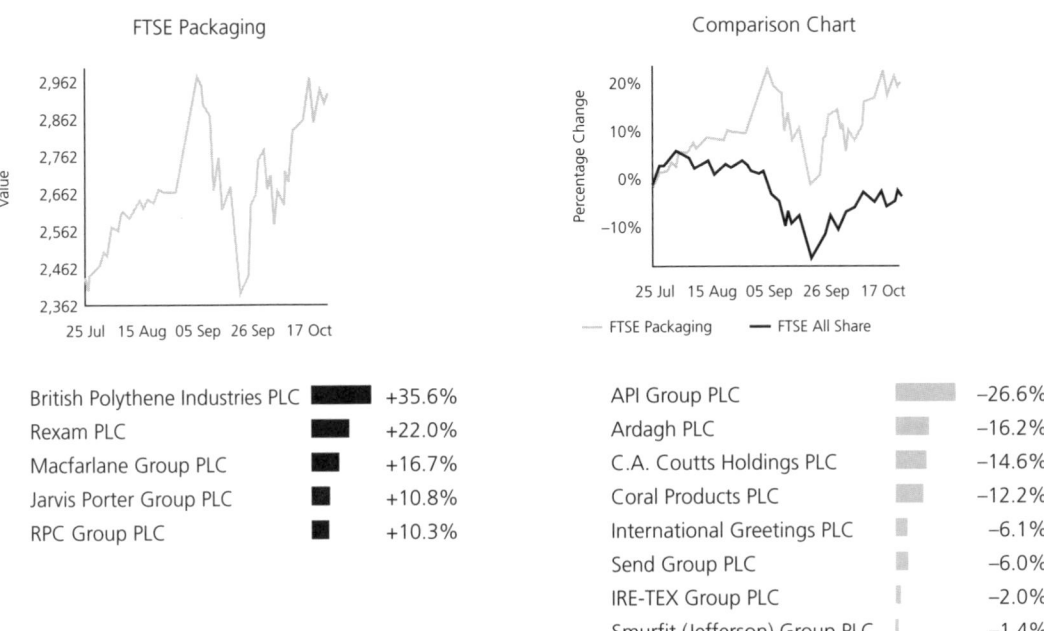

Percentage Change in Price over 3 Months

FTSE Packaging

Comparison Chart

British Polythene Industries PLC	+35.6%
Rexam PLC	+22.0%
Macfarlane Group PLC	+16.7%
Jarvis Porter Group PLC	+10.8%
RPC Group PLC	+10.3%

API Group PLC	−26.6%
Ardagh PLC	−16.2%
C.A. Coutts Holdings PLC	−14.6%
Coral Products PLC	−12.2%
International Greetings PLC	−6.1%
Send Group PLC	−6.0%
IRE-TEX Group PLC	−2.0%
Smurfit (Jefferson) Group PLC	−1.4%

You are definitely not alone

For those worried that such an activity may be a little risky for its 'frontier-type' nature, you are definitely not going to one of a few online traders trying out untested technology (see Table I.1).

According to IDC, there were 6.4 million online broker accounts in the US alone as far back as the end of 1998 and there will be 24.7 million by the end of 2002.

TABLE I.1 Online trading forecast

	1998	2002
Commission Revenues	$1.3 billion	$5.3 billion
Accounts	6.4 million	24.7 million
Individual Investors	5.6 million	22.7 million
Percent of Total Investors	8%	30%

In Europe, online trading is going to have an exponential increase. According to JP Morgan, by 2002 there will be 8 million people trading online in Europe (Table I.2). The message must be that there is going to be a mad rush, so join in or be left out.

TABLE I.2 Online trading accounts in Europe

1997	1999	2002
Under 100,000	900,000	Over 8 million

I don't do that kind of thing

Of course, online trading is not for everyone. But a common misconception is that you have to trade short term to justify opening an online account. Wrong! Even if you buy shares only once a year, you could save in commission charges. And even when the markets are falling, the number of online trading accounts increases – just see Fig I.18 for the UK market.

You need not be put off from opening an online account by the false belief that you should shift your entire holdings to your online account. In the UK and US it appears most online traders are being quite shrewd and trading online with a small amount of the overall capital they have devoted to trading and investing (see Fig I.19).

A common **misconception** is that you have to trade short term to justify opening an online account.

FIGURE I.18 | Internet investors in the UK

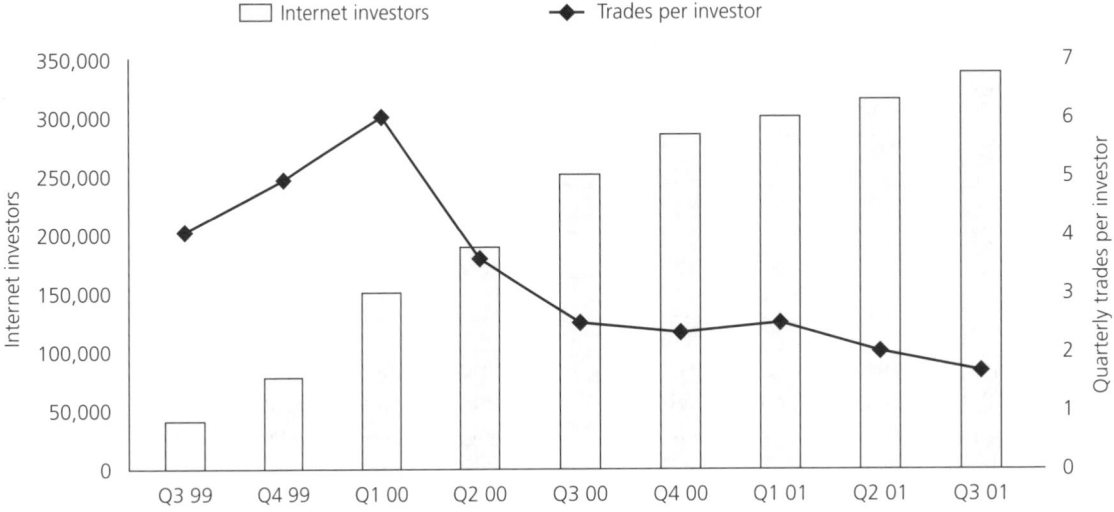

In the US, according to one recent survey, most people trade online with less than $10,000 in their accounts. In the UK, the Association of Private Client Investment Managers and Stockbrokers findings appear in Fig I.20.

Truly global

Online trading is truly global. You can buy Sony and China Telecom stock in dollars as easily as Coca-Cola and IBM. In September and October 2001 I travelled to Miami, London, Beijing, Kuala Lumpur and Puerto Rico – everywhere I have been able to trade and everywhere I have met online traders.

If you have a bank account, you should have an online trading account.

> Online trading is truly **global**. You can buy Sony and China Telecom stock in dollars as easily as Coca-Cola and IBM.

But this is not just about online trading

Online trading is like offline trading in many respects. That's why this book takes a holistic view and teaches you the skill all traders have to avoid common trading pitfalls. See Fig I.21 which illustrates a major market failing.

FIGURE I.19   Start small

**What size is your
average trade?**

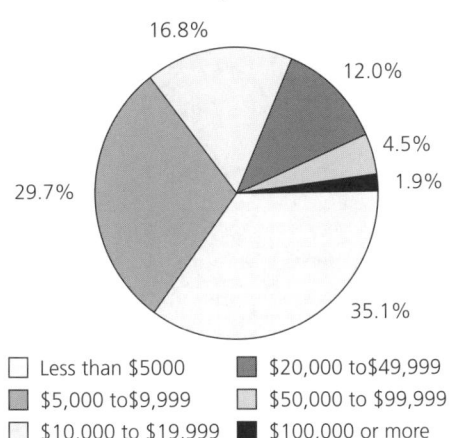

16.8%

12.0%

4.5%

1.9%

29.7%

35.1%

☐ Less than $5000   ◼ $20,000 to$49,999
◼ $5,000 to$9,999   ☐ $50,000 to $99,999
☐ $10,000 to $19,999   ◼ $100,000 or more

☐ Internet trade size (£)   ☐ Non-internet trade size (£) (execution only)

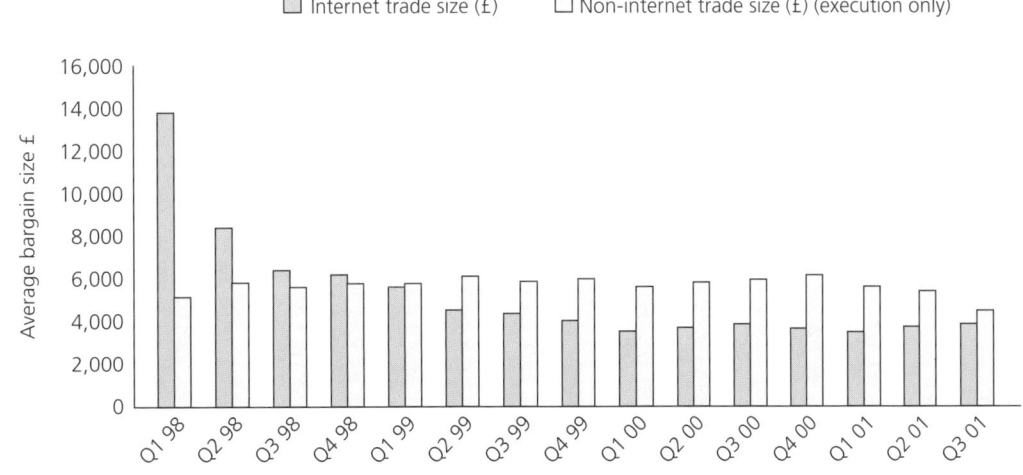

Average bargain size £

FIGURE I.21   A major market failing

"In investing, what is comfortable is rarely profitable."
Robert Arnott
Active Asset Allocation

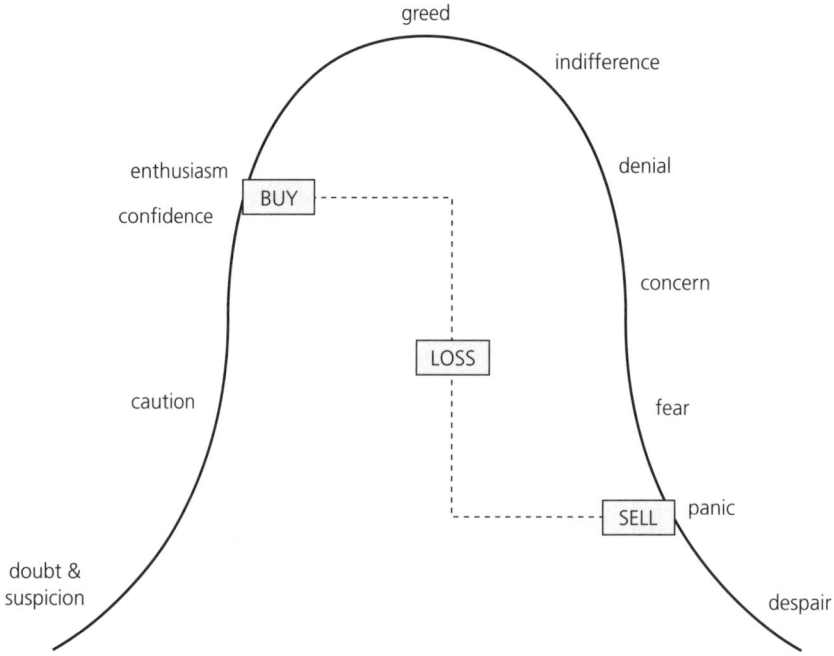

We trust you'll find the book both an enjoyable read and a valuable source of revenue.

Alpesh B. Patel
Priyen Patel

Getting **online**

Essential hardware

You can't trade online unless you are online. Besides, online trading can at times be a frustrating venture – you'll need something to kick, and that's where hardware comes in.

Before you can connect to the internet we need to discuss some basic hardware requirements. You could, of course, go for higher specs, depending on how much performance you require – the sky's the limit. However, there are certain essentials that we should focus on in this module.

What you will learn

Having worked through this module you will understand the types of hardware needed to trade online. These will include the following:

- computers
- modems
- monitors
- internet service providers (ISPs)
- printers
- browsers.

Most people have these already, but this chapter will be useful for those thinking of upgrading or who want to know if they have the right equipment.

The brains – computers

PC or Mac?

You must decide which type of personal computer suits your trading needs.
The two giants are the PC and the Apple Mac. You may have strong views on
this already. Sure, it sounds like the VHS/Betamax showdown of folklore.
People will tell you one's better than the other; that it's a case of what you
get used to; even that Mac, as urban myth has it of Betamax, is the superior
machine, unjustly suppressed by big corporate interests. Whatever.

The critical issue for the online trader is compatibility. Windows operates
on the PC and far more software is written for PC users. Outside the US the
PC is even more dominant than the Mac. For these reasons I would suggest
you go for the PC – most trading software is not Mac-compatible.

The processor

The central processing unit (CPU) is one of the most important factors to
consider when buying a computer. It will determine in part the speed at
which programs operate and therefore how quickly you can work.

The safest option among the plethora of processors is Intel's Pentium
range. Pentium IV are now entry level and well able to handle multiple
online trading tasks.

The speed of a processor is measured by its clock speed. Obviously, you
should weigh price against performance.

The critical issue for the
online trader is
compatibility.

A guide for minimum requirements

Fortunately, for trading, even a humble 266 MHz Pentium processor is sufficient

Most entry level PCs have fast enough processing speeds to undertake all trading tasks. Speed becomes a problem only if you have many applications open simultaneously and are also playing Doom while trading.

64 MB RAM (random access memory) is minimum requirement

RAM is the temporary memory in which your computer runs programs, a little like room to play. The more room the computer has, the quicker it can get things done. However, 256 MB is more than enough. If you want you can buy more, but you do not strictly need it for your trading.

3 GB hard drive or larger is best

The hard drive is where all the programs and other things you save are stored. Storage space is useful as over the years we all tend to collect clutter, such as bric-a-brac, spouses, etc. A 3 GB drive would probably last most traders until they decide to upgrade their computers (and their spouses).

Windows 2000 operating system is recommended

When it comes to programming trading software, most programmers use the latest version of Windows. The problem with Windows 98 is that it crashes more often than a crash-test dummy. Windows 2000 is based on the industry standard, 'hard as a rock' Windows NT, which is far more difficult to crash. XP also meets this task

CD drive useful, x16 or faster

Most programs and much data are provided on compact disks. A 16-speed one is more than adequate, although many computers now come with nothing slower than a 32-speed. DVD players are not needed as yet.

What you have learned

Your choice of computer hardware will depend on your preferences for performance and therefore you must ask yourself how committed you are to trading online and what other uses you may have for your computer.

▶

Nevertheless, a **PC** with the **Pentium IV** processor, **128MB RAM** and **3GB hard drive** are not too demanding specs. **Windows 2000** and a 16-speed **CD drive** are highly recommended. Remember that it is better to be conservative with such purchases and to then **upgrade** as the need arises.

Modem

Internal or external makes little difference

It does not matter from a trading point of view whether the modem is some electronic wizardry inside the computer or a separate attachment outside it. The latter option may be better if you are not keen on opening up the computer. 56k external modems cost around $40–60.

At least a 56k modem

You do not want to be waiting all day to receive trading news and information. The speed of your modem is important to ensure you can have an outside life, too. Therefore at least a 56k modem is recommended.

Consider ISDN or ADSL/cable broadband

These offer digital connection that is faster than a normal modem. They are lightning fast, but can be expensive. However, if you can afford them or get them, they are worth considering.

Cable

About 25 times faster than a dial-up modem, cable uses the standard cable TV connection. The only problem is that it's a shared line, so the more people online, the slower the connection. This is just like dial-up modems today, only faster. Despite this, it still looks like being the best home option. Availability is limited at present. Check with your local cable provider.

ADSL

You do not want to be **waiting** all day to receive trading news and information.

Asynchronous Digital Subscriber Line (ADSL, sometimes called DSL) is a service provided by some local phone companies. ADSL transmits compressed digital data down part of your standard phone line. The advantage over a modem is that you can still make and receive calls on your phone while being online. Okay, 'so get a second line' you might say. True, but ADSL is also impressive, being similar to cable (i.e. 25 times the speed of a modem).

ISDN

You may well have heard of the Integrated Service Digital Network (ISDN). It's not as advanced as ADSL but it can be up to twice as fast as a 56.6k modem. Consider it if you can afford the extra cost and cannot get ADSL or cable.

T-1 lines

What most businesses have. Pretty much instantaneous connections with high-capacity data lines.

T-3 lines

Very expensive – i.e. what very big businesses have. Currently unavailable for home use but, as ever, it must surely be only a matter of time …

Satellite

Currently about seven times the speed of a 56.6k modem. The problem is that you'll need both a dish to receive data *and* a satellite service provider by phone line in order to send e-mail. Only really worth considering if you have no cable or local digital services such as ADSL or ISDN.

Monitor

17" preferred – twin flat panels even better

Beyond 15", monitors start getting very pricey. Less than 15" and you start needing a magnifying glass. With 17" screens becoming standard, you could even go to 19".

I have two flat panel monitors which not only save on desk space but also increase productivity since I can monitor share prices on one screen and research on the other. Speak to your computer vendor about these. Dell is particularly good in my experience, (www.dell.com). You can't, of course, just buy a separate monitor and plonk it on. You need a graphics card and preferably 64 or 128Mb RAM.

Anti-glare and anti-radiation filter essential

The radiation emitted from the trading screen that is on all day may cause you to grow a second head, but there is no evidence that two brains would improve your trading performance. So buy a filter, and keep your uni-head good looks. (Most modern flat panels would not require such filters.)

> There is no evidence that two brains would **improve** your trading performance.

Printer

Laser printer

These printers may be the most expensive but they have dropped dramatically in price and are best when it comes to printing out all those trading charts and for reading text.

Inkjet minimum requirement

If the purse strings are tight, an inkjet is likely to be adequate for printing charts and text.

What you have learned

Again, you can go to town when it comes to throwing money at modems. **56k** is a requirement for the tasks demanded for online trading. Anything faster than 56k will require some introspection on your part – do you really need the performance given the price, are you going to use the internet for other things, etc., etc.?

A **17" monitor** with an anti-radiation filter is preferred.

When it comes to printers, an inkjet is a minimum requirement and a laser jet is best for intricate graphs.

Internet service providers and access providers

Choosing an internet service provider

Asking an online trader what 'ISP' stands for is a bit like asking a journalist what BBC means. But although many people will have heard of ISPs, not everyone will know what an ISP is and, more importantly, what it does. An internet service provider provides access to the web from a PC using your modem (see above). An internet access provider (IAP) just provides dial-up while an ISP also provides access to exclusive online content, e.g. AOL.

Well-known ISPs are AOL (AmericaOnLine), Freeserve, Microsoft Network, Virgin and BTclick. They're a bit like your phone company but instead of providing you with a line they give you an entrance into the web – a doorway, if you like. The major ISPs offer a vast range of information and web links to their subscribers, including search tools or 'engines' as they're usually known.

Don't worry about finding an ISP – the biggest, like AOL, will find you. If you've just bought a new PC, you'll probably find two or three ISPs ready-loaded onto your hard drive. ISPs differ in what they offer and how much they charge. If you go for the ADSL or ISDN option outlined above, you will be given an ISP connection automatically.

If you don't have your desired ISP on your PC already, you'll have to get hold of their dial-up software. This is mostly free – usually with PC magazine CD giveaways or as a free mailing. Once you've found the software, follow the instructions that come with it. Alternatively, you can sign up to another ISP if you're already online, but this gets a little 'chicken and egg', so I'm assuming you're not already online. Once you've downloaded the software and signed up with the ISP, you're ready to go online – or 'surf' as your dad no doubt insists on calling it.

Remember

1 Oversubscription: try out the ISP before you subscribe. If it's slow it may be because there are too many subscribers for the ISPs to handle. This is particularly so at peak times such as midday and early evening. Try out the service at different times of the day.
2 Do they allow you to have more than one member per account? You may find this useful for family use.
3 If you use a laptop and travel, how accessible globally is the ISP?

■ **An unlimited online time plan is required**

ISPs and internet access providers (IAPs) usually have different charging plans, many charging by the number of hours spent using their services. Since we traders may spend a lot of time online, the cheapest pricing option is almost always the 'unlimited' time plan, since there is only a monthly flat fee for access.

Take a free trial.
Try before you buy is the advice here. Almost all ISPs and IAPs permit a one-month free trial, and it is best to use this to test their reliability.

Browsers

Internet Explorer or Netscape Navigator

If you are looking for a browser then you want the most sophisticated one and one catered for by almost all internet sites. So Internet Explorer and Netscape Navigator are highly recommended. They are available free from cover CDs of most internet magazines.

Make sure you regularly check for upgrades and consider having the 'add-ons' when you download the software. All those bells and whistles are sometimes used by trading sites (www.microsoft.com; www.netscape.com).

Bookmarks

It is essential to familiarize yourself with Bookmarks in Netscape Navigator or Favourites in Internet Explorer for the purposes of managing information.

PC TV

If you are trading from home, you could have a TV playing in a small section of your monitor, such as CNBC or Bloomberg, to keep you up to date with the markets. Not essential, but I like it. Also great for watching 'The Simpsons' while you write books – only kidding: you, the reader, have my undivided attenti …

Exercises

1 List the minimum hardware requirements you will need to trade online. (See the summary below for suggested answers.)
2 Find a search engine site on the net and find out what the price and product range is for the hardware minimum requirements needed to trade online. (See the website section below for help.)

Summary – what you have learned

When buying hardware keep in mind minimum requirements, and remember that you can upgrade. Here are some numbers: Pentium IV processor, 128 MB RAM, 3GB hard drive, Windows 2000, 56k modem, 17" monitor, inkjet printer.

Go for ISPs with an unlimited time plan, and as many free trials as it takes to find one that suits you. Get the latest version of Explorer or Netscape. Specs a bit better than the minimum will stand you in good stead, but do remain conservative.

Most entry-level PCs will accommodate all the aspects mentioned here and you will not have much to worry about. People with older systems may need to upgrade, however.

Websites

| Microsoft | www.microsoft.com |
| Netscape | www.netscape.com |

Listed below are some manufacturer websites. However, the best way to find pricing and specs info on computer hardware is to use a search engine (e.g. www.yahoo.com, www.lycos.com, www.google.com, www.ask.com, www.altavista.com). Type in something like 'computers', 'modems', 'desktop' etc.

Apple	www.apple.com
Compaq	www.compaq.com
Dell	www.dell.com
Hewlett-Packard	www.hp.com
IBM	www.ibm.com
NEC	www.nec-computers.com
Sony	www.sony.com
Toshiba	www.toshiba.jp

Trading **online**

Do you really want **to trade online?**

Online trading is a skill. And as with all skills, it must be developed. Developing competence is hard. But it is also rewarding.

What you will learn

Having worked through this module you will:

- understand what online trading involves. Online trading is often portrayed as a simple way of making money – it is not;
- appreciate the pitfalls. The market is quite fickle – what the market may give the market can take away;
- understand the three golden rules;
- know what basic ideas you should bear in mind when trading and creating a trading system.

Module outline

I will help you to achieve the broad objectives bulleted above by:

- first, examining some presumptions about online trading;
- second, outlining the three golden rules of online trading;
- third, explicating a few key practices that every online trader should carrry out;
- fourth, looking at types of trading systems.

> If you are looking to make **money** every day, you will have to trade every day.

Don't fall foul of misconceptions

Everyone seems to have some preconceptions about what online trading involves. These claims are often misguided or over-simplified. I shall pose the following assertions and then try to explain to you how they are flawed. When reading the assertions, try to think of a retort before reading my opinion.

I shall present the claims again at the end of the module in the form of self-assessment questions. By then, having worked through the 'golden rules' and the 'key practices' sections, you should be able to breeze through the self-assessment.

The preconceptions	Some replies
1 Online trading is the way the few who dare make a fortune.	**a** There is no more to online trading than there is to buying books from Amazon. The mechanics are relatively easy – that is why so many people are starting to get involved. However, knowing what to buy and when, and then when to sell, is where the skill lies. Whether you trade online or not you will have to master the skills of investment. These lie in the right direction and practice: I hope to give you the former, while the latter is the fun part I have left to you.
2 Online trading allows rapid short-term gains.	**b** While with online trading you can trade relatively short term because orders are transmitted electronically, online brokers are not intended to be used as a substitute to your being a floor trader. Online brokers confirm your orders as quickly as they can, but this is nowhere near quick enough for day trading, where you are looking to buy and sell in a few seconds. By the time you get the price, place an order, get confirmation, review the new price, place a new order, get a confirmation, the market will have moved on. Day trading and online trading are very different.
3 There is so much free information about stocks on the internet that you have an advantage over everyone else in making profitable trades.	**c** There is a lot of information, but information without an understanding of how to use it is useless and even detrimental. I will show you what I consider to be the best places to get information, but that is just the starting point. We must then know what to do with it to make money.

4 The costs you save in placing an order online make it far easier to come out ahead at the end of the year.

d Discount online brokers do offer very low brokerage rates, saving you a lot of money compared with placing trades with a full-fee broker. But you still need to be good at picking stocks.

5 Online trading offers an instant daily incom from a small capital start-up.

e The more money you want to make, the more capital you need. If you are looking to make money every day, you will have to trade every day. That will be expensive in commissions, let alone time, and soon you may find yourself without any trading capital. That's why most short-term traders look to place two trades a week instead.

6 You can give up your day job and work from home.

f If you want to trade for a living you will have to understand what you're giving up. But also to trade you will need capital and experience. Without capital you will not earn enough. Without experience you will make mistakes that the pressure to perform intensifies.

7 You can make profits off the back of more knowledgeable traders' postings on chat sites and bulletin boards.

g The best places for research are reputable sources of company information such as Hoover (US) or Hemmington Scott (UK). Chat rooms are not places to form opinions about stocks because you are not guaranteed advice from those with good enough experience – this is obviously dangerous to your pocket.

Notes

_____

_____

_____

_____

_____

_____

_____

_____

_____

_____

The three golden rules

One of the mysteries of human conduct is why adult men and women are ready to sign documents which they do not read, at the behest of salesmen they do not know, binding them to pay for articles they do not want, with money which they do not have.

GERALD HURST

The above 'mysteries' will be very costly in the stock market, where uncertainty is naturally all-pervasive and the stakes are high (your capital). No matter how much you are sure of your trading system, no matter how much research you do, no matter how successful you have been, you are never 100% certain.

Given the intense uncertainty, ignorance is very costly and the benefits of gaining knowledge very great. You should take this into consideration when you start putting your hard-earned cash on (the) line. Do not forget that you must:

- know what you are buying – research the stock using various tools – fundamentals and technicals (see later);
- know the ground rules for all investors under which you buy and sell a stock or bond;
- know the level of risk you are undertaking. Any analysis of returns must be taken with serious analysis of risk. Risk and return are part of the same whole.

While the manner in which orders are executed may be changing, the time-honoured principles of evaluating a stock have not.

ARTHUR LEVITT, CHAIRMAN SEC

The key is evaluation

Merely gaining information is grossly insufficient and not particularly demanding. What is required of you is evaluating information for significance, knowing how to employ it, and when. You do not need to know every piece of information about a stock and the market, but you have to analyze what the important information is and why it is significant. If you can think critically and independently of city analysts, your trading will become sharper and more enjoyable. We will come to the tools you'll need in later modules.

Practice makes perfect

There are critical practices online traders should undertake to avoid the problems of trading on the internet.

Question, question, question...

Questioning will provoke independent thought. Question incessantly. Your most important device is the question: 'Why?' Like a child, pose it on all occasions. Always question advice and try to find independent advice. If you hear someone talking up a stock, ask yourself why they are doing that, then find out for yourself.

Keep accounts

The more often you trade, the more information you will receive. You must keep it in a safe place. I recommend keeping a file on a spreadsheet which provides a running list of purchases, sales, profits, losses, commissions paid. That way you know how much you are paying and what kind of profits or losses you are making.

Plan B

Contingency plans are integral. You must always be aware of your options before placing a trade if you cannot gain access to your account online. A good major reputable broker will always be able to offer telephone back-up in case of a technology failure. There is no point planning to go online to find the appropriate information if it is not available because the site is 'down'.

Sleep at night – get confirmation

If you cancel an online trade make sure you get confirmation of the cancellation, rather than assuming it has been cancelled. Otherwise, you may place other orders in the erroneous belief that your previous trade was cancelled.

Take care with your clicking ways

The trouble with the internet is that procedure is so simple – click, click and then click some more. You could have bought anything ... twice. Be careful not to click away like crazy on the 'place order' button just because you do not get instantaneous feedback. Otherwise, two things will happen: you'll be sinking into the 'red' and you'll be afflicted by repetitive strain injury.

> The more often you trade, the more **information** you will receive.

> The trouble with the **internet** is that procedure is so simple – click, click and then click some more. You could have bought anything ... twice.

What you have learned

- Online trading deserves our respect or it will have our money.
- There is more to it than placing an order. It is **a skill**.
- **Do your homework** – get a lot of quality info and think about it independently of other opinions.
- Beware of procedure and be disciplined enough to engage in key procedure from the start.
- Online trading is not electronic day trading.
- Know what you are giving up as you expand your commitment to online trading.
- Fruitful and enjoyable trading demands clear and **critical thinking** about the raw information. Information is easy to obtain; evaluation is the hard part.
- Remember the **three golden rules**: know what you are buying/selling, know the ground rules, have a clear understanding of the risk you are undertaking and your preferences.
- **Question trading opinion using the data**, keep accounts, **prepare for contingency**, get confirmation, do not over-trade simply because the procedure is easy. Do not trade on a whim.

Notes

Key terms

Trading online: this is when you trade using an internet broker. Like any other product on the Internet, it is easier, faster and often cheaper.

Electronic day trading: this is intra-day trading. That means you open and close a trading position on the same day to make a profit from your trading. Day trading requires very fast responses to market conditions because the time frame is so short. You cannot do this online with an internet broker, it is not quick enough. You will need a special electronic account. Moreover, you will have to have a lot of expertise – not for the beginner.

Day trading requires very fast **responses** to market conditions because the time frame is so short.

Self-assessment test

Unlike other self-assessment tests on this course, this one will not be marked. The point of it is for you to think for yourself about online trading as an important and serious skill.

1 Does online trading allow rapid trades and short-term gains?
2 What is necessary if you want to trade for a living?
3 Why is it not easy to make money hand-over-fist by online trading given the amount of information and opinion, and the low commission charges?
4 Why is risk analysis important?
5 Try to think of the important practices that should be imbedded in your mind when you are trading.

Some suggested answers

1 Online brokers confirm your orders as quickly as they can but this is nowhere near quick enough for day trading, where you are looking to buy and sell in a few seconds. By the time you get the price, place an order, get confirmation, review the new price, place a new order, get a confirmation, the market will have moved on. Day trading and online trading are very different. Online trading is flexible, and applicable to a large range of possible trading time frames (between the opening and closing of a trade) – anything from maybe a couple of weeks to four years.

2 If you want to trade for a living you will have to understand what you're giving up. But also to trade you will need capital and experience. Without capital you will

Without **experience** you will make mistakes that the pressure to perform intensifies.

not earn enough. Without experience you will make mistakes that the pressure to perform intensifies.

3 It is not easy to make money because uncertainty is inherent in any investment. Some part of stock market volatility is wholly unpredictable. That part of share price movement that can be predicted requires you to gain information and evaluate significance – you will have to judge the merit of a trade for yourself. Your judgement is not the truth, it is merely one interpretation among many. However, there is hope, because your judgement will improve with knowledge, experience and critical thought.

4 Following on from the above question/answer, risk analysis is important because share prices are volatile. It is important that you quantify, as much as possible, the probability that the share price will move up and down from its present position, that you evaluate how much capital you are willing to stake, and your preferences towards risk in general.

Here is a very simple gamble that you can use to try to evaluate your preference to risk:

■ Option A: You get £100 for certain.

■ Option B: I flip a fair coin and you get £200 if it lands heads (probability ½) and nothing if it lands tails (probability ½).

Do you prefer A or B, or are you indifferent? The expected value of both options is £100:

■ A: £100 * 1 = £100.

■ B: £200 * ½ + £0 * ½ = £100.

If you chose A then you are risk-averse as defined by Expected Utility Theory because you went for the option with a lower possible 'variance in outcome' (i.e. £100 for certain over a half chance of £200) even though it has the same expected value as the other option. Now ask yourself how much you would have to be paid to just switch from A to B; what is your risk premium with regard to the two options? In answering the question you will be evaluating how much you value the certain option, A, vis-à-vis the gamble, B.

If you chose B then you are risk-loving. How much would you have to be paid to take A?

If you are indifferent then you are neutral with regard to risk.

The above exercise is clearly too simple for most tasks of risk evaluation in everyday life and especially trading – the values of gains and losses and the probabilities themselves are not known with certainty and trades are not pure gambles. But market risk can be evaluated as the value of historic volatility of the share price/s, i.e. how much the price deviates from a historic trend line or relative to the rest of the market (the beta is a measure of volatility and therefore pure risk).

Moreover, thinking about risk in a quantifiable way, as in the simple example above, will help you realize what your preferences to risk are. You must have a clear perception of your tolerance to risk when trading – that's the nature of the game. Try to think of some possible gambles.

There will be a more extensive analysis of risk in Module 14.

> You must have a clear perception of your **tolerance** to risk when trading – that's the nature of the game.

5 Here are some things to think about: risk assessment, question opinion, think independently using the data, the three golden rules, contingency plans, keep accounts, get confirmation.

Mechanical or discretionary?

Many online traders ask whether they should have a purely mechanical trading system or a discretionary one. A mechanical system is one in which, by a strict set of rules, for every market eventuality you know whether to be in or out of the market. For instance, a very simple system may involve being long (i.e. being in the market) if the price is above the 50-day moving average and being out (i.e. out of the market) if it is not.

With a discretionary system the ultimate decision is down to the trader who may consider all the facts before him plus gut instinct and try to incorporate experience, etc. So, which should you go for? (See Table 2.1.)

TABLE 2.1 Discretionary system or mechanical system?

Discretionary system	Mechanical system
■ No amount of programming can incorporate human experience into a mechanical system.	■ No emotions in decision making. Should lead to a less stressful life.
■ Can never be as thoroughly back-tested because the trader cannot put himself back in time to decide how he would have felt about a particular trade and whether he would have placed it.	■ Since it can be mathematically back-tested you can have a fairly good idea, albeit inconclusive, about future performance.
■ Do not need to know how to program trading software.	■ No constant decision making. Relatively stress-free.

There are certain personality-related issues to resolve too before you decide the type of **strategy** you should go for.

There are certain personality-related issues to resolve too before you decide the type of strategy you should go for. Here is a simple test. It meets the highest standards in psychometric testing and has been designed with cunning subtlety – so you should take it very seriously.

- How disciplined are you when it comes to executing trades?
  1 My name is General Colin Powell.
  2 Very disciplined, always take a signal, no problems.
  3 Sometimes disciplined, but occasionally go for a wild shot.
  4 Not very disciplined at all, trade on whim.
  5 My name is Homer Simpson.
  Total points _____

- Are you mathematical by nature?
  1 I've lost count of my age.
  2 Hate maths.
  3 Intermediate, competent.
  4 Very good.
  5 I work for NASA.
  Total points _____

- Do you like programming computers?
  1 I can't program the microwave.
  2 I could probably learn but wouldn't really enjoy it.
  3 I wouldn't be bad.
  4 I could do it and would enjoy it.
  5 I taught Bill Gates all he knows.
  Total points _____

- Are you more logical or more emotional?
  1 I cried through *Star Wars*.
  2 Pretty emotional and feeling-based rather than strictly rational.
  3 Probably a bit of both most of the time.
  4 I think things through clearly and methodically, logic is my light.
  5 My name is Spock, I work on the *Starship Enterprise*.
  Total points _____

- What do you enjoy about trading?

    1 Soros comes to me for my opinion on the markets.

    2 I like being involved, part of the game, plus want to profit, too.

    3 I want to make money, but want to enjoy trading, too.

    4 I want to make lots of money. Period. I don't care too much about the trading.

    5 Greed.

    Total points _____

- What type of trader do you admire most?

    1 George Soros.

    2 The type who has to make choices and work hard.

    3 I don't know.

    4 The type who can put his feet up.

    5 John Merriwether.

    Total points _____

- How good are you at decision making?

    1 I told you, my name is General Colin Powell.

    2 Quite good. I like to make them, stick by them and watch them succeed or fail.

    3 All right most of the time. Have difficulties occasionally.

    4 Pretty indecisive.

    5 I have just spent an hour on this question.

    Total points _____

- How lazy are you?

    1 I don't do sleep.

    2 Not very, I like to work hard, play hard.

    3 As much as the next guy. I like my short-cuts.

    4 If there is a quicker way of doing something I would like to know it.

    5 I am answering this in bed. It is 4pm.

    Total points _____

- How do you handle stress?

    1 I am a space shuttle commander when I am not sailing naked down the Amazon, coated in honey.

    2 Quite well. It gives me a buzz.

3 Sometimes I dislike it.

4 Hate it.

5 On my wedding night I had to use Viagra. I was 22.

Total points _____

Now tot up your scores and use the following guidelines to determine whether you are more suited to a mechanical system or a discretionary one.

9–23: You would handle a discretionary system well given your personality, and would probably enjoy it, too.

24–36: You could probably handle both quite well. You may want a very mechanical system with occasional override discretion.

37+: Better do it by the book. Mechanization for you, my friend, is the best option.

Your very own system: you just gotta have one

Since this is a book about trading systems, I feel obliged to give you a few reasons why you should have one, although it is arguable that if you have bought the book, you do not need converting.

Trading Valium: a stress reliever

Trading gets frustrating. Whoever you are. It gets stressful if you have had a string of losses. It can consume your waking hours, and your sleeping ones. You can get to a stage where you think of nothing but how you have been trading.

With a trading system some of that stress can be alleviated, if not avoided altogether, if you have the knowledge that your system was tested for profits and that despite some losses you will make money by following it.

Plan A, Plan B ... Plan Z

While a plan cannot predict the future, it can lay down how you will react to the possible outcomes. This is why a plan is essential. It is a list of strategic responses to events beyond your control. You control the only thing you can control – yourself.

A system removes much uncertainty, which itself is the cause of anxiety, confusion, anger and frustration. A good plan should therefore release psychological energy that is being expended unnecessarily on uncertainties. The flip side is that trading should become effortless, you should be more relaxed and possibly even enjoy your trading more!

> You can get to a stage where you think of **nothing** but how you have been trading.

Don't chase me

Strategically, too, a good plan improves trading. It assists in identifying opportunities and so stops you from chasing the market. It tells you when to exit, so you are not left clinging to the mast of a sinking ship. You gain some control instead of being swept along and buffeted around.

Expert advice

Pat Arbor, former chairman, Chicago Board of Trade

As a trader you must decide what you are. You are either a speculator, spreader or local scalper. You have to fit into one of those categories. Me, I am suited to spreading. To find what suits his personality, he just has to see whether or not he makes his money at what he's doing. I have had people come into the office saying, 'I am a great trader.' I say, 'You're right.' They say, 'Know how to trade.' I say again, 'Right,' and they say, 'I predicted that the market was going to go up or down,' and I say again, 'You are right. But the bottom line is whether you make any money.'

Save me from temptation

A system makes it easier for you to resist the temptation of doing what is comfortable, because in trading, doing what is comfortable is often the wrong thing. Think of how many times you have let a loss run or cut a profit short because it was the comfortable thing to do. Eventually, as you get used to following your system, it will become second nature. So, too, a plan is a means of changing your trading behaviour for the better. A kind of trading straitjacket, protecting you against your wilder emotions.

> Think of how many times you have let a loss run or cut a profit short because it was the **comfortable** thing to do.

> Good traders have **confidence** in their abilities to the point they know they are destined to make money.

I am in charge

Your own trading strategy is going to give you the independence to test your ideas without having to wait for a particular market guru to give you his opinion. The buck can stop with you, for profits and losses.

Pick and choose

When you are building your own trading system, you can pick and choose which fits your trading personality and preferences instead of choosing someone else's system, designed for their particular foibles. For example, you may want a profitable system, but with very few losing trades. You may be happier with such a system than one which is 10% more profitable but has double the number of losing trades.

Confidence

With your own creation, you know you have tested it for profitability. That can mean a lot when it comes to actually 'pulling the trigger', when you are unsure whether or not to place a particular trade. Good traders have confidence in their abilities to the point they know they are destined to make money. Part of this confidence comes from having spent hours developing their own systems. Once they execute the trade, confident in the system, they can focus on the trade itself, and not have to waste time on whether it was a mistake, or whether 'expert' Joe Shmoe in the newspaper was right in his opinion about the trade.

Emotions are out, certainty is in

For many online traders deciding when to place a trade and when to get out can be an agonizing experience. With a system, you can almost automate the process. The additional benefit is that you can remove the fear of cutting a loss and the hope that comes from hanging onto losers when you should have cut them.

System is friend, me is enemy

> You are your own worst **enemy** when it comes to trading.

You are your own worst enemy when it comes to trading. You are human and inevitably make irrational decisions based on tips, fear, greed. The system is like a port in a storm. It keeps you safe and makes sure you remain on track and do not get sidetracked.

Exercises

1 What is the difference between a discretionary and a mechanical system?
2 What are the merits and demerits of both?

What you have learned

Much anxiety in trading, as in life, stems from uncertainty about the future. It is when we do not know what the future holds that we become anxious. That's where a trading system comes in.

Discretionary *trading systems are more flexible but can never be as thoroughly back-tested because the trader cannot put himself back in time to decide how he would have felt about a particular trade and whether he would have placed it.*

Mechanical *trading systems can be mathematically back-tested. You can have a fairly good idea, albeit inconclusive, about future performance.*

While a plan cannot predict the future, it can lay down how you will react to the possible outcomes. The advantages of developing your own system are clear.

- You can have a system that is made to measure by picking and choosing which signals fit your trading personality and preferences.

- You will gain confidence from having spent hours developing your own systems. Once you execute the trade, confident in the system, you can focus on the trade itself and not have to waste time on whether it was a mistake.

- Deciding when to place a trade and when to get out can be an agonizing time. With a system, you can automate.

- You can control inappropriate, ill-planned trades.

Notes

_____

_____

_____

_____

_____

_____

_____

News – how to get it and how to **use** it

News is important. It allows us to get a feel for why the market is moving, then why a sector may be moving, and downwards onto an industry then into a stock (see Fig 3.1, p. 34). News has many functions for the trader (see Table 3.1, p. 32).

There is a lot of information on the web and you have little time. Therefore you will have to know where to go to get the knowledge you need and how to use it once you have it.

What you will learn

Having worked through this module you will know:

- what type of news and information you need;
- where the best sources are;
- how to use this knowledge in your trade evaluations as a whole.

Module outline

- First we shall see what general information you should look for and why, e.g. economic news, market news.
- Second we will examine how you should research individual companies.
- Third we will familiarize ourselves with the workings of search engines.

There is a lot of **information** on the web and you have little time.

TABLE 3.1   What the trader can glean from news

Type of News	Uses
Market news	■ Is the market in trouble? ■ Is there much negative news that will stop stocks soaring? ■ Are there economic problems in the economy, such as high inflation, low growth, strikes, political uncertainty, low productivity, all of which will impact stock price rises?
Sector	■ Which sectors are rising and which are falling? ■ Is there sector rotation, i.e. some sectors accelerate while others fall? ■ Is there growth in certain sectors, e.g. technology, and trouble with others, e.g. consumer goods?
Industry	■ More specifically, which industries in a sector are enjoying good growth? ■ Is there news about positive telecoms development or negative tobacco issues?
Company	■ Is the company generating a sound, positive stream of news? ■ Or is it warning of earnings problems? Good news flows should be reflected in strong upward price moves. How is the price faring?

General news

Question, question and ... then question some more

As a trader, at the outset you must have a general idea of what parts of the economy are doing well. Your aim as an online trader is to invest in those projects that will present you with the highest possible return relative to the plethora of other available investment projects, over a given period of time. 'But there are so many different areas to invest in,' I hear you say. Therefore you need to have a starting point, otherwise you will be swamped. A good place to begin is to ask general questions about the markets and stocks and then proceed to answer those questions. As you work your way through this chapter, answer the following questions:

- Which markets am I interested in?
- Is the general economy doing well?
- Which sectors am I interested in?
- Is the US telecoms sector (or other sector you may be interested in) suffering?
- Which telecoms stocks have been popular?

All this questioning – what purpose does it serve? Questioning is the first stage of analysis. It helps to focus your thoughts so that you can create an efficient plan of action. However, it's not enough to ask questions. Here is where the general market news comes in. Financial and market news is crucial because it answers your queries, and it encourages further questioning. Also, if you wish to trade on the market index, e.g. the FTSE 100 or the Nasdaq, rather than any particular company, general market news is, of course, directly important.

Types of news

All news is not the same. And each type of news has different uses for the trader. We need to appreciate the different types and how to use them – see Table 3.2.

FIGURE 3.1 The news hierarchy

Company news

Industry news

Sector news

Market news

TABLE 3.2 The different types of news

Type of news	What it provides	How to use it
Newswire (also called market pulse) – see Fig 3.2	A quick-fire summary of a news item. Limited analysis. Mainly just describes what has happened. We have to do most of our own analysis.	Can give us advance warning of impending price moves. Most useful to short-term active traders because of its likely impact on prices in the short term.
Columns (commentary) – see Fig 3.3	A daily or weekly piece from a regular writer on a particular issue such as telecoms stocks or emerging market stocks.	The columnist is usually taking the recent newswires and adding a bit more analysis and opinion to them, explaining their significance to us. They give us a clearer picture of which stocks we should investigate further.
Feature – see Fig 3.4	An infrequent, very detailed special feature on a sector.	For the longer-term trader as usually identifying longer-term prospects. Often identifies value stocks whose present stock price does not accurately reflect future prospects yet or which will gradually rise over time as the company 'proves itself'.

FIGURE 3.2 Newswire

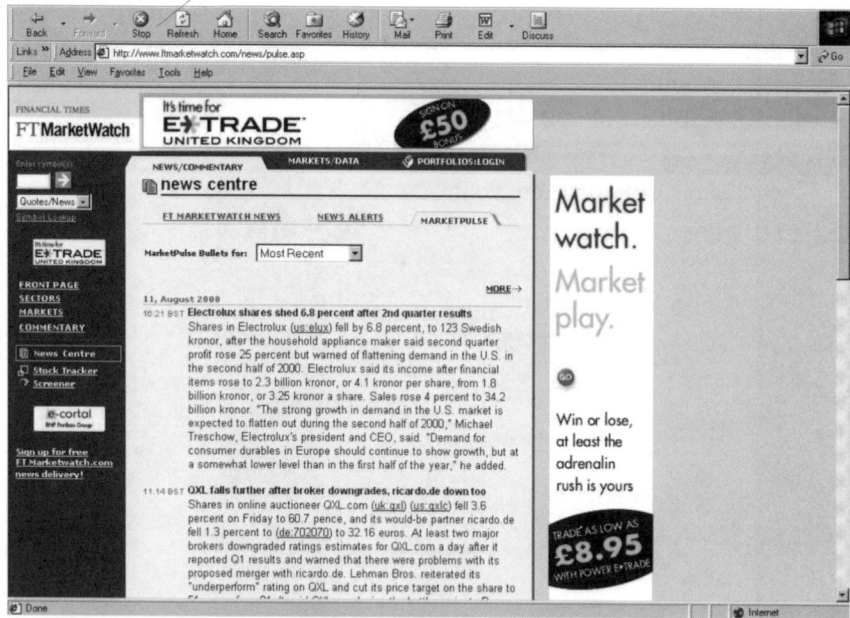

FIGURE 3.3 Column

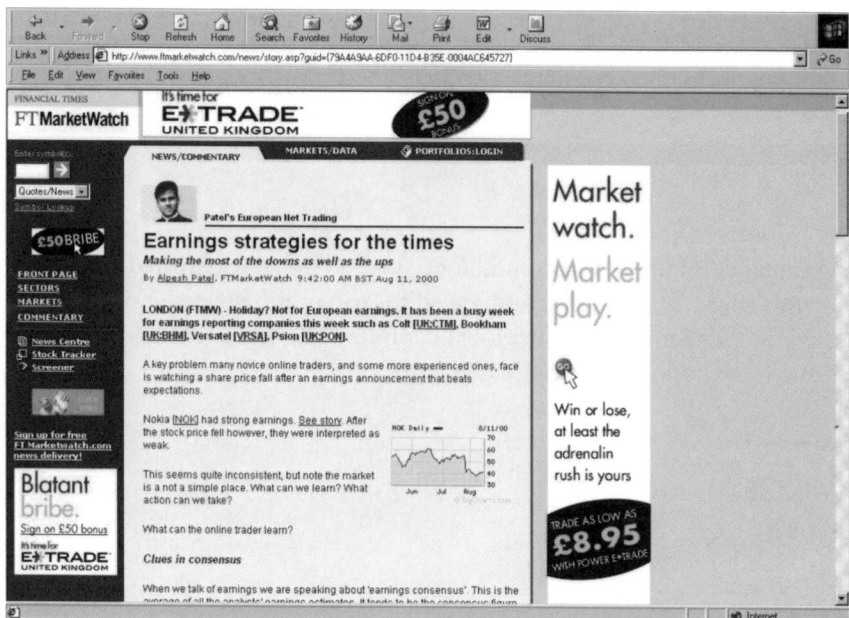

FIGURE 3.4 | Special feature

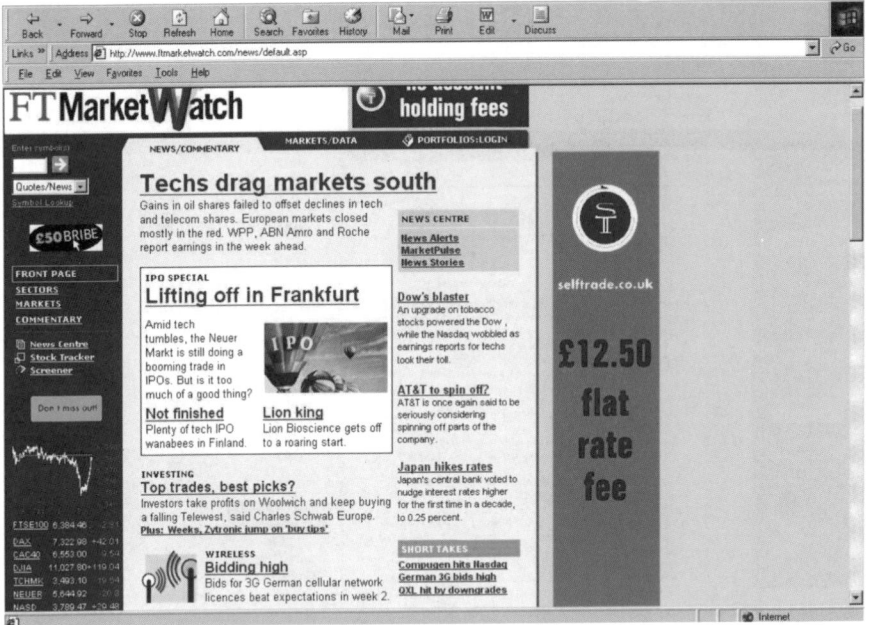

Where to look

Here are some of the best news sites. The sites listed in the next section on researching individual companies will also be useful for general news.

Bloomberg ✱✱✱

www.bloomberg.com

An abundance of news and commentary in a no-nonsense format. Excellent reporting, sharp presentation and speed for top-notch coverage of industry, markets, hi-tech stocks and the global economy. The site is cleanly designed. Valuable information delivered well.

Each type of news has **different** uses for the trader.

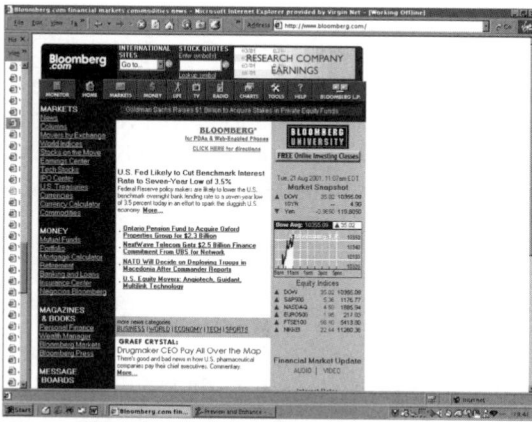

CBS Market Watch ***

www.cbs.marketwatch.com

Front page packs essential breaking stories on the market and companies. The information is well organized and easy to navigate, with keyword searches. Links in articles are well thought out. Free tools include company research, charts and delayed quotes.

CNNfn ***

www.cnnfn.com

With its reporters worldwide, the site is able to break news and offer a very fast newswire service. Its writers also do more in-depth thoughtful analytic pieces which we as traders can use, too.

European Investor **

www.europeaninvestor.com

A good site for quotes, charts and news for European exchanges. Design is attractive and the site is easy to navigate. Free registration gives you 25 real-time quotes a day. The company profiles could be more in-depth but are sufficient, especially if you want information about European stocks in one place.

Financial Times **

www.ft.com

The reliable pink pages online has full access to its leading companies and markets news. It also has a searchable archive and you can get news e-mailed to you. Also see FT Market Watch at www.ftmarketwatch.com – decent market coverage and analysis. Offers an assortment of model portfolios. Well-written articles. The design is uncluttered.

LatinFocus ***

www.latin-focus.com

Sharp site for investors in select Central and South American countries. Pull-up detailed economic profiles packed with data. An excellent place for initial research.

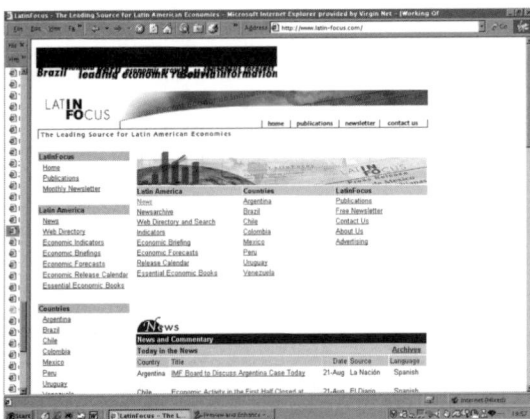

Money.net ***

www.money.net

Free streaming real-time quotes. Recently added improved market news and message boards. Very valuable.

Reuters Moneynet **

www.moneynet.com

Market commentary is very good. Breaking news, category news and companies prominent in the news today will all be very helpful to get you started. But little visual variety makes it a bit monotonous.

Wall Street Journal **

www.wsj.com

The main problem with this site is the annoying registration aspect. Other than that the news content is best for thoughtful pieces, not necessarily the newswire aspects.

WorldlyInvestor ***

www.worldlyinvestor.com

An excellent collection of columns and in-depth features from industry practitioners, which means they are especially insightful and helpful to the trader. The site is well organized so you can focus on sectors you are most interested in.

411 Stocks ***

www.411stock.com

This is a simple megasite for finding information about a stock. Provides price data, news, discussion groups, charting, fundamental data, income statements. A lot of information in one place.

I want to see which sectors the **websites** are picking up on.

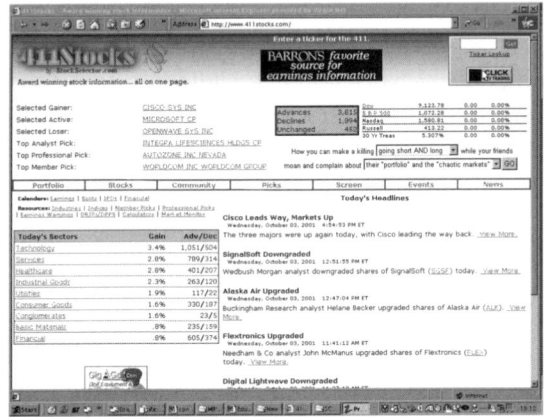

Case study: getting sector news

I want to see which sectors the websites are picking up on. Are there any sectors they think are particularly interesting? So I click on the CBS Market-Watch site (Fig 3.5) which always has useful, insightful commentary – the type that knows what is really happening in the markets and is written for traders to profit from.

FIGURE 3.5   CBS Marketwatch headlines

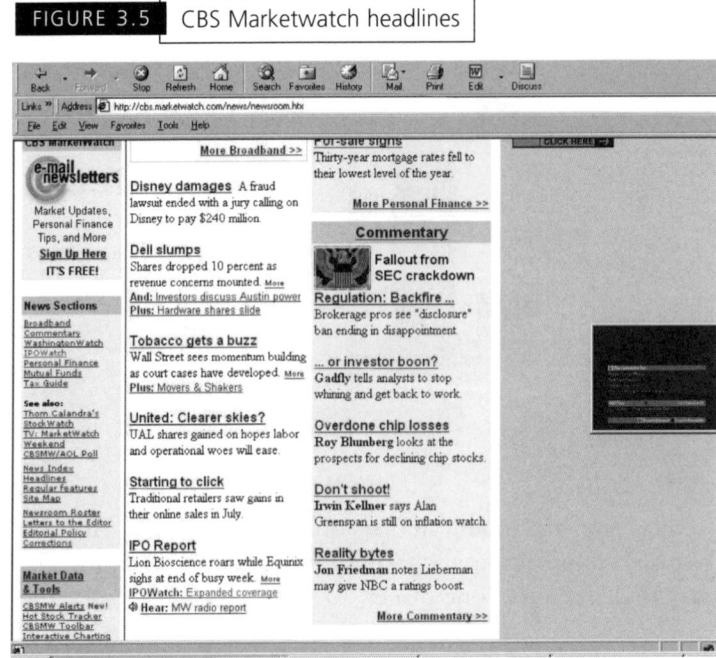

Visiting the site, the headline which catches my attention is 'Tobacco gets a buzz'. Clearly there has been some positive news surrounding tobacco issues and I may want to investigate this sector further. So I read on (Fig 3.6)

FIGURE 3.6 The news gets more detailed

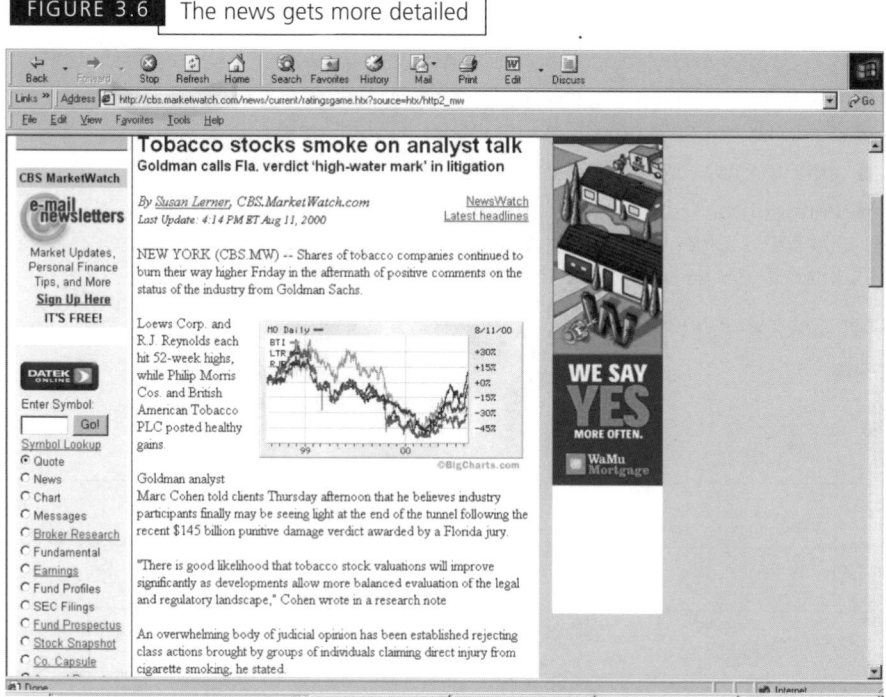

But how do you know if you should listen to that one commentator on that one site? Easy.

1 Is it a well-respected site such as the ones I have listed here? If it is not listed above, is it one whose brand you have come across before?

2 Scan a few other sites. Do any of them pick up a similar theme, e.g. tobacco stocks likely to rally?

3 Make a note of the stock names and the reasons the site gives, then use them later for when we do our own research and confirm for ourselves whether we agree these stocks are a good buy or a goodbye. A good trader doesn't take anyone's word for it but his own.

> A good trader doesn't take **anyone's** word for it but his own.

Exercise

You have a go. Visit four of the sites listed above, and scan for two major economy or sector stories that suggest that further investigation may lead to good stocks to research.

Remember as you do this:

- the clue is in the headlines;
- it should not take time – the headlines should jump out at you;
- after the headline see which subtitle looks the most promising;
- Print out the story for later cross-reference to assist in your research. Also to keep in a folder so that it can help with your trade planning (more about this later) if you decide to buy the stock.

Jot down your findings here.

Site: Headline: Potential stocks
                to investigate:

_____

_____

_____

_____

But surely if the story is in the headlines the stock price will already have jumped?

This can sometimes be true for very immediate price moves, but if you are a longer-term holder it need not be a problem. We are looking for the types of news stories that suggest the price is still to move up, that are forward looking, for instance something headed:

'Telecoms undervalued'
'Pharmaceuticals still further to ride'
'Housebuilders may end slide'

We would not be looking for headlines which report what has already happened to the share price, with little inkling of what may happen next:

'Tobacco stocks popped up yesterday'
'Good morning for retailers'

The firm

How do you **gauge** whether you should invest in this company?

Let's presume you have heard about a company and are interested in it as a potential investment – you may have heard about it on one of the sites above, the newspaper, from a friend. How do you gauge whether you should invest in this company? The news is a starting point, but it's time for you to consider whether the company looks good enough for *you*.

Starting with news to research individual companies

What kind of things would you want to know about a potential investment? Here are a few suggestions:

■ What exactly is their business?

■ How big is it?

■ Any major items of recent news about them.

■ How much profit analysts think they will make in the future; the firm's business strategy.

■ What other investors have thought of them.

■ How their share price has performed in the last few years.

■ How their accounts look – how profitable they are and how profitable they can be.

Most of these questions will be answered in Modules 6 and 7. For now let us focus on company-specific news.

To find out news about a specific company using any of the excellent sites mentioned above is relatively easy as they all follow a similar format.

Ticker box

The first thing you need is the company's ticker symbol, which is an abbreviation for the stock, e.g. Microsoft's ticker is msft. The symbol lookup link under the ticker box will help you find the ticker symbol for your stock. You then enter that into any appropriate box – Figs 3.7 and 3.8 show boxes where tickers can be entered.

You will then be taken to more detailed information about the stock and this usually includes most recent news (Figs 3.9 and 3.10).

Story

Often, however, whenever a company is mentioned in a story the company name is underlined, meaning if you click on it you will be taken to more information about the company, including news (Fig 3.9).

News search

Some sites allow you to search for news, but the same principle applies as for a first search (Figs 3.10 and 3.11).

Question: What about news about non-US stocks?

Answer: Simply go to a site that caters for this. For example, FTMarketWatch and ADVFN will give you stock symbols and news for UK and European companies as well as US ones. ADVFN has a helpful site at www.advfn.com.

FIGURE 3.7 Showing symbol lookup link and ticker box symbol

FIGURE 3.8	Symbol lookup box for searching company tickers

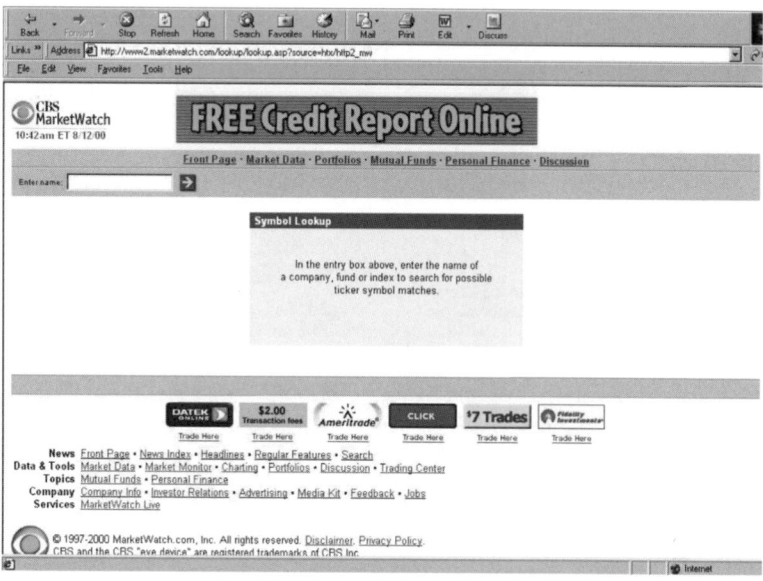

FIGURE 3.9	Clicking on highlighted stock names takes you to more information about those companies, including news

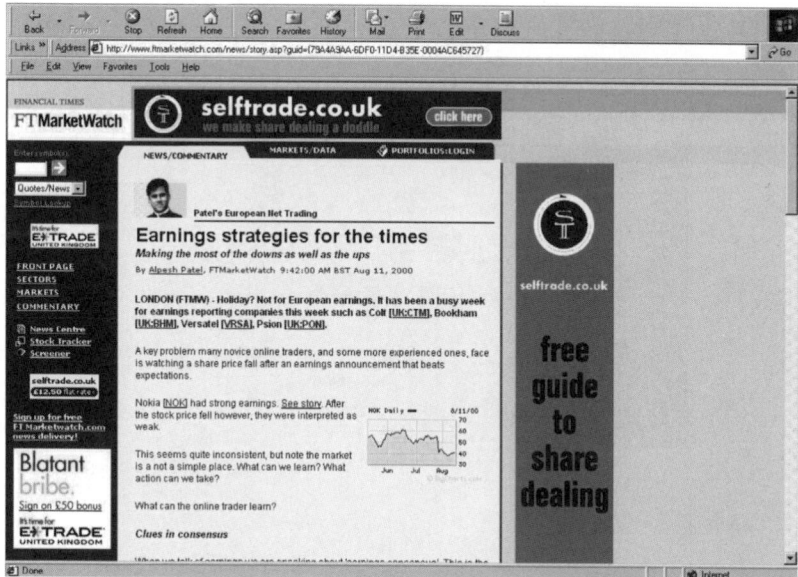

FIGURE 3.10   All the news from Microsoft

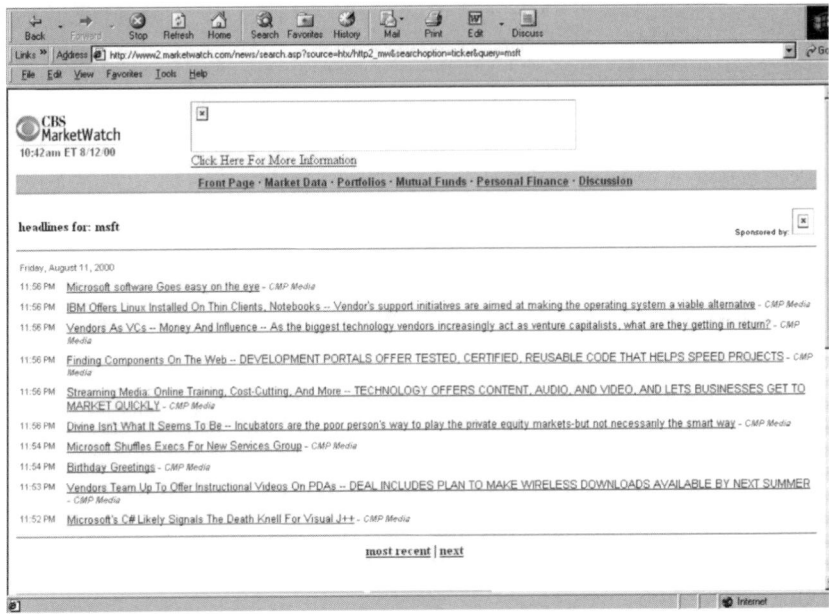

FIGURE 3.11   FT.com and Moneynet.com have good search facilities

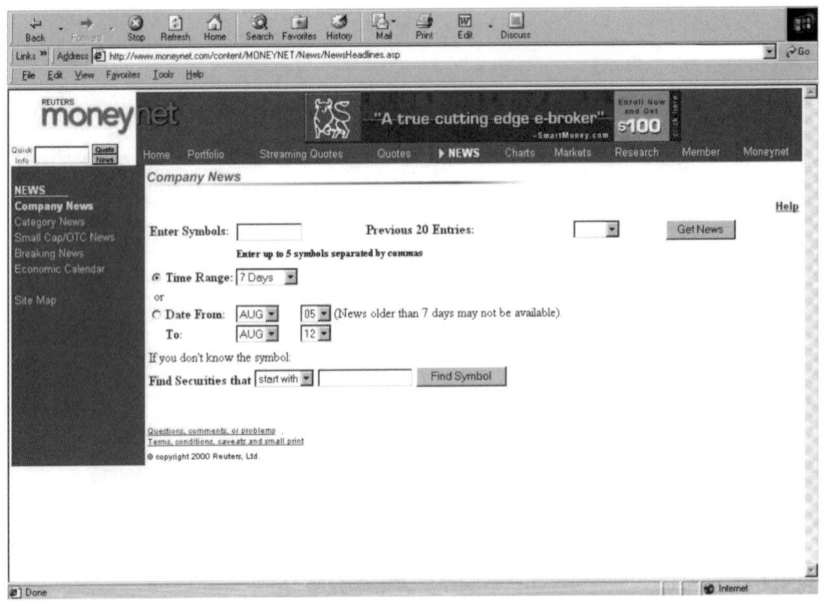

Definitions

RNS – a term you will find when searching for news on UK companies. Stands for regulatory news service. It will be bland, basic news, with no interpretation. However, this news is useful precisely because it is an impartial primary source of information.

AFX – news articles from the Associated Financial Press. It is a newswire and therefore opinionated, so maybe not an adequate option.

Exercises

1 Find the ticker symbols for the following four stocks:
Cisco (US)_____
Sun Microsystems (US)_____
Atlantic Telecom (UK)_____
France Telecom (French)_____

2 For each of these companies find both the latest and historical news using one of the websites mentioned above.

What we are looking for in company newsflow

We are looking out for positive news items about the company:

- winning new orders;
- increasing orders;
- entry into new sectors;
- new product developments;
- good strategic alliances;
- accelerations in current business model.

We also want to know what the analysts are forecasting upcoming profits to be. This is worth knowing because they receive regular private briefings from the company on how things are going and so are usually on the mark with their estimates.

> If there is some aspect of the company you are **wondering** about or cannot understand, other people's opinions will be helpful.

Finding out what other investors have thought of the company, through chat rooms and 'share picks', is interesting since you gauge other people's opinion. If there is some aspect of the company you are wondering about or cannot understand, other people's opinions will be helpful. However, there are various warnings that are stamped on these sorts of prescriptions. I discuss these in Modules 11 and 14.

Remember …

An investor's opinion is just one estimation, one outlook, not the last word.

How to scan newsflow

Since there are many news items, and we want to be as efficient as possible so we can make our money and actually have time to spend it, instead of being in front of the computer all the time, we need to know how to scan these news headlines.

The general rule is that news companies try to tell as much as possible in the headline. Consequently, I tend to focus on those headlines which common sense tells me are likely to include some information of the above type I am looking for. In Table 3.2 I have highlighted the ones I consider to be in that category out of a series for Sun Microsystems. However, I may examine some of the others, too, if I think I need more information about a stock.

Friday, August 11, 2000

11:56 PM	Startup Axient Bets On Private Fiber Network — WITH A 60-CITY NETWORK, AXIENT GETS DEAL FROM NBC TO DELIVER BROADBAND OLYMPIC COVERAGE – *CMP Media*
11:56 PM	Vendors As VCs — Money And Influence — As the biggest technology vendors increasingly act as venture capitalists, what are they getting in return? – *CMP Media*
11:56 PM	Finding Components On The Web — DEVELOPMENT PORTALS OFFER TESTED, CERTIFIED, REUSABLE CODE THAT HELPS SPEED PROJECTS – *CMP Media*
11:52 PM	The New Developer Portals — BUYING, SELLING, AND BUILDING COMPONENTS ON THE WEB SPEEDS COMPANIES' TIME TO MARKET – *CMP Media*
11:51 PM	Vendors Partner With Venture Capitalists To Fund Startups – *CMP Media*
11:50 PM	The Two Faces Of E-Biz Management – *CMP Media*
11:50 PM	Sun teams with vignette – *CMP Media*
11:50 PM	Stealing Java's Thunder — Microsoft's upcoming Visual Studio.net offers an integrated development interface, a new programming language, and programming shortcuts that should result in more-efficient Web development. A secondary, unstated aim is to slow Java's progress. – *CMP Media*
11:39 PM	AMD, Intel draw 64-bit battle lines – *CMP Media*
11:37 PM	XML GAINS MOMENTUM — ebXML emerging as EDI alternative for B2B transactions – *CMP Media*
6:05 PM	GSA Awards FirstGov Contract to GRC International – *PRNewswire*
4:14 PM	WRAP: Dell shares fall 11% on concerns about future sales growth (Update1) – *Futures World News Select*
3:46 PM	LinuxWorld Conference & Expo Exhibitor Profiles A to Z; Conference and Expo to Start Next Week in San Jose, Calif. – *BusinessWire*
2:47 PM	Stock picks of the week: EMC, Pfizer, Sun, Johnson & Johnson and H-P – *Deborah Adamson © CBS MarketWatch.com*
12:54 PM	First Ecom.com Inc. Announces Second Quarter Financial Results – *BusinessWire*
11:02 AM	Robinson-Humphrey Analyst Interviews On RadioWallStreet.com – *BusinessWire*
9:45 AM	Planet City Software Teams With CRD Capital – *PRNewswire*

Thursday, August 10, 2000

11:01 PM	Sun, Microsoft Java Battle Delayed – *Unknown (cmtx-pc)*
8:23 PM	James J. Whitney Named Forsythe Solutions Group's E-Business Solutions Technologist – *BusinessWire*
8:13 PM	PVI, Sportvision, Inc. Named Winners Success Story Receives Recognition from Sun Microsystems, Computerworld Competition – *PRNewswire*

Exercise

Find and highlight the most important news items for the Indian technology company Satyam, which is listed in the US under ticker code SIFY.

■ Did you learn anything about US corporate investment in India?
■ Did you find out the names of major US companies investing in India?
■ Did you discover Indian economic conditions?
■ Has Satyam entered into recent alliances?
■ What other interesting stock moving news was there for the stock?

Key terms

Technical analysis: methods used to forecast future prices using the price data alone (for example by plotting it as a chart and noting direction) or using the price as an input in mathematical formulae and plotting the results. Contrast this with fundamental analysis.

Fundamental analysis: forecasting prices by using economic or accounting data. For example one might base a decision to buy a stock on its yield.

Market capitalization: this is the product of the number of shares outstanding and the current price.

Director dealings: whether the directors have been buying or selling shares in their company.

Search engines

The internet is a huge expanse of information and if you want to navigate it and find the information you want, you will have to search.

What is a search engine?

A search engine is simply a site that 'searches' other sites depending on keywords entered by a user. Search engines are therefore of general use, not just for the online trader.

The **internet** is a huge expanse of information.

How to search

Simple: type in the keyword and press enter. If you want to be technical, most search engines have options which allow you to specify whether the engine is to provide results that contain the keywords as a phrase or any one of the keywords.

- Since pages on the internet change quickly, a search engine is unlikely to be up to the minute and some results may be out of date.
- Just because an engine does not find a site does not mean it doesn't exist.
- Because of the different ways search engines work each will return different results.
- If you are not satisfied with the results, try a different engine.
- Results are ranked according to the closeness of the match to your request, and not according to the best available site in terms of content.

Top search sites

Use these sites to search for information on specific areas of trading:

- Altavista   www.altavista.com
- Excite   www.excite.com
- Lycos   www.lycos.com
- Yahoo!   www.yahoo.com

Summary

You now have a good idea of what basic information you need for your trading and where to get it. You will need general and company-specific news. However, remember this is not a one-off process. Researching potential areas for your investments is an ongoing and dynamic process. As you learn you will fill in gaps and gain insights. By building a body of knowledge and experience, you will gain confidence.

In Module 4 we go on to look in more detail at how to pick stocks.

Self-assessment

1 Which one of these is not something you would find a useful piece of market news?
   a inflation projections;
   b last year's inflation figures;
   c expected growth rates;
   d possible foreign armed conflict.

2 What is sector rotation?

3 What is another name for a newswire service?
   a market wire;
   b market rotation;
   c market pulse;
   d market beat.

4 To what type of trader is a newswire most useful?
   a active short-term traders;
   b medium-term traders;
   c long-term traders.

5 Which has the least analysis?
   a market pulse;
   b column;
   c special feature.

6 Does stock price always react to news?

7 Name a site that provides news on non-US securities by allowing you to enter their ticker symbols.

Answers:

1 **b** – because they are backward looking. While they are relevant in shaping this year's expectations, they are too far in the past to have market influence.

2 Where sectors that were not increasing in price start growing as money rotates into them and out of previously leading sectors.

3 **c** – market pulse (used for instance by FTMarketWatch.com).

4 a – active short-term traders as such news is purely factual and tends to influence the immediate price, although it can often have longer-term ramifications, depending on how it is interpreted.

5 a – market pulse – it tends to be factual, not with opinion.

6 No – that is one reason why trading is so difficult.

7 One answer could be www.ftmarketwatch.com.

Choosing stocks – **technical analysis**

Tools and – **strategies**

MODULE

4

Don't gamble: buy some good stock, hold it until it goes up and then sell it – if it doesn't go up, don't buy it!

WILL ROGERS

The eternal question, the question that bears on the mind of every trader, is:

Will this stock rise?

This question is at the heart of any choice about a stock - all other questions flow from this one. One way of evaluating whether a stock price will rise is to analyze how the price has moved in the past. Technical analysis (or TA to its friends) is a basis for forecasting future prices using (recent) past price data.

What you will learn

Having worked through Modules 4–6 you will:

- have an understanding of many of the TA strategies;
- know when and how to use them as tools in your overall trading;
- have information about what sites to look at for TA tools online and for TA education;
- have an idea of what software you will need, depending on how much TA you want to do.

Module outline

- First I shall look at some online trading problems and the rationale for TA.

> One way of evaluating whether a stock price will rise is to **analyze** how the price has moved in the past.

- Second I shall take you through some tools used to evaluate price moves (this is a large section).

TA: What? Why?

You will face many queries when trading.

- How do I know which securities to buy?
- Even if I know what to buy, when is the best time to buy it so I reduce the chances of the stock going down right after I have bought it?
- What are the signs that a security is 'tanking', i.e. ripe for a fall?

However, you have the ability to tackle such problems. The reason for using TA is to get a good idea about when to buy low and sell high. It tends to work best over a time frame of a few days to a few months, so is ideal for short-term to medium-term trading. Many of the indicators and methods of analysis we will examine are trying to determine when traders may have overreacted and have sold too much stock too quickly or vice versa and therefore afford us the opportunity to enter or exit the market at the best time to maximize profits.

Definition

Technical analysis is a method of determining opportune buying and selling points. It involves methods used to forecast future prices using the price data alone (for example, by plotting it as a chart and noting direction) or using the price as an input in mathematical formulae and plotting the results. Contrast this with fundamental analysis, which looks at a company's accounts, reports, etc. in order to evaluate price moves.

TA does not always work. It cannot explain everything in the market.

But TA does not always work. It cannot explain everything in the market, since the market does not behave in a necessarily consistent manner. Whenever we use TA, or any other form of analysis, we are, in fact, looking for points where there is an increased probability of a price move. We look for areas into which it is highly probable that the price will move.

The tools and the strategies

I am not going to go through every single analytic method known to man and beast. I am going to focus on the techniques I use, those which are the most popular and which the major institutions use. At the end of this module you won't have a PhD in TA, but that doesn't matter – you're going to use TA, not lecture on it.

The basics

Charting The first thing all technical analysts will do is put up a price chart. There are many types – see Figs 4.1–4.3 for a few examples.

FIGURE 4.1 Bar chart

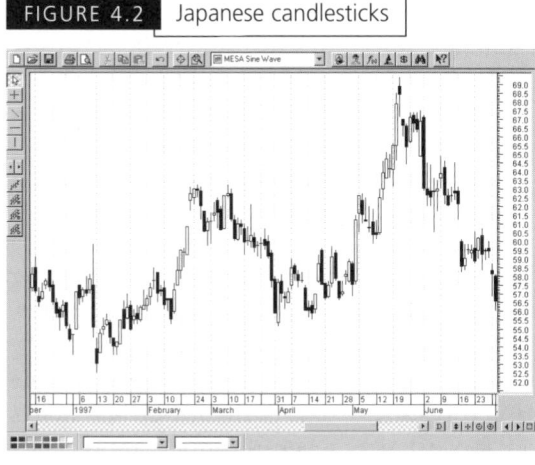

FIGURE 4.2 Japanese candlesticks

FIGURE·4.3   Line chart

Bar charts (Fig 4.1) are the most popular way of depicting prices. The extremities of the price high and the low determine the length. The horizontal line on the left of each vertical line represents the opening price, and the horizontal line on the right represents the close.

In Japanese candlesticks (Fig 4.2) there is a 'body' and a line (like a wick). The body is a rectangle drawn between the open and close of the day. It is shaded black if the close is lower than the open, and white if the close is above the open. The wick is added to join the high and low of the day. Of course, if there is no price movement after the open then there will be no body or wick, just a horizontal line.

There are many more, but you get the point.

Trendlines A trendline simply joins a series of higher lows and lower highs. Uh? Look at Fig 4.4. We see the line joining higher and higher lows. What trendlines try to represent are areas where there is a relatively increased probability of a price move off the trendline. Drawing trendlines is an art and you should not look for exact points but a feel of where prices are hitting the approximate narrow area around the line and then moving back up. You would not trade off the trendline, but rather use it as one piece of evidence when determining likely price moves.

Drawing **trendlines** is an art.

Support and resistance – the last frontiers By drawing support and resistance levels we are again trying to determine areas where prices are probably, but not certainly, going to behave in a particular way (see Fig 4.5). This shows support and resistance levels, the lower line being the support. So, for instance, when the price approaches

The trend is your friend

Support and resistance

the resistance area it has greater difficulty getting past that area and you may decide you want to exit your position (if you are holding one) at that point.

Like trendlines, they are not set in stone. They are liable to move, and can be penetrated intra-day or over a couple of days. They are zones of probable price action.

With trendlines and supports and resistances, the probability of a price move in a particular direction increases the longer the trendline has been in 'force', i.e. not been significantly penetrated. For example, if the price has hit the trendline on five occasions and then moved up, it should do the same the seventh time it hits the trend.

With supports and resistances what we are seeing is a battle between buyers and sellers. For instance, at a resistance level sellers may have decided they will start selling a security at that level because it is over-priced and buyers are too few to do much about it. So the price has to retreat as selling increases. If buyers increase in number and size at the crucial point, the price may break through with the force of a broken dam, marauding buyers pushing the price higher and higher. This is one reason why price often jumps at breakouts with a sharp rise, a leap up in price and large volume. Watch out for these things.

- Look for penetration or breakthrough of the resistance – if there is one it should be followed by a big move.
- An alternative method of trading is to wait and see if the trendline or support is not broken and then trade in the direction of the rebound.

What counts as penetration? Given market volatility you could get price piercing a trendline or support or resistance but then close back above. For this reason, some analysts only draw trendlines and supports based on closing prices, because intra-day prices are too erratic. Others say the price must close for two or three days in the penetration position.

- When a support or resistance level is broken it tends then to reverse its role and become a resistance level or a support level respectively. See Fig 4.6. This is a common occurrence known as a 'reversal pattern' and the same rules apply as before.
- After a breakthrough of a support or resistance the price will often 'pull back' to the trendline it just broke through. You have to be careful of this as you may think the move has just ended, in which case you may exit an otherwise profitable trade prematurely.

Exercises

1 What is technical analysis?
2 Define and outline the significance of the following indicators:
   a bar charts;
   b Japanese candlesticks;
   c Supports and resistance.

What have you learned

Technical analysis is a method used to forecast future prices using the price data alone or using the price as an input in mathematical formulae and plotting the results. Contrast this with fundamental analysis, which looks at a company's accounts, reports, etc. in order to evaluate price moves.

Bar charts are the most popular ways of depicting prices. The extremities of the price high and the low determine the length. The horizontal line on the left of each vertical line represents the opening price, and the horizontal line on the right represents the close.

In **Japanese candlesticks** there is a 'body' and a line (like a wick). The body is a rectangle drawn between the open and close of the day. It is shaded black if the close is lower than the open, and white if the close is above the open. The wick is added to join the high and low of the day.

Supports are trendlines that join previous lows. **Resistances** join highs. When a support or resistance level is broken it tends then to reverse its role and become a resistance level or a support level respectively. This is a common occurrence known as a **'reversal pattern'** and the same rules apply as before. After a breakthrough of a support or resistance the price will often 'pull back' to the trendline it just broke through. You have to be careful of this as you may think the move has just ended, in which case you may exit an otherwise profitable trade prematurely.

Notes

_____

_____

_____

_____

_____

_____

_____

_____

_____

_____

_____

_____

Reversal pattern strategies

Reversal patterns are chart patterns which historically have tended to precede a reversal in prices. Again, they are added to our overall evidence of what the price may do, which gives a better idea of whether we should exit a position or enter one.

Head and shoulders strategies   An anatomical pattern this. Take a look at Fig 4.6. It is not always as clear-cut. This is a common pattern on bar charts and fairly reliable. The horizontal line represents the 'neckline' and you always wait for it to be broken for it to be a head and shoulder position. The pattern can occur on a slope. The position can also occur as a bullish (rising share price) pattern if it appears as an opposite or mirror reflection.

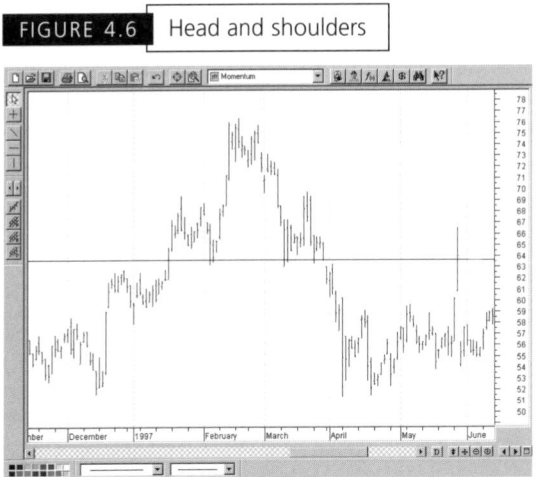

FIGURE 4.6   Head and shoulders

Triangle strategies   Figure 4.7 shows a triangle. For a price reversal on the upside the horizontal line appears above the ascending diagonal line. We are then looking for a breakout of the horizontal line. To trade the pattern you can treat it very much like a breakout pattern from a resistance level. Volume should be decreasing to the apex and then increase on breakout as the marauding purchasing invaders impeach the sellers' line of defence.

Figure 4.7 shows an ascending triangle; the descending triangle is a mirror reflection and would represent a price breakout on the downside.

> To trade the **pattern** you can treat it very much like a breakout pattern from a resistance level.

Triangle pattern

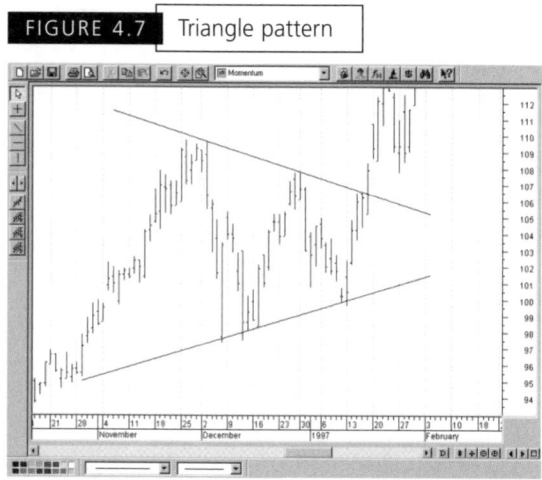

Saucer strategies   The pattern for this is shown in Fig 4.8. It represents a gradual change in opinion about a stock. Although saucers are rare, if you can spot them as the price is rising they can be an additional confirmatory indicator of a trend change. There are no price targets for this pattern so exit needs to be determined more by rising percentage stop-losses or exit points determined by other technical methods.

Saucer pattern

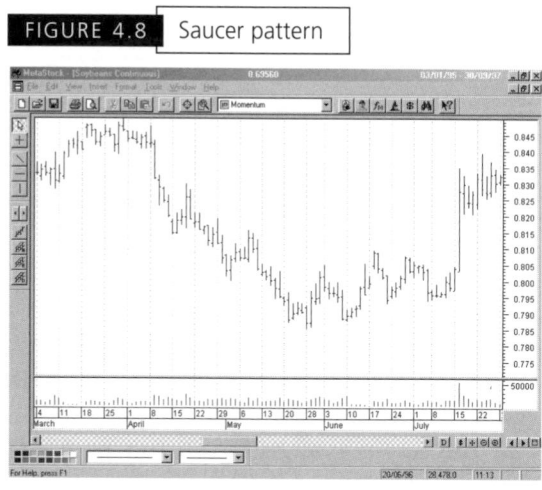

Percentage stop-losses – with this, a floor is maintained a fixed percentage down from the share price. Naturally, as the share price rises, this floor also rises. The floor value is never lowered when the share price falls, since it is penetration of this floor by the share price that is the selling signal. As the share price rises, the profit so far is consolidated by this constant rising of the floor.

Continuation patterns

These patterns confirm that the current direction of price movement will continue. They can represent a pause in price and so can be used as a good point to step on before the escalator starts moving up again.

Rectangles   The rectangle is simply where the price action moves sideways between a support and resistance level after a rise. It can be thought of as a resting place where buying and selling troops stop to reconsider the price levels.

A strategy for this is to trade it in the same way you would any other breakout of a resistance. Unlike a normal breakout, the fact that price has risen to the rectangle formation adds to the likelihood of the breakout.

Flag strategies   A flag can appear in an uptrend or downtrend (see Fig 4.9). The flag looks like a rectangle rotated diagonally upwards and is preceded by a downtrend. The flag is where, instead of a sideways move after a downturn, buyers for a while outgun sellers and cause prices to rise, as they believe prices have oversold. But the sellers soon return as price rises. The flag is important only after the bottom of the flag is pierced – so wait for that. If it is not pierced, you simply have a reversal.

> It can be thought of as a resting place where buying and selling troops stop to **reconsider** the price levels.

Pennant strategy   The pennant shows a rising trend followed by a price move where low boundary lines converge – representing the battle between buyers and sellers. Volume should decrease to the apex and increase on the breakout of the upper boundary. You can treat the breakout of the upper boundary in the same way for trading as we discussed before about trading breakouts generally (see Fig 4.10).

FIGURE 4.9 Flag pattern

FIGURE 4.10 Pennant pattern

HOT TIPS

Before moving on we should make a general point about how the TA tools examined are to be used as part of your overall trading strategy. Remember:

- any single tool is not sufficient as the basis of a trading decision;
- the tools must be used in conjunction, each providing further confirmation or not. Find out which tools are best for you;
- the TA tools must also be used to precisely time your entry or exit from a position. Timing your entry or exit is crucial, since it is not enough to think the price will rise or fall in the next couple of weeks. TA is a fine-tuner.

Exercise

What is:

- a head and shoulder pattern?
- a triangle pattern?
- a continuation pattern?
- a percentage stop-loss?

What you have learned

There is a plethora of reversal pattern strategies. You should keep in mind the most important.

Head and shoulders is a common pattern on bar charts and fairly reliable. The horizontal line represents the 'neckline' and you always wait for it to be broken for it to be a head and shoulder position. The pattern can occur on a slope and can appear in a bullish market as well.

Triangle patterns can mark a price reversal on the upside when the horizontal line appears above the ascending diagonal line. We are then looking for a breakout of the horizontal line.

A **saucer** represents a gradual change in opinion about a stock.

Continuation patterns confirm that the current direction of price movement will continue. They can represent a pause in price and so can be used as a good point to step on before the escalator starts moving up again.

The **rectangle** is simply where the price action moves sideways between a support and resistance level after a rise. It can be thought of as a resting place.

A **flag** can appear in an uptrend or downtrend. The flag looks like a rectangle rotated diagonally upwards and is preceded by a downtrend. The flag is important only after the bottom of the flag is pierced – so wait for that. If it is not pierced, you simply have a reversal.

Percentage stop-losses are an important tool to protect you on the downside. With this, a floor is maintained a fixed percentage down from the share price. Naturally, as the share price rises, this floor also rises. The floor value is never lowered when the share price falls, since it is penetration of this floor by the share price that is the selling signal.

Notes

A little more sophisticated **analysis**

Continuing on from the last module, and now that you've had a chance to catch your breath …

Momentum-based strategies

Momentum is a generic term I am using here to discuss four similar indicators: stochastic, momentum, MACD and RSI. The reasoning behind all momentum indicators is that a security price moving in a particular direction tends to slow down before reversing direction. A ball thrown in the air will slow down before it plummets to earth. So will security prices.

Therefore, if we can pinpoint where it has started slowing, we can be ready for the reversal and plan our strategies accordingly. Plotting these indicators is simple on either the software or the charting websites detailed later.

Time frames

All the indicators mentioned so far are based on mathematical operations undertaken on price. These formulae have one or two, sometimes three, variables that affect how the indicators are displayed and the time frame for which they will give the best signals. Again, most software and sites already incorporate as default settings the most popular values for the variables and so, again, you do not need to worry about that either.

So onwards to the issue of how to interpret these indicators so that you can base some strategies around them.

> A ball thrown in the air will slow down before it **plummets** to earth. So will security prices.

Overbought/oversold strategies

All momentum indicators can be used to indicate how
overbought or oversold a security is. Let's stick with oversold. We say a security is oversold when selling has forced
the price down so much that it should bounce back. Overbought is the opposite.

So how do we measure this? Look at Fig 5.1 which plots
the momentum indicator. We would say that the security is
oversold when the momentum indicator is near its extreme
lows relative to its other lows. Now you can get more precise and say that
the security is oversold if the momentum is below a specific figure.

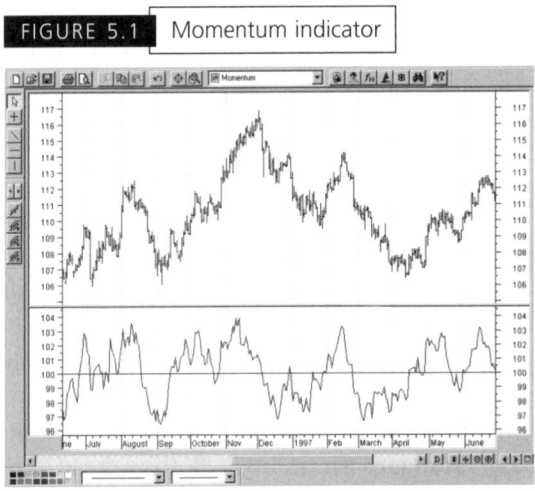

FIGURE 5.1 Momentum indicator

The strategy One way to trade oversold signals is to buy the security
when the momentum indicator moves up from being oversold. Why is it so
simple? Even though it is too simple a strategy in itself, it is a useful piece of
evidence. It is too simple because momentum indicators often go oversold,
go up a little out of oversold territory, and then become oversold again. Also,
we want price to be our ultimate indicator and we therefore wait for price
to move up also – momentum indicators could continue up but price could
continue down.

One way to use momentum indicators in tandem with other evidence of
an impending price move may be if the momentum is oversold and just
starts moving up, the price is in a rectangle formation and just starts to break
out. You will be more confident in the move because you will have two
independent strategies.

Positive divergence

Improving on oversold signals is positive divergence. A positive divergence occurs when the momentum indicator makes a higher low but price does not.

The strategy   One popular strategy is to buy as the momentum and the price rise after the price makes its higher low. This is not foolproof, but it is more reliable than simple oversold signals.

Negative divergence

Figure 5.2 illustrates negative divergence. The momentum indicator makes lower highs while the price does not, or makes even higher highs. As the momentum indicator then starts to fall from its high (overbought territory), the price should also start to fall. Again this is a stronger signal.

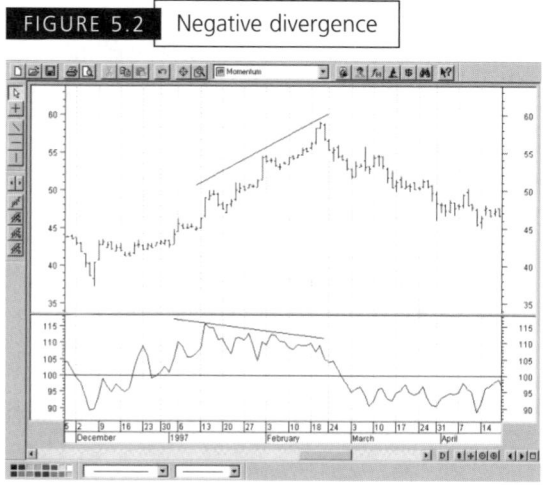

| FIGURE 5.2 | Negative divergence |

The strategy   Go short or exit a long position as the price and momentum start to dip lower. To avoid a bad signal, you could incorporate a rule like 'the momentum has to fall from an oversold position and the price has to break the previous day's low before you exit'.

Definition

Long – a position, opened but not yet closed, with a buy order.

Short – an open position created by a sell order, in the expectation of a price decline and so the opportunity to profit by purchasing the instrument (so closing out) at a lower price.

Reverse divergence

The reverse divergence is a variation on the negative divergence theme. It occurs when the price makes lower highs but the momentum makes higher highs, deeper into oversold territory. The price should fall with the momentum indicator now.

The strategy   You can decide to exit or go short as the momentum and price both move downward from the momentum's oversold position.

Momentum trendlines

Trendlines on momentum indicators can sometimes give clues to possible price movement where no trendline can be drawn on the price chart.

The strategy   The trendline on the momentum can be used in the same way as in a normal price indicator. So, for instance, a resistance level on the momentum indicator may give a good indication that a price reversal is imminent.

| Exercises

1 What is the reasoning behind momentum indicators?

2 What is positive divergence?

3 What is negative divergence?

4 What is reverse divergence?

5 Look at the bar charts and momentum indicators below (a–c). Note I have used MACDs (a type of momentum indicator) here – MACDs will be discussed in more detail later, but just read MACD as momentum for the time being. What do the charts suggest?

Answers

For answers to questions 1–4, look back on the relevant areas of the module.

For question 5, charts (a) and (b) suggest positive divergence in the middle of the time frame, as the price remains near static and the momentum indicator is moving out of oversold territory and the price is then strengthening (draw in some trendlines to help you). Note, however, the price chart could be interpreted as moving on a slight downtrend in both charts (a) and (b) – this would suggest reverse divergence and imply an imminent price collapse. Therefore the significance of analyzing charts a and b is that momentum patterns are not clear-cut and their associated strategies are not fully sound; we must look at trading as an art and use many more indicators as supportive evidence. Remember, no indicator is robust enough to make trade on.

Chart (c) suggests negative divergence as the price chart can clearly be seen to move on an uptrend between February and June and with the momentum indicator moving into oversold – the price then plummets – you should have gone short in June.

(a)

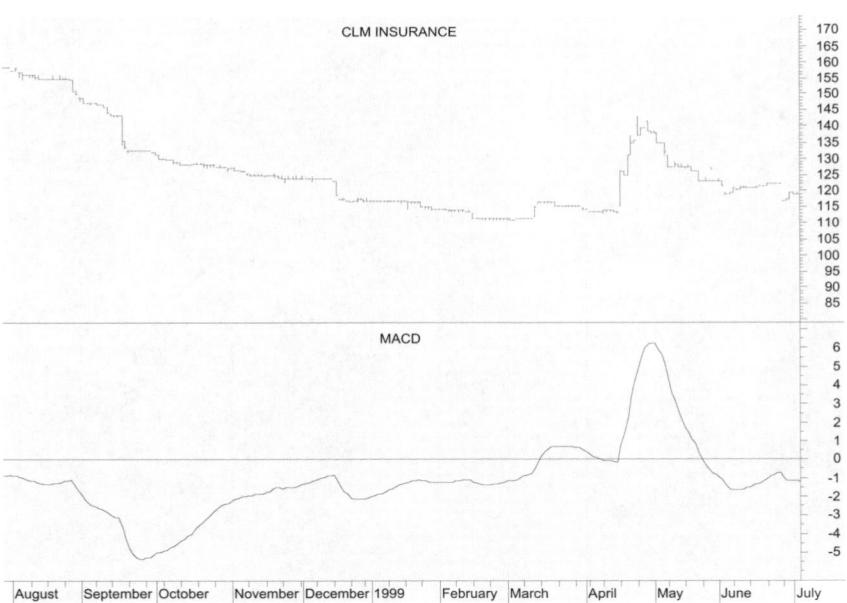

(b)

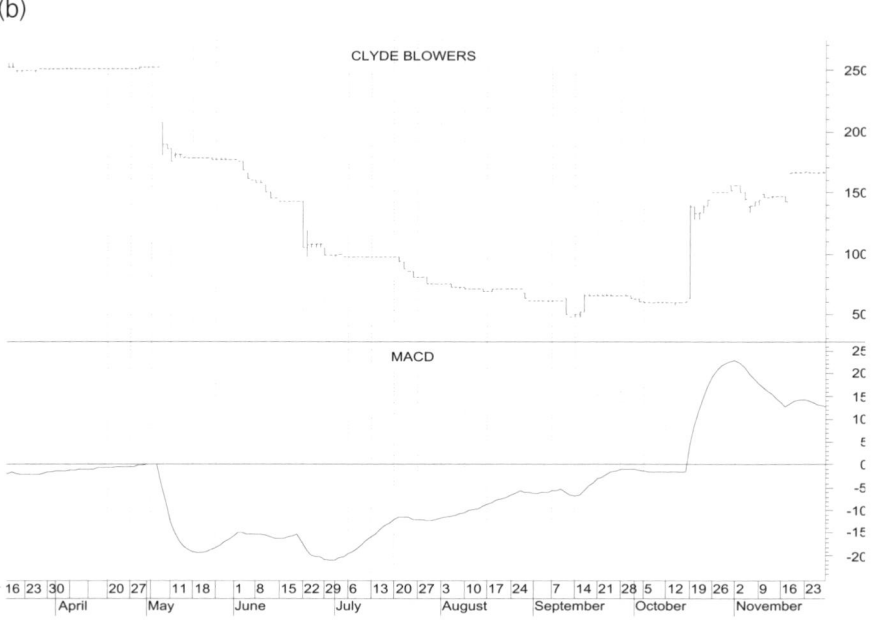

CLYDE BLOWERS

MACD

(c)

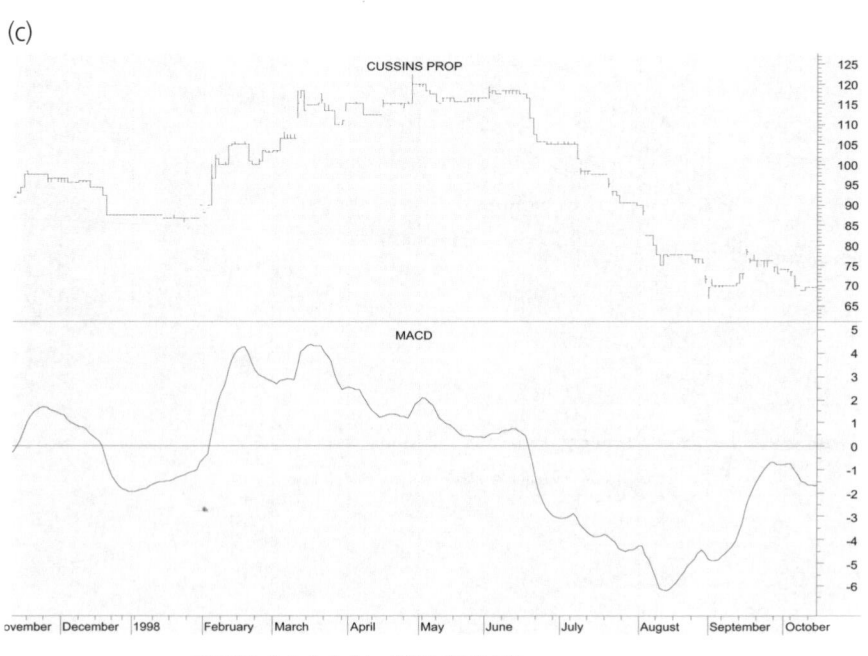

CUSSINS PROP

MACD

Momentum   Stochastic Oscillator   Relative Strength Index

What you have learned

The rationale behind all **momentum indicators** is that a security price moving in a particular direction tends to slow down before reversing direction. So, if we can pinpoint the slowing down of the price, we can try to predict reversals.

The purpose of all momentum indicators is to **indicate how overbought or oversold** a security is. One way to trade oversold signals is to buy the security when the momentum indicator moves up from being oversold. This is too simple since momentum indicators go oversold often, but it can be useful evidence. (NB: **momentum indicators can go up but price could go down**.)

Use momentum in tandem with other evidence, for example if the momentum is oversold and just starts moving up, the price is in a rectangle formation and just starts to break out. You will be more confident in the move because you will have two independent strategies.

A **positive divergence** occurs when the momentum indicator makes a higher low but price does not, and a popular strategy is to buy as the momentum and the price rise after the price makes its higher low. This is not foolproof, but it is more reliable than simple oversold signals.

Negative divergence occurs when the momentum indicator makes lower highs while the price does not, or even higher highs. As the momentum indicator then starts to fall from its high (overbought territory), the price should also start to fall. Again this is a stronger signal.

Reverse divergence occurs when the price makes lower highs but the momentum makes higher highs, deeper into oversold territory. The price should fall with the momentum indicator now. You can exit or go short as the momentum and price both move downwards from the momentum's oversold position.

Trendlines on momentum indicators can sometimes help.

Notes

_____

_____

_____

_____

_____

_____

_____

_____

_____

The final **instalment** – nearly there

N ow for the technical analysis the pros use. There is no reason why even a beginner should not be able to get up to speed with this.

Stochastics

While the stochastic is a momentum indicator and the interpretation and strategies already examined can be applied to it, there are also some features specific to it because of its design. Figure 6.1 shows a stochastic and price chart.

FIGURE 6.1 Stochastic and price chart

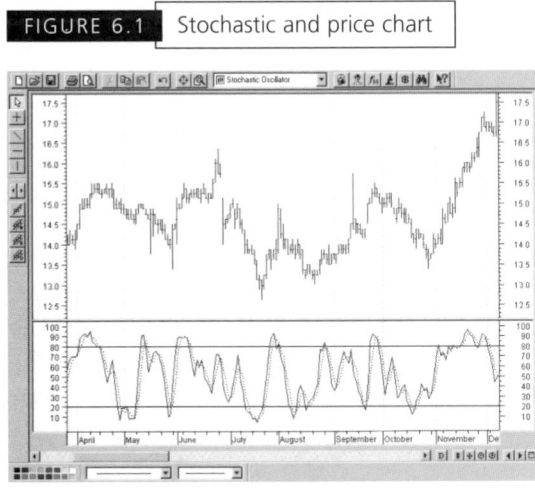

I tend to find the **stochastic** less prone to false signals which see me enter only to have the price not do as expected.

%K crosses %D With the stochastics you can see there is a solid line (%K) and a dotted line (%D). Don't worry about the mathematical formulae that generate them. Stochastic followers will consider a buy signal when the %K crosses up through the %D in an oversold territory. A sell signal is when the %K crosses down through the %D and both are in overbought territory. When combined with the other pattern above, such positive divergences can be quite a powerful indicator.

False divergence This pattern occurs when the %K approaches the %D, looks as if it is going to cross it and be a buy signal, but instead just teases us by kissing it and rebounding off it. This can be a strong signal of a price continuing to fall. Figure 6.2 shows an example.

FIGURE 6.2   False divergence with a bullish pattern

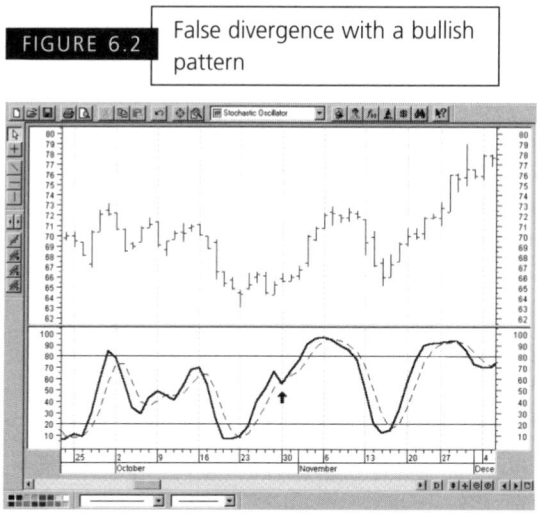

Stochastic compared to the RSI and momentum indicator Relative Strength Indicator (RSI) is a measure of momentum in the price index. The RSI is designed to oscillate between zero and 100. I tend to find the stochastic less prone to false signals which see me enter only to have the price not do as expected (Fig 6.3). The stochastic is not a volatile indicator and gives smoother, easier-to-read lines. I like it.

FIGURE 6.3 False sell signals in stochastic

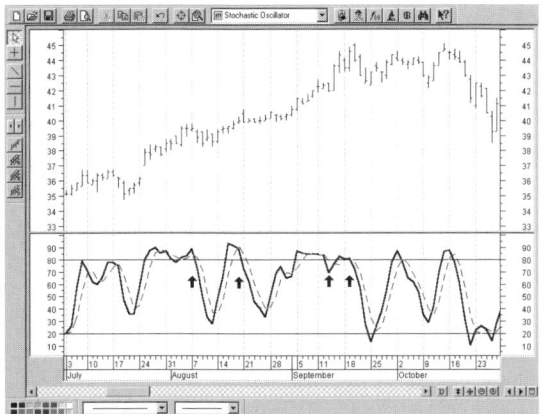

Insight

The weakness of stochastics, momentum and RSI

If we can understand the weakness of certain indicators, we can then, hopefully, avoid traps of poor trades, and compensate for those weaknesses by adding new indicators which do not suffer the same weaknesses.

The above indicators can all waver in the oversold or overbought regions for prolonged periods when a trend is continuing onwards in the same direction. So you could get a false signal to sell prematurely during an uptrend, as the oversold indicator suggests a sell signal (see Fig 6.3).

How do we solve this?

- One way is not to act on a signal until the price confirms it.
- Another way to avoid the premature signal is to observe both the momentum indicator and the MACD.

MACD (or Mac-D if you're hungry)

Not the name of a Scotsman or a burger chain, but standing for the moving average convergence divergence, the MACD by its mathematical construction tends not to suffer from the problems of the other momentum indicators.

> The **MACD** tends to give fewer buy or sell signals than the other momentum indicators.

The strategy The MACD tends to give fewer buy or sell signals than the other momentum indicators. I tend to use it to avoid the problems with the momentum indicators giving premature signals.

Why not use the MACD all the time? Well, I think it works best when combined with other momentum indicators because the MACD is a little slow and tends to give buy signals a bit too late. The best strategy is buying based on other momentum indicators so long as the MACD is not falling sharply and possibly has just started moving sideways (see Fig 6.4).

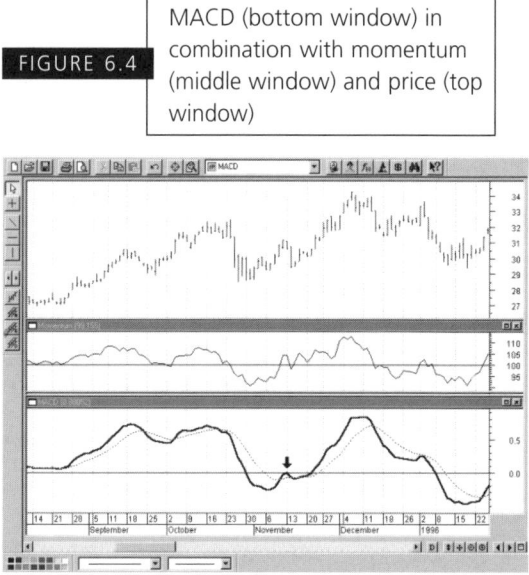

FIGURE 6.4 MACD (bottom window) in combination with momentum (middle window) and price (top window)

A quick round-up of the tools and strategies

We have looked for indicators of relatively high probability that the stock price is going to move one way and not another, and the rest is detail. It is something you should re-read, as one read is unlikely to be enough.

Remember:

- when using TA tools, bear in mind that how stocks move in reality is not an exact science. Therefore TA will not be on the ball all of the time;
- price movement reflects investor psychology;

■ TA should be used to 'time' a purchase or sale – the more you use it, the better your timing will become.

Another little self-assessment exercise …

… to stop you dozing off. This is a long section and by now you probably have a heap of TA tools messing with your normal brain functions. So in order to have a good look at the momentum indicators while you're working through this module, try to analyze QXL.com and BT stock prices. Using the sites, find the momentum, stochastic and MACD charts for the share price over the last year.

■ What is the share price doing at the moment?

■ Is there any positive or negative divergence with the momentum indicators?

■ Does the stochastic and MACD support any buy or sell signals generated by the momentum indicator?

■ Would you buy, sell or just walk away?

■ Try to look at how the price moved earlier on in the year and how the indicators performed in predicting what actually happened later in the year – just play about with the tools. It might be fun, honest.

Exercises

1 What is a stochastic indicator?

2 What is considered a possible buy signal and a possible sell signal in stochastics?

3 What are the characteristics of a false divergence pattern?

4 What is a MACD?

What you have learned

Stochastic is a momentum indicator and the interpretation and strategies already examined can be applied to it. With the **stochastics** there is a solid line (**%K**) and a dotted line (**%D**). Stochastic followers will consider a buy signal when the %K crosses up through the %D in an oversold territory. A sell signal is when the %K crosses down through the %D and both are in overbought ter- ▶

ritory. When combined with the other pattern above, such positive divergences can be quite a powerful indicator.

The **false divergence** pattern occurs when the %K approaches the %D, looks as if it is going to cross it and be a buy signal, but instead just teases us by kissing it and rebounding off it – a strong signal of the price continuing to fall.

The stochastic is not a volatile indicator but it is important not to act on a signal until the price confirms it.

Another way to avoid the premature signal is to observe both the momentum indicator and the **MACD**. The MACD tends to give fewer buy or sell signals than the other momentum indicators. I tend to use it to avoid the problems with the momentum indicators giving premature signals.

The best strategy is buying based on other momentum indicators so long as the MACD is not falling sharply and possibly has just started moving sideways.

Notes

Technical sites and software

There are numerous TA resources on the web. The major choice is between using software and a data download or using an online charting service. The latter, with its inherent limitations, is a better choice for the fundamental analysts or the dabbler in TA. The former is the choice of the serious technical analyst, since TA software is quicker and has more sophisticated tools.

> The major choice is between using **software** and a data download or using an online charting service.

The sites

Which are the best websites for doing technical analysis online if I don't want to buy the software?

Educational sites Below are some good places to learn more about TA.

DecisionPoint
www.decisionpoint.com
A good educational site with lots of free stuff.

Equis
www.equis.com
The specialist software company that does a neat line in online education.

Market Technician Society
www.mta-usa.com
The site for the society of technical analysts.

Trading Tactics
www.tradingtactics.com
Each major indicator is hyperlinked and explained. Quite good.

Charting websites This section contains some of the best online charting sites. Performing TA on an online website is not as easy as on a dedicated software, but it is a good starting point. The best sites tend to be the ones with 'Java' charting, as this makes them more interactive.

Alpha Chart **
www.alphachart.com
A very good site for real-time charting. One of the first internet sites to provide charting and still going strong with pretty good design and ease of use.

Askresearch **
www.askresearch.com
A very good charting site, allowing multiple windows. Could be a little easier to use. It is one of the original internet sites.

Big Charts ***
www.bigcharts.com
Charting is not an add-on feature to this site. Here you can click and compare your favourite stock with other stocks or with a number of different indices. Choose from a variety of chart types. You can also customize your time frame and indicators. The website maintains three data centres to improve reliability.

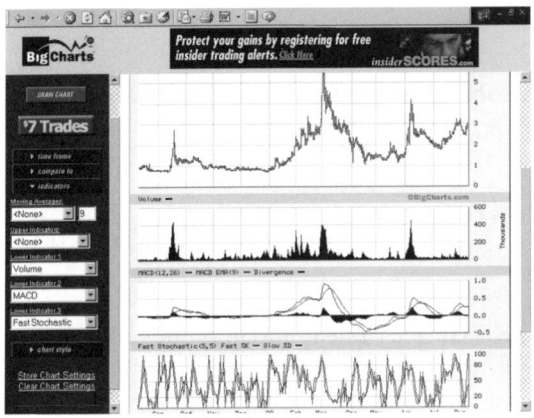

E*Trade UK ***
www.etrade.co.uk
Although this is a brokerage site, a lot of effort has gone into making the charting aspect of it best of breed. Charting sites that open up a new screen on the browser permit multiple screening, plus all the main indicators are covered. The site is not Java-based but design means it is user friendly.

MetaStock Online ★★★

www.equis.com/msonline

There is a learning curve here, but once you master this Java application, you'll be able to call up some of the web's best technical charts. Not for beginners.

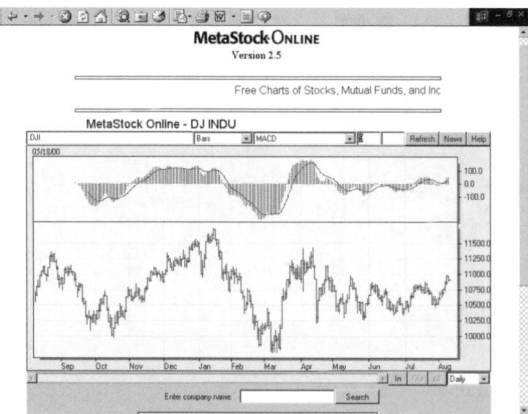

Outer Curve Finance ★★★

www.outercurvefinance.com

This site gives a free and fast read on companies' technical outlook, using 22 indicators.

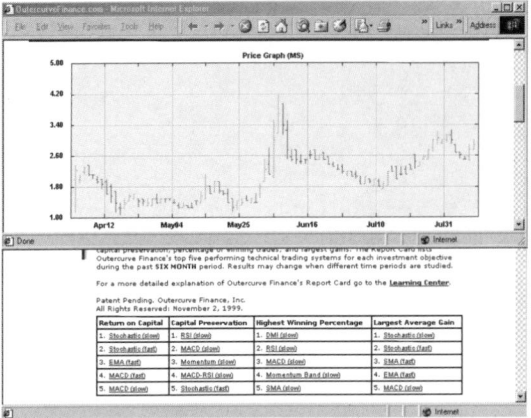

Patagon ***
www.patagon.com

This is a very good super-site for those interested in trading in Latin American stocks. The charting facility is excellent, offering all the tools mentioned above, and the design and layout make the site easy to use.

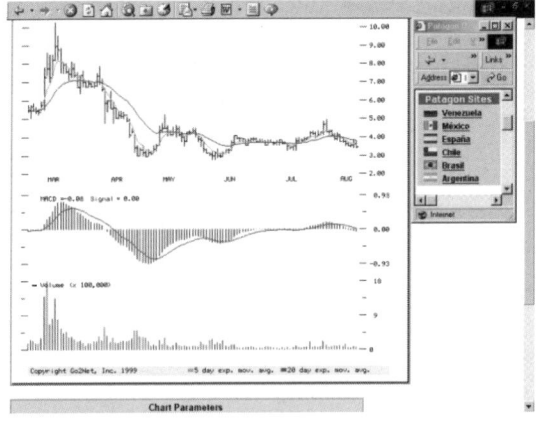

Prophet Charts **
www.prophetfinance.com/charts

This is another Java-based site. Cool feature shows current-day priced data on chart and lets you add room on the right to do prospective charting. It is good quality and some users may prefer its layout.

Wall Street City **
www.wallstreetcity.com
An excellent site, crisp and clear, just the way I like it. Not Java, though.

The software

Numerous companies provide software which can then be used to download quotes from quote vendors and perform technical analysis (see Table 6.1). Few permit you to download their software from their websites, but you can preview and download demos.

TABLE 6.1 Software for downloading quotes from quote vendors

Product	Company	Address	Ranking	Cost
MetaStock 6.5	Equis	www.equis.com	***(recommended)	$349
Omnitrader 3.1	Nirvana	www.nirv.com	***	$395
SuperCharts	Omega	www.omegaresearch.com	**	$200
TeleCharts 2000	Worden Bros	www.worden.com	**	$29
TradeStation	Omega	www.omegaresearch.com	**	$200
Window on Wall Street	Window on Wall Street	www.wallstreet.net	**	$295

Look out for:

- data included – are data included in the cost or do you need to go to a supplier?
- data downloader – do you need extra software to download data?
- data cleaner – does the software come with a feature that scans all downloaded data for errors?
- features – how many indicators and types of charts can be drawn?
- system development – is there a programming language permitting you to produce your own system?

Summary

There are many TA tools to choose from. There are many which are more sophisticated than the popular ones detailed in this module. Check these out

> Do not use technical analysis **blindly** – it is not foolproof and is not going to make you money all the time.

if you are interested through the recommended reading listed at the end of this course book.

You do not have to use all the available technical tools. Experiment to find out which you prefer to use together as part of your overall trading system. And do not use technical analysis blindly – it is not foolproof and is not going to make you money all the time, the market does not work like that. Technical analysis is only a tool; you will have to employ it well.

Exercises

1 Triangle patterns in trendlines generally represent:
- **a** a slow change in opinion about the share price with the price reversing slowly;
- **b** a sharp change in opinion with the price reversing dramatically;
- **c** a strong indication that the price will continue on an uptrend;
- **d** a strong indication that the price will continue on a downtrend.

2 With stochastics the best indication of a buy signal is when:
- **a** the %K (solid line) crosses up through the %D (dotted line) in overbought territory;
- **b** the %K (solid) crosses down through the %D (dotted) in overbought territory;
- **c** the %K (solid) crosses up through the %D (dotted) in oversold territory;
- **d** the %K (solid) crosses down through the %D (dotted) in oversold territory.

3 False divergence occurs when:
- **a** the %K approaches the %D as if there is a sell signal but then rebounds; this is a strong signal of a continued price rise;
- **b** the %K crosses through the %D and then both lines diverge;
- **c** the %K approaches the %D as if there is a buy signal but then rebounds; this is a strong signal of a price fall;
- **d** the %D approaches up towards the %K as if there is a buy signal but then rebounds; this a strong signal of a price fall.

4 Saucer patterns in trendlines generally represent:
- **a** a slow change in opinion about the share price with the price reversing slowly;
- **b** a sharp change in opinion with the price reversing dramatically;
- **c** a strong indication that the price will continue on an uptrend;
- **d** a strong indication that the price will continue on a downtrend.

Look back on the modules if you are not satisfied with your answers.

Answers: 1 b, 2 c, 3 c, 4 a.

Notes

_____

_____

_____

_____

_____

_____

_____

_____

_____

_____

_____

_____

_____

_____

_____

_____

_____

_____

_____

Choosing stocks – **fundamentals**

Key ratios
and statistics

I **n the** next five modules we're going to look at fundamental information about stocks – fundamentals for short. Fundamentals take us under the bonnet of a company: they show us not just how well the stock is performing but how different aspects of the company are bearing up (what the profits are, how much money the company is investing in assets, whether the stock is overpriced, whether company earnings are better or worse than expected). We're in the business of shopping for stock, so these fundamentals are a prime source of ideas.

Several websites offer information about a company's fundamentals in the form of profiles or a 'snapshot report' – a checklist, if you will, of how a company and its stock is performing in various areas. We shall examine these sites and their relative merits later on, but for the present we are going to focus on one as our example: Market Guide (www.marketguide.com).

Each fundamental tells us something different, but on the whole fundamentals are broken up into groups, e.g. fundamentals that tell us about cash flow, fundamentals that tell us about company earnings. These groupings take the form of tables. We will examine each table in turn as it's presented at Market Guide.

What you will learn

- How to find your way around a fundamentals profile.
- What each fundamentals table represents about a company.
- How to read the information they offer and how it was arrived at.

Each fundamental tells us something **different**, but on the whole fundamentals are broken up into groups.

- How to get trading ideas from this information – what to look for and how to act on it.

Module outline

- Getting started
- Price and volume
- Company growth rates

Getting started

To get to the Market Guide snapshot report we have to do five things:

1 Choose a company.

2 Write down the company's name and its ticker symbol.

3 Log on to Market Guide (www.marketguide.com).

4 Type the name or ticker symbol of the company into the box that says 'Enter names or symbols'.

5 Press 'Go'.

And hey presto, we're looking at our company's snapshot report. At the heart of the report is the key ratios and statistics section. This is a huge chart and pretty daunting at first until you realize that it's not one large table, but a collection of smaller fundamentals tables under one roof – hence the title. See Table 7.1. *These are the key data necessary for fundamentals analysis.*

TABLE 7.1 Key ratios and statistics

Price and volume

Recent price $	43.63
52-week high $	47.38
52-week low $	25.00
Average daily volume (mil.)	4.09
Beta	0.97

Share-related items

Market capital (mil.) $	59,029.73
Shares out (mil.)	1,353.12

Dividend information

Yield %	0.46
Annual dividend	0.20
Payout ratio (TTM) %	87.43

Financial strength

Quick ratio (MRQ)	0.39
Current ratio (MRQ)	0.58
LT debt/equity (MRQ)	0.71
Total debt/equity (MRQ)	0.79

Valuation ratios

Price/earnings (TTM)	39.55
Price/sales (TTM)	4.93
Price/book (MRQ)	6.60
Price/cash flow (TTM)	24.61

Per share data

Earnings (TTM) $	1.10
Sales (TTM) $	8.85
Book value (MRQ) $	6.61
Cash (MRQ) $	0.23

Management effectiveness

Return on equity (TTM)	17.34
Return on assets (TTM)	8.30
Return on investment (TTM)	9.45

Profitability

Gross margin (TTM) %	36.16
Operating margin (TTM) %	23.20
Profit margin (TTM) %	12.48

Note: TTM = trailing twelve months
MRQ = most recent quarter

So let's go through the snapshot report and break it down step by step.

Price and volume

This table starts off with the very basics: the latest price of the stock, how much it has sold for in the past year, how much of it has been selling and how stable the price is.

Price and volume

Recent price $	43.63
52-week high $	47.38
52-week low $	25.00
Average daily volume (mil.)	4.09
Beta	0.97

Recent Price: *the most recent price of stock.*

The nature of the stock market means that stock prices are variable – they are always changing. In fact, the whole point of looking at fundamental information is that we're trying to get an idea of what direction the stock price will take in future. Recent price is the latest available price Market Guide has for that stock.

52-week high: *the highest amount the stock has sold for over the past year.*

52-week low: *the least amount the stock has sold for in the past year.*

Ideally we want the recent price to be closer to the 52-week high than it is to the 52-week low. This shows us that the stock price is good in that it is on an uptrend and that the company is in favour with the market.

Average daily volume (ADV): *the average amount of stock traded in a day.*

The size of the average daily volume reflects the liquidity of the stock, i.e. how much demand there is for shares in this company and therefore how easy it is to sell those shares. In turn, this liquidity indicates the 'size' of the company, i.e. how wealthy and powerful it is. The higher the average daily volume, the more liquid the stock and the 'larger' the company. The lower the ADV, the less liquid the stock and the 'smaller' the company.

Of course, it helps if we have some way of gauging ADV. Unofficially you can break it down into four levels, each representing a different class of stock – see Table 7.2.

Ideally we want the recent price to be **closer** to the 52-week high than it is to the 52-week low.

TABLE 7.2	Gauging ADV

Average daily volume	Size of stock (i.e. company)
over 4 Mil	Macro capitalization
1.6 Mil	Large capitalization
1.0 Mil	Small capitalization
less than 1.0 Mil	Micro capitalization

(Note: Market Guide places the average daily volume for stocks at 0.20 mil.)

Why is ADV important?   Well it isn't, but it can be useful to know if a stock has an ADV below .01 mil – you may have difficulty selling your shares. It can also give a clue as to whether your sale or purchase will affect the stock price. Suppose you want to buy or sell a large amount of shares in a company whose ADV is low. A sale that big could set off alarm bells in the market and affect the material price of the stock. In this case you have to spread out your purchase over a longer period of time.

Why does size matter?   In theory, large companies that are well diversi-fied and that have a larger financial collateral should be more stable than smaller ones. Larger companies with overseas branches and multi-market presence may be able to withstand cyclical shocks better, whereas small specialized companies are much more vulnerable. However, the reverse is also true – small growing companies that are more volatile are prone to larg-er upturns in share price changes than large conglomerates. Obviously, when choosing stocks you must have a clear perception of your tolerance to share price volatility. So let's discuss betas.

> **Beta:** the volatility of a company's stock price in relation to the volatility of the stock market.

Beta doesn't measure the volatility of the stock. It measures how volatile it is in the context of the market (which itself is volatile); it measures its relative volatility. This measure-ment is made over a five-year period. Here's how it breaks down:

When choosing stocks you must have a clear perception of your **tolerance** to share price volatility.

■ Beta value – relative value to the market.

> If your **investing** is income orientated you might want to look at companies with a low beta value.

- More than 1.00 – the stock price is more volatile than the market.
- 1.00 – the stock price is no more or less volatile than the market.
- Less than 1.00 – the stock price is less volatile than the market.

So how does this help us? If your investing is income orientated (i.e. family shares, nest egg for your grandchildren) you might want to look at companies with a low beta value. But a higher beta number indicates that this is a growth company, and that's what we should be looking for as equity investors. Some companies have high share prices far above their here and now liquidation values. They aren't doing spectacular business – they may be new and so aren't doing much business at all – but they're perceived to have a healthy future. And that, to the serious investor, is the Holy Grail.

HOT TIP

Check that the recent price is strong; ignore ADV, ignore beta.

Exercises

1 What does a beta greater than 1 signify?
   a The company has a large capitalization.
   b The share price is less volatile than the market.
   c Average daily volume is above average.
   d The share price is more volatile than the market.
   e The 52-week highest value of the share is the same value as the current share price.

2 Larger multi-product companies
   a are more able to absorb cyclical shocks in the economy than smaller companies;
   b tend to have a more volatile share price than smaller companies;
   c will always have a rising share price relative to small companies;
   d have very low ADVs.

3 A daily trading volume of about 1.2 million characterizes a
   a macro cap;
   b large cap;

c small cap;

d micro cap.

4 When looking at the recent price, we want it to be

    a close to the year low because this means it must go up now;

    b sitting nicely in the middle of the range between the year low and year high;

    c close to the year high;

    d above 1000 cents.

Answers

1 d, 2 a, 3 c, 4 c.

What you have learned

Recent price shows us how much the stock costs, while the **52-week high** and **52-week low** figures tell us how good this price is. **Average daily volume** tells us how much buying and selling of the stock has been going on – not that important but it adds context – while **beta** tells us whether the stock price has been steady or volatile compared with the rest of the market (again this isn't essential). From this we can get a rough – rough! – idea of what direction the stock is going in.

So now we've made a start.

Exercises

1 Compare the recent price to the 52-week high and the 52-week low of ten different companies in the telecoms sector. Is the price performing above or below average?

2 Looking at the average daily volume, estimate the size of the company – macro, large, small or micro?

Beta can give a clue to growth but it's like trying to calculate the time by the position of the sun when you're wearing a perfectly good wristwatch. So let's leave the key ratios and statistics section at the moment and look at a more useful guide to growth at Market Guide…

Growth rates

We know a few basics about the stock. We now want to get a few basics about the company; specifically what its sales are, what its shares are actually earning, and what it's having to spend to stay in business. We should now look at growth rates, in Table 7.3.

Sales: the amount of a company's product that has been purchased over a given period.

What's the most obvious way of finding out how well a company is performing? By its sales of course. Table 7.3 charts those sales for the most recent quarter (MRQ), the trailing 12 months (TTM), and the last five years.

TABLE 7.3   Charting a company's sales

| | | Growth rates (%) | | |
	Company	Industry	Sector	S&P 500
Sales (MRQ) vs qtr 1 yr ago	5.03	9.08*	7.92	19.47
Sales (TTM) vs TTM 1 yr ago	4.93	8.88*	8.30	23.89
Sales – 5-yr growth rate	5.52	9.85	13.15	22.43
EPS (MRQ) vs qtr 1 yr ago	3.34	–13.79*	5.39	24.43
EPS (TTM) vs TTM 1 yr ago	3.22	–13.79*	3.84	23.49
EPS – 5-yr growth rate	4.56	12.66	14.13	21.84
Capital spending – 5-yr growth rate	15.30	14.20	15.81	28.30

We're looking for a company whose sales are growing – again, pretty obvious stuff. But don't just glance at these figures and move on. Sometimes a drop in sales may prompt a company to cut costs and actually become more profitable (though admittedly, that company will still have to face the problem of reversing its sales drop).

A company might also have completely changed its product – something the table won't tell you but which may affect future performance. There might also be a sudden rise in sales followed by an equally sudden slump as consumer tastes change or the product receives bad publicity (e.g. British beef).

> Sometimes a drop in sales may **prompt** a company to cut costs and actually become more profitable.

Earnings per share (EPS) growth: how much profit each share earns over a given period (after taxes).

This shows you how much money you, the shareholder, would have earned over the most recent quarter, the last 12 months, and the last five years. The figure is arrived at after taxes and other payments (payments to preferred shareholders, depreciation allowances) have been subtracted so it's a real, money-in-your-hand figure.

As traders, we're looking for a company whose EPS is rising – that means profits for us, but more importantly, an investment that has the potential to go the distance.

Capital spending: money spent on purchasing and/or expanding company assets.

Why does a company decide to spend more money on its assets (e.g. a new computer system, a bigger office)? Because it thinks that if it improves these assets it will either cut production time and costs, produce a better quality of product, or produce more of a given product. Ergo, it will increase sales.

The capital spending entry shows you how much a company is spending on assets relative to the rest of the industry. Sometimes an increase will match that of the industry, indicating, say, that a new technology has become an essential purchase (e.g. the need for every company to have its own web-site). If the amount is less, it could be that the company is saving up for a spending increase in the future (perhaps a major new project is in the pipeline). If the increase is greater than the industry, the company may already be putting that project into action (a car company may have bought new technology to help it produce a new, cutting-edge model). It could also be that, having made that investment, the company won't have to spend so much over the following years, which means that capital spending will drop, thereby freeing up the amount of cash the company has to do business with.

It's also useful to compare capital spending with sales. This will give you an indication as to whether past capital expenditure has resulted in increased sales as planned – an indication in turn that a company will or won't continue to grow.

HOT TIP

Look for rising sales, rising EPS and rising capital spending.

Exercises

1 The EPS represents:
  a the total amount of turnover a company makes divided by the share price;
  b how much profit each share earned over a given period after taxes;
  c how much a company spends on acquiring assets per share over a given period of time.

2 The level of capital spending is defined as:
  a the level of earnings per share;
  b the spending on the creation or acquisition of assets;
  c the value of the company's product being bought;
  d an increase in efficiency.

3 Sales are defined necessarily as:
  a the measure of the quality of the company's product;
  b the total spending on company assets;
  c the total operating profit of a company;
  d the value of company product sold over a given time period.

Answers
1 b, 2 b, 3 d.

What you have learned

Now we've started to learn more about the company. **Sales** tells us how much of its product the company is selling. **Earnings per share growth** shows us how much money the shares are making for the company's shareholders. And **capital spending** shows us how much money the company is spending on improving or expanding its operations. All of these figures relate to company growth: the first two show us how the company has been growing; the third indicates whether this growth will continue.

Exercises

1 Looking at Table 7.3, see if you can tell whether the company's sales have risen or fallen over the past year.
2 Define capital spending.

So we've got a rough idea of whether the shares are performing well and whether the company is doing well as a business. But there's something else we need to know: Are we getting value for money? And how do forecasts for growth look?

Definition

Growth is important but in itself means little if future earnings cannot be sustained. To identify value there must be a consistency of earnings and a correspondingly attractive price to earnings ratio (P/E ratio). Many analysts will classify shares as 'growth' only if they can forecast at least four years of growth.

Forecasts are not always essential however. Where it's not possible to estimate, the growth rate assessment is based on the average growth in historic normalized EPS over the last two years, although where the following year's growth is lower, forecasters go by the most recent year. The growth rate is then reached by apportioning the figure from the current and following financial periods covered by estimates.

Let's go back to the key ratios and statistics section and take a look at the valuation ratios on Table 7.1.

Valuation ratios

It's all very well knowing whether the stocks or the company are performing well, but we still need to know whether we're paying the right price for the shares – are we being overcharged or undercharged? Valuation ratios give us a yardstick by comparing the price of stock to earnings, sales, the book value and cash flow respectively.

Valuation ratios

Price/earnings (TTM)	39.55
Price/sales (TTM)	4.93
Price/book (MRQ)	6.60
Price/cash flow (TTM)	24.61

Price to earnings ratio (PER): the multiple you're paying for each dollar of earnings of the company.

Or in plain English, a figure that tells you whether you're being overcharged for your shares.

How is it worked out? You divide the price of the stock by the annual share earnings. When do we need this? It's always useful, but it can be particularly helpful when comparing companies that are in the same industry – companies which don't seem to be much different to one another. What do

> Rules of thumb can be a **dangerous** thing in trading – they breed complacency.

we look for? Obviously a company with a lower price to earnings ratio rather than a company with a higher P/E ratio.

BUT … as with sales, it's not that simple. A company with a high P/E ratio may be just the ticket because it's going through a period of rapid growth – hence you appear to be being 'overcharged' for your share. Likewise, a company may have a low P/E ratio because it's having difficulties with competition, a cyclical downturn or a lawsuit, i.e. it's being 'forced' to sell cheap. Rules of thumb can be a dangerous thing in trading – they breed complacency – but it tends to be the case that an attractive stock is one whose P/E ratio is lower than its long-term compound earnings per share growth rate.

Price to earnings growth (PEG): the price to earnings ratio of a share divided by the estimated future growth rate in earnings per share.

The price to earnings ratio of a company is not the best way of assessing the investment opportunity offered by a company's shares. It merely tells you the price of the share relative to future earnings. It doesn't tell you whether the price constitutes a bargain investment.

The price to earnings growth (PEG) factor is a more sophisticated method of assessment because it ties in the price to earnings ratio with future earnings growth rate. This gives a much better insight into the true potential value of a company. PEG shows how high the PER could be and whether the shares are a realistic bargain or an expanding bubble.

Example One

Take the situation in the UK in May 1998. The average UK share had an estimated multiple of 15 and was tipped to have increased coming-year earnings growth of 8%. This meant that the estimated PEG was 1.9 (15 divided by 8). A low PEG value reveals that investors are paying a relatively low price for future earnings growth, whereas a high PEG indicates that the shares are relatively more expensive.

A lower than average PEG may at first seem attractive but in fact this means the market is still at a relatively high level. Ideally, and for the best bargains, you should be looking for a PEG below 1. Time has confirmed this again and again. A company growing at 15% pa would be very attractive on a multiple of 15 or less. Correspondingly, a multiple of 20 would also be good value.

Example Two

Here's a hypothetical example to give a clearer idea of how PEG works. A company growing at 25% pa on a forecast PER of 16 would present the attractive PEG of 0.64. When the estimate becomes a reality with an actual 25% growth, the shares gain a double benefit: first the higher earnings figure used by the analysts in coming to their conclusions; and second from a change in status as the market accepts that a higher PER is justified. So the PER might rise from 16 to 20, marking an earnings gain of 25% on top of another 25% increase from the status change. The total gain would therefore be 56.25%. In this way PEG can have a dramatic effect on share price.

PEG can also be used defensively and not simply to maximize share potential. The lower the PEG below average, the less vulnerable. It can be a good idea to regularly assess the PEG average of a growth portfolio to see how defensive it would be in a bearish climate. Of course, PEG shouldn't be seen in isolation as a litmus test of profitability. Nonetheless, as a single financial statement it gives a quick guide to the relative value of growth shares.

Price to sales ratio (PSR): the price of stock relative to the sales generated by the company.

How is it worked out? PSR is calculated by dividing the company's market capitalization by total sales, ex VAT. It's just like dividing share price by sales per share. Again, what use is this? P/E ratios are all very well, but some companies don't have earnings and don't pay dividends either (e.g. some internet companies). In this case you have to look at multiples of sales and the level of growth rate – the higher the better.

Of course, it could be a company that does have earnings but experiences wild swings of peaks and troughs (e.g. a toy manufacturer that specializes in merchandising that ties in with the annual summer Hollywood blockbusters – you know, those toys that sell like hot cakes in July but are in the bargain bins by Christmas). In both cases price to sales ratios offer a more stable indicator of the company's health.

> In both cases price to sales ratios offer a more **stable** indicator of the company's health.

Low PSR is often regarded as the best indication of share value by many analysts. Wall Street figures for 1954–94 reveal that low PSR companies outperformed the market average at the rate of 15.5% against 12.5%. The average rate for a high PSR company was a meagre 4%.

HOT TIPS

- PSR is a great method of analysis when it comes to spotting potential recovery in otherwise slumping companies. In a slump, a company will often have no PER and even no dividend yield against which to value its shares in the traditional way. PSR is a handy means of assessing potential value in the event that the company recovers. And usually it's true to say that the lower the PSR the better.

- Turnover must be profit convertible if it is to add value to a company. Profit margins and their trends should be studied in comparison with PSR figures. Compare companies within their sectors to discover those anomalies that might just indicate a brilliant investment opportunity.

- Debt is an important factor. A company with no debt and low PSR is better placed than one with debt and a high PSR. Debt will need to be repaid and further equity will inevitably have to be issued. The extra shares will then be added to the market capitalization and this will increase the PSR level accordingly.

Price to book value (PBV) ratio: the value of stock compared to the value of the assets it owns (clear of debt).

> PBV is a **theoretical** ratio. It gives an estimate of how much money would be left if a company liquidated its assets and settled all its debts.

PBV is the share price of a company divided by net asset value per share – another way of saying this is to divide capitalization by net assets. This is a theoretical ratio. It gives an estimate of how much money would be left if a company liquidated its assets and settled all its debts.

There is a problem, though, with that word 'theoretical'. For a start, this doesn't apply to a services company because the assets don't generate the revenue. Second, assets are valued on the books at the prices the company paid for them, minus cumulative depreciation/amortization charges, the idea being to reduce their value to zero over the period of use in which they approach obsolescence.

But this 'period of use in which they approach obsolescence' is calculated through a specific accountancy formula. It does not necessarily reflect the 'real world' slide into obsolescence (e.g. the unforeseen invention of a new technology that makes certain assets obsolete 'overnight').

The major problem with relying on PBV is the indeterminacy of the notion of 'value'. Patents and other intangibles such as copyrights and brands can be given a value only when placed up for auction to test the market. Yet another complication is that companies tend to deal with intangibles in a variety of ways. They can write them off entirely or in part and do so over a period or straight away. Some even revalue their intangibles in their balance sheets.

Even tangibles can be difficult to value in abstract. Plant can soon become outdated and/or may be idiosyncratic to the business and therefore of little value on the open market. Book values are notoriously subjective. So approach with caution.

HOT TIP

The upshot is that PBV is not the most reliable comparable to use when assessing competing stocks. But you can adopt a general rule: don't buy a share at a price above its book value.

Price to cash flow (PCF) ratio: the value of stock relative to the level of cash flow.

Cash flow represents the amount of money a company generates in a year. It's not the profits (i.e. revenues after expenses) generated in a year, so you could be pedantic and argue that it's not strictly speaking a measure of how well a business is doing. It's the amount of money generated by the company as it went about its business. In short, how much cash it had to hand to pay its expenses.

PCF is calculated by dividing market capitalization by cash flow. This is often represented by a cash flow statement, as required by the Accounting Standards Board. This statement categorizes different cash streams by economic source. For example, there will be a heading for net cash inflow from operating activities - this figure must be reconciled with operating profits. The other entries will include ups and downs in stocks, debt levels and credit levels.

The term cash flow conjures up images of circulation - the circulation of blood around the body - and that's a

> The term cash flow conjures up images of **circulation** – the circulation of blood around the body.

handy way to think of it: as a sign of the company's health. A company with high cash flow has plenty of money circulating to pay its expenses. A company with low cash flow may have to borrow money or sell assets to meet its costs.

So what are we looking for in a price to cash flow ratio? A high PCF reflects that cash flow is low in comparison with share price. Ideally we are looking for a company with a low ratio relative to that of other companies. But we also want to see a cash flow that is rising from year to year. Be particularly wary of a company with a PCF higher than its price to earnings ratio – be sure to look into why this is so.

However, PCF does not tell you how strong that cash flow is; all it reflects is the relative position of the share price.

HOT TIPS

- Ignore P/B ratios; go for low P/S, P/E and P/CF ratios.
- Low ratios mean good VFM.

Exercises

1 The significance of a very low price-earnings ratio must:
   a be that the share price is a bargain investment as it will go up;
   b be that the share price is overvalued;
   c depend on other specific factors as well but may suggest well-valued shares;
   d mean the company is experiencing poor growth in earnings.

2 PEG shows:
   a the value of the price-earnings ratio divided by the value of the company's assets;
   b the value of the stock relative to earnings;
   c the value of stock relative to the cash (liquid assets) generated by the company;
   d the value of the price-earnings ratio divided by the future growth rate of earnings per share.

3 Ideally we are looking for PEGs of about:
   a less than one;
   b between one and two;
   c greater than the price to earnings ratio;
   d greater than five.

4 The P/CF ratio is:

   a price of the stock relative to the cash revenue minus costs;

   b price of the stock relative to the money generated from selling the company's product;

   c price of the stock relative to the cash generated (liquid assets) of the company;

   d price of the stock relative to the total value of assets clear of debts of the company.

5 The P/S ratio is:

   a price of the share relative to total earnings;

   b price of the share relative to securities;

   c price of the share relative to the total stock of assets;

   d price of the share relative to revenue generated from selling the company's product/s.

Answers

1 c, 2 d, 3 a, 4 c, 5 d.

What you have learned

Valuation ratios tell us whether we're getting value for money for our shares. They work by comparing the share price to the company's earnings, its sales, its book value, and the level of its cash flow.

    Price to earnings ratios compare the share price to company earnings, thereby telling us whether we're paying too much for our shares – given the amount the company is earning – or too little.

    Some companies don't have earnings, so we work out the value for money of our shares by comparing the price to the amount of sales the company is generating. This is the **price to sales ratio**.

    The **price to book ratio** compares the share price to the amount of money the company would have left after it liquidated, sold all its assets and paid all its debts.

    The **price to cash flow ratio** compares the share price to the amount of money the company generates, i.e. the amount it has to pay its bills and running costs.

Exercises

1 What is the difference between price to earnings ratio and price to sales ratio?

2 Compare the price to earnings ratio and price to sales ratio of five companies in the same industry.

3 In what situation would a price to sales ratio tell us more than a price to earnings ratio?

In the last point we touched briefly on cash flow – and with good reason. Cash flow, along with net income, offers a whole new vista of information, one that's too big to cover just in a footnote on valuation ratios. It's a different kind of information too – if the key to valuation ratios is knowing how to compare figures, the key to cash flow is how to read between the lines.

Picking stocks based on 'cash is king'

Cash flow and net income

Cash flow and net income figures examine the amount of money a company generates as it goes about its business. As we discovered in the previous module, cash flow represents the total amount of money a company generates. From this money it has to pay all its bills and expenses. The amount left over represents the company's profits or, to use a more precise term, its net income.

Net income: total revenues minus expenses incurred.

In other words, how much money a company gets to keep after all its bills have been paid.

This sounds like a pretty foolproof way of finding out how well a company is doing. After all, this isn't abstract, on-paper profits. This is a real-world, 'how much money have we really made?' statistic.

But there's a catch: it's an annual figure. And not all capital spending yields results by the end of the financial year. Suppose a manufacturer decides to expand its production base by building a $10 million factory. When we come to calculate the net income for that year, we will be deducting a whopping $10 million builder's bill – not a good year for profits. But the next year the new factory is up and running, and doubling production. Profits that year are high and continue to be high for the rest of the decade. They're high because that $10 million bill has already been accounted in the first year's net income. But on paper it looks like one bad year for profits followed by nine pretty-darned-good ones.

What we need to do is try to match revenue as closely as

What we need to do is try to match **revenue** as closely as possible with the expenses incurred to generate it (link cause and effect).

possible with the expenses incurred to generate it (link cause and effect). In this case, we spread the cost of the factory evenly across the decade, paying it off at $1 million a year. We call this kind of evenly spread expense a depreciation charge (depreciation refers to payments for assets; if it was another, non-asset-related expense, we would call it an amortization charge). By spreading the cost like this, we can now get a more accurate picture of how profitable the company has been.

Cash flow: net income after you've added back non-cash depreciation and amortization charges.

A company's ability to pay its investors dividends is determined by its profitability – officially. But in truth, cash flow is the key factor. Cash flow is the key measure of a company's capacity to fund loan repayments, capital expenditure and dividend payments.

What does 'cash flow' represent? The amount of free cash a company has, say, to pay in dividends or use to make other investments. Well, almost. We've added back the depreciation charges and amortization charges we subtracted, but other costs are subtracted when we calculate net income, such as non-operating cash outlays, capital spending and dividend payments. Ideally we want to put that money back too and come up with a purer form of cash flow ...

Free cash flow: cash flow after you've added back 'non-operating' cash outlays, capital spending and dividend payments.

So now we really have got the amount of money the company's operations generated in a given year – its capacity to generate cash. But what does it tell us?

> Net income shows how much a company has made in **profits**, i.e. after it has paid its expenses.

Net income shows how much a company has made in profits, i.e. after it has paid its expenses. These expenses include production costs, payment of dividends and capital investment. But we don't know how the company paid these expenses. Free cash flow gives us a clue as to whether the company was able to generate enough money to pay for these things internally, or whether it had to sell equity (which will dilute your holdings), borrow money, sell assets, or use its working capital more efficiently.

But who cares? Surely profits are the surest mark of success? Not necessarily. Suppose two rival companies in the same industry announce similar profits. Externally there's not much difference except when we take a look at free cash flow. Here we find that one is able to pay its expenses through the cash it generates as a business (i.e. it has high cash flow) while the other goes to the bank or sells off assets to pay its bills (low cash flow). Both companies are making the same amount of profit, but we might assume that the first one is healthier.

Remember, we aren't looking to make a fast buck, we're looking to invest in a company with potential for growth. Health is the watchword here. Better a modest, steady, growing company than one that achieves profits by burning the candle at both ends.

It helps if we can take a closer look at cash flow, though, to see whether the company is using it wisely. Market Guide does that for us with its statement of cash flow table (Table 8.1).

TABLE 8.1 Market Guide's statement of cash flow table

	Annual			Year to date	
	12 months ending 31/12/98	12 months ending 31/12/99	12 months ending 31/12/00	9 months ending 30/09/00	9 months ending 30/09/01
Net income	1,427,300	1,572,600	1,642,500	1,231,600	1,201,600
Depr'n & amort'n	709,000	742,900	793,800	557,000	648,300
Non-cash items	−4,200	32,900	−110,700	0	0
Other operating CF	164,100	112,600	116,700	−68,400	147,500
Total operating CF	**2,296,200**	**2,461,000**	**2,442,300**	**1,720,200**	**1,997,400**
Capital expenditures	−2,063,700	−2,375,300	−2,111,200	−1,444,000	−1,350,100
Other investing CF	−45,300	−195,000	−106,000	−102,200	−50,100
Total investing CF	**−2,109,000**	**−2,570,300**	**−2,217,200**	**−1,546,200**	**−1,400,200**
Dividend paid	−226,500	−232,000	−247,700	−184,300	−179,500
Sale of stock	−314,500	−599,900	−1,113,100	−568,400	−1,049,100
Net borrowings	445,100	779,300	1,001,500	415,000	390,100
Other financing CF	63,600	157,000	145,700	146,000	204,200
Total financing CF	**−32,300**	**104,400**	**−213,600**	**−193,700**	**−634,300**
Exchange rate effect	0	0	0	0	0
Net change in cash	**154,900**	**−4,900**	**11,500**	**−19,700**	**−37,100**

(Note: units in thousands of US dollars)

Yes I know – what a lot of numbers. But don't panic. The columns across the page speak for themselves: the first three cover successive years; the last two cover successive nine-monthly periods (with a three-month gap between them). The rest of the chart is divided into four sections:

- Operating: this tells us how a company's basic business is performed.
- Investing: this tells us how the company is investing its money for the future (capital expenditure, acquisitions).
- Financing: this shows whether the company is borrowing money or if it issued or repurchased shares to raise cash.
- Net change in cash: this shows the net effects of what a company generates in operations, spends to invest for the future, how it finances itself, and the impact of foreign currency adjustments.

Fairly simple then (although that last section is a bit of a mouthful!). But what are we looking for on this chart? First, we have to do some arithmetic: we want to add net income to depreciation and amortization (both in section one). Then we want to add capital expenditures (section two) to dividend payments (section three). This gives us two figures. We're looking for a company in which the first figure (net income + depreciation and amortization) is greater than the second (capital expenditures + dividend payments).

If a company has this then it has free cash flow. If it has free cash flow, it can finance both its growth and its dividend payments from internal sources. If it doesn't have free cash flow then (at the risk of repeating myself) it may have to sell equity, borrow money, sell assets or use its working capital more efficiently.

The question is, which sources did it use to finance its growth and dividend payments? Here are some clues to look out for:

- positive and growing cash from operations;
- large and growing capital expenditures – a sign that the company is investing in its future;

- repurchase of stock is represented by a negative number – this is a good sign. The sale of stock is represented by a positive number; this is usually a bad sign unless the company is experiencing rapid growth and needs additional equity capital;
- a negative number next to net borrowings is usually another good sign – it shows that a debt has been paid. But taking on a debt can also be a good sign if it is done

by a profitable company with low financial leverage. However, if the company is a highly leveraged one, it could be dangerous.

Net gearing: the ratio between what a company owes and what it owns, the company's borrowings and its capitalization.

Cash may be king, but excessive gearing brings home the value of a constitutional monarchy. Too much cash can be a threat to a company's survival. Highly geared companies are more vulnerable to changes in interest rates and to sudden recessions or industrial action. The reason is simple – they tend to be operating at a maximum level of commitment. As a rule, be wary of any company with net gearing over 50%. Analysts calculate net gearing by comparing the total borrowings less cash as a percentage of shareholders' funds, including intangibles such as brand names and goodwill. Remember that cash figures don't include marketable securities because these can be difficult to convert into cash at short notice.

Do consider gearing in the context of the company's business plans. If interest rates are low, a well-managed company can make good use of its debts.

Exercises

1 If a company has free cash flow it can finance growth from internal sources, otherwise it has to sell equity, sell assets or borrow. A company has free cash flow, properly defined if:
   a capital expenditure is less than net income + dividend payments + depreciation + amortization;
   b net income is greater than capital expenditure + dividend payments + depreciation + amortization;
   c capital expenditure + dividend payments is less than net income + depreciation + amortization;
   d net income + dividend payments is greater than capital expenditure + depreciation + amortization.

Too much cash can be a threat to a company's **survival**.

2 Analysts calculate net gearing by comparing the total borrowings less cash as a percentage of shareholders' funds, including intangibles such as brand names and goodwill. Which one of the following is important when considering net gearing?

   a Interest rates.
   b New projects by the firm.
   c Management expertise.
   d How much borrowing the company has undertaken.
   e All the above.

3 Under the 'sale of stock', the repurchasing of stock is measured by a:

   a negative number and is a bad sign;
   b positive number and is a bad sign;
   c negative number and is a good sign;
   d positive number and is a bad sign.

Answers
1 c, 2 e, 3 c.

What you have learned

Net income represents the profits a company has left after it has paid all its expenses. Among those expenses we include depreciation and amortization charges so that profits always appear relative to the drop in income incurred to achieve them.

If we add back the non-cash depreciation charges and amortization charges we just subtracted, we get **cash flow**. And if we add back 'non-operating' cash outlays, capital spending and dividend payments we get **free cash flow** – the amount of money a company generates in a year.

Free cash flow shows us how much money a company has to pay its expenses, which in turn shows us its health and potential for growth. We're looking for a company with high cash flow relative to its rivals, and a cash flow that is rising steadily year by year.

All in all we're using cash flow to tell us not how well a company performed but how well it will perform; whether it has the potential for the kind of growth we're looking for.

The **net gearing** of a company may indicate a number of things, but as a rule you should find out why a company is highly geared before you invest, particularly if interest rates are high, because servicing the debt could cause considerable strain.

Exercises

1 Define cash flow.
2 What is the difference between cash flow and net income?
3 What does the level of cash flow indicate about the way a company might be paying its costs?

Share-related items

Share-related items (see Table 7.1) give us a little more background on the shares themselves. They tell us how many shares were issued, how many are owned by the company, its employees and owners, how many are realistically available for trading, and what the status of the company is in the market.

Share-related items

Market capital (mil.) $	59,029.73
Shares out (mil.)	1,353.12
Float (mil.)	1,339.60

To make sense of this table, we're going to start with the second entry (the reason for this will soon become apparent).

Shares outstanding: the number of shares issued by a company less the amount the company bought back.

When a company issues shares, it often buys some back for itself. Shares outstanding is the amount of shares left after this deduction has been made – the amount of shares that aren't held by the company.

Float: The number of shares held by everybody other than officers, directors and 5% or more owners.

If you take shares outstanding and deduct the shares held by the company's officers, directors and owners, you get the float. The thing to remember here is that if the float is small, there's probably little trading volume so anyone looking to buy or sell stock could impact the price significantly (as in the case of a company with a low ADV).

Market capitalization: the current price of a stock multiplied by the number of shares outstanding.

> When a company issues shares, it often buys some back for **itself**.

Unsurprisingly, large cap companies tend to represent a safer, more **conservative** investment.

Basically, this is the value that investors have assigned to the company by the act of purchasing stock in that company. It's often referred to as the 'size' of the stock because it refers to the status of the company. The larger the market capitalization, the wealthier and more powerful the company, i.e. the 'larger' the company.

Like the average daily volume of stocks, market capitalization is divided into different levels (see Table 8.2). The larger the market cap, the higher the liquidity and the lower the risk.

TABLE 8.2	Levels of market capitalization

Level	Size of capitalization
Large cap	greater than $5 billion
Mid cap	between $1 billion and $5 billion
Small cap	between $300 million and $1 billion
Micro cap	below $300 million

Unsurprisingly, large cap companies tend to represent a safer, more conservative investment. The smaller cap ones are therefore riskier investments. But smaller cap companies tend to outperform their larger counterparts over a given period of time. Since both types offer benefits, a shrewd trader will go for a mixture of micro and large cap companies.

HOT TIP

Buy micro and large cap companies to balance potential losses. Tread carefully if the float is small.

Exercises

1 The float is:
   a the number of shares issued by a company less the amount the company bought back;
   b the number of shares held by everybody other than officers, directors and 5% or more owners;

c the current price of a stock multiplied by the amount of shares outstanding;

d how much money a company has to pay its expenses.

2 A company with a market cap of $700 million can be regarded as:
  a a large cap;
  b a mid cap;
  c a small cap;
  d a micro cap.

3 The larger the capitalization:
  a the higher the liquidity and the higher the risk;
  b the lower the liquidity and the lower the risk;
  c the lower the liquidity and the higher the risk;
  d the higher the liquidity and the lower the risk.

4 The shares outstanding are:
  a the number of shares issued by a company less the amount the company bought back;
  b the number of shares held by everybody other than officers, directors and 5% or more owners;
  c the current price of a stock multiplied by the amount of shares outstanding;
  d how much money a company has to pay its expenses.

Answers
1 b, 2 c, 3 d, 4 a.

What you have learned

Shares outstanding shows us the amount of shares that aren't held by the company – the amount left to the rest of us to trade with.

  Float is the amount of shares on the market that aren't owned either by company directors, company officers or company owners (those who own 5% or more of the company).

  Market capitalization represents the price of the stock multiplied by the amount of shares outstanding. It shows us the size of the stock, i.e. the wealth and power of the company, its liquidity, and its risk. The larger the market cap, the higher the liquidity and the lower the risk. The smaller the market cap, the lower the liquidity and the higher the risk.

Exercises

1 In what way does shares outstanding differ from the total amount of shares issued by a company?

2 What kind of shareholders does float represent, i.e. what are these shareholders not?

3 Do larger companies have higher or lower liquidity?

4 What is the implication of this for the stock?

Picking stocks based on dividends, management **effectiveness** and **profitability**

Dividend information

When you purchase stock, you are essentially giving money to a company so that it can operate. Your share certificate acts as a receipt for this. As the company goes about its business, this money will help it to generate more money, so that in a sense your money is earning interest. That 'interest' is then paid back to you, the shareholder, on an annual basis. This is your dividend.

Dividend information

Yield %	0.46
Annual dividend	0.20
Payout ratio (TTM) %	87.43

Annual dividend: the amount of dividends you would expect to receive if you held the stock for a year and there was no change in the company's payment.

In loose terms, this means the amount the company would pay you, the shareholder, per year (the figure is derived from the current quarterly dividend payment projected forward for four quarters). What are we looking for? The truth is ambiguous. The knee-jerk response would be 'a high dividend'. But we're growth investors, and generally a growth company will reinvest its dividend rather than pay it out to investors. And since growth companies are what we're looking for, a lower annual dividend may be the most tempting.

Yield: the annual dividend rate expressed as a percentage of the price of the stock.

> When you purchase stock, you are essentially giving money to a company so that it can **operate**.

> The more favoured companies are subject to the whims of mass-market attention – **whims** that are essentially over-reactions to good or bad news.

This tells you how much income you can expect per $ or £ investment in this stock, which means you can compare it with similar stock. What are we looking for – high yield or low yield? As with annual dividend, it depends on what kind of investor you are. We happen to be looking for growth companies, so that may suggest low-yield companies.

However, the truth can often be argued both ways.

- High-yield portfolios often outperform the market on a total return basis. This is because they are often less favoured companies. The more favoured companies are subject to the whims of mass-market attention – whims that are essentially over-reactions to good or bad news. This drives up the prices of growth shares to exorbitant level. The less popular shares are left at lower, more consistent and arguably fairer prices.

- Another reason why high-yielding shares can perform well is that dividends have, historically, accounted for 40–50% of the total return on the Dow. This means a higher annual payout represents a considerable cumulative benefit to investors. But the benefits can be seen in the UK as well. The BZW 1994 Equity-Gilt study revealed that dividends had amounted to 42% of the total return on equities over the previous 75 years. And dividend yield is a more reliable investment return than, say, share growth which is based on potentially highly fluctuating earnings figures.

- High dividend-yielding stocks are also a good bet because they provide a large dividend income in addition to the potential capital gain. This cash could be reinvested.

There are compelling reasons for buying shares in high-yielding companies. But as with any investment, things can go down as well as up. When interest rates fall, investors look to preserve their income streams and, correspondingly, high dividend-yielding companies do well. But it's a bad idea to seek out high-yield shares just because they seem high yield. High yield may just reflect market fears that the dividend rate may be cut. To be on the safe side, it's best to avoid companies whose dividends are very poorly covered or for any other reason seem likely to be reduced.

Here are some key things to bear in mind when weighing up the risk of dividend cut.

1 Poorly covered dividends are more likely to be cut.

2 Cash flow per share is a better forecast of dividend capacity than profits.

3 Watch out for heavy borrowing companies – even if profitable they may not be able to pay dividends.

Payout ratio: the percentage of company earnings given to shareholders (as cash dividends) over the past 12 months.

Again, growth is our criterion so we're looking for a company that reinvests rather than pays out its dividend. And that means a low payout ratio. That may seem like a funny approach given that we're potential shareholders – why go for a company that pays us less? Why, because we're equity traders. We look at the big picture. We look to the future. We look at growth.

Exercises

1 The dividend yield is:
  a the amount of dividends you would expect to receive if you held the stock for a year and there was no change in the company's payment;
  b the amount of dividends you would expect to receive if you held the stock for a year expressed as a percentage of the price of the stock;
  c the percentage of company earnings given to shareholders (as cash dividends) over the past year;
  d none of the above.

2 The payout ratio is:
  a the amount of dividends you would expect to receive if you held the stock for a year and there was no change in the company's payment;
  b the amount of dividends you would expect to receive if

We look at the big picture. We look to the future. We look at **growth**.

you held the stock for a year expressed as a percentage of the price of the stock;

c the percentage of company earnings given to shareholders (as cash dividends) over the past year;

d none of the above.

3 Which of the following is a good reason for going to low dividend-yield shares?

a Low yield suggests that the company is undervalued as the price is very low relative to the dividend payout.

b Historically low-yield shares have outperformed the market on a total return basis.

c Low yield suggests the company is reinvesting profit in the company.

d Low-yield shares have a higher annual payout and this suggests a higher cumulative benefit.

Answers
1 b, 2 c, 3 c.

What you have learned

Annual dividend is an estimate of how much money a company will pay us, per year, for every share we hold. **Yield** tells us how big that dividend is compared with the price of the stock, i.e. how profitable it is for us.

Payout ratio shows us how much of its earnings the company is giving us and how much it's keeping to reinvest in its business. The more it keeps for investment, the greater the possibility of future growth.

| Exercises

1 Define dividend.

2 What is the difference between annual dividend and yield?

3 Why might a company keep most of its earnings instead of passing them on to the shareholder?

4 And why might this be a good sign?

By now you should be finding these tables easier to read. The fog is lifting. This is another simple table, as is the one that follows. But don't race through it because it seems easier to understand – the information it contains is no less important for that.

Management effectiveness

This table shows not so much how the company is performing as how the people who run it are performing – the management.

Management effectiveness

Return on equity (TTM) %	17.34
Return on assets (TTM) %	8.30
Return on investment (TTM) %	9.45

Return on equity: how well a company has managed the equity (capital) given to it by the shareholders.

Equity is that portion of the company's assets that would be distributed to the shareholders if the company were liquidated and all its assets were sold at values reflected on its balance sheets. In short, what the company itself – and therefore the shareholders – own (as opposed to, say, money loaned from a bank).

Return on investment: how well a company has managed the money provided by the company's owners (equity) and long-term creditors.

This sounds not unlike return on equity, but there is a difference – return on equity relates to capital provided by shareholders. The problem with this figure is that the company has other sources of money at its disposal too, so this doesn't give a complete picture of how the management is handling funds.

Return on assets: how well a company is using everything at its disposal (equity, long-term credit and temporary capital) to produce profits.

This is much better. It's the best measure of how a company is using the funds provided to it, for obvious reasons – it includes everything the management have at their fingertips. For instance, as well as shareholder capital and long-term money granted to it, a company has access to shorter-term loans of capital, e.g. an internet company may borrow money to buy some routers for its website – money provided on a short-term (i.e. less than one year) basis.

Return on capital employed (ROCE): the percentage of pre-tax operating profit relative to capital invested ('employed') in that year.

> It's the best **measure** of how a company is using the funds provided to it, for obvious reasons – it includes everything the management have at their fingertips.

The higher the ROCE, the greater the company's competitive advantage. Companies with a high ROCE provide the market with something that can command a high return – with correspondingly above-average margins.

It's best to compare ROCE levels of different companies within the same sector rather than looking to the whole market. But don't assume that a high ROCE necessarily means best. A high ROCE figure can mean that a company's products will face excessive competition and find it difficult to sustain previous levels. But of course a low ROCE suggests the company may be in danger of making a loss.

A company's ROCE should always be compared with the current cost of borrowing.

It's also worth bearing in mind that low ROCE companies often face changes in management control and this often leads to a rights issue. Any new management will be tested by its ability to lift the ROCE percentage. A high ROCE has the attraction of meaning that a higher than average amount of profit can be reinvested for the benefit of shareholders. This reinvested money is then 'employed' again at an even higher rate of ROCE and this helps to boost continued EPS growth. This is why, when you look at consistently good growth stocks, they usually share a high ROCE.

HOT TIP

Look at high return on assets – this means management knows how to use your cash wisely.

| Exercises

1 The return on investment can be defined as:
  a how well a company has managed the money provided by the company's owners (equity) and long-term creditors;
  b how well a company has managed the equity (capital) given to it by the shareholders;
  c percentage of pre-tax operating profit relative to capital invested ('employed') in that year;
  d how well a company is using everything at its disposal (equity, long-term credit and temporary capital) to produce profits.

2 The return on assets can be defined as:
  a how well a company has managed the money provided by the company's owners (equity) and long-term creditors;

b how well a company has managed the equity (capital) given to it by the shareholders;

c how well a company is using everything at its disposal (equity, long-term credit and temporary capital) to produce profits;

d percentage of pre-tax operating profit relative to capital invested ('employed') in that year.

Answers

1 a, 2 c.

What you have learned

Management effectiveness tells us how well a company is using the money at its disposal – how profitable it has been with it. The table reveals this by breaking down the money into different types and seeing how each one is being used.

Return on equity shows how well the company has been using the money given to it by shareholders.

Return on investment shows how well the company has used the money given to it by its owners and long-term creditors.

Return on assets shows how well the company has been using all the money given to it by shareholders, owners and long-term creditors as well as other kinds of money not included in the first two figures, such as short-term loans.

Return on capital employed shows the percentage of pre-tax operating profit relative to capital invested ('employed') in that year. It's best to compare ROCE levels of different companies within the same sector rather than looking to the whole market. But don't assume that a high ROCE necessarily means best.

Exercises

1 What is the difference between return on equity and return on investment?

2 Which of the four figures is the most comprehensive, and why? (Return on equity, return on investment, return on assets and return on capital employed.)

Profitability

The ratios on this table show you how much of the company's revenue is being turned into profit. This sounds simple: profit equals revenue minus costs, right? But there are different kinds of costs, and these ratios follow the effects on revenue as each of these costs is subtracted from it to reach that final profit figure.

Profitability

Gross margin (TTM) %	36.16
Operating margin (TTM) %	23.20
Net margin (TTM) %	12.48

Gross margin: the percentage of each revenue dollar remaining after deducting the *direct* costs that went into producing the good or services involved.

Revenue is the amount of money a company gets for selling its goods and/or services. Gross profit is the amount of revenue it has left after it has paid the *direct* costs it incurred to produce those goods and services. Gross margin, then, is a percentage figure that shows the difference between gross profit and revenue. Let's say that for every dollar of revenue a company earns it spends 90 cents paying its direct costs. That leaves 10 cents in the dollar. So its gross margin is 10%.

Operating margin: the percentage of each revenue dollar remaining after deducting the direct and *indirect* costs that went into producing the good or services involved.

We subtract the direct costs from revenue to get gross profit. We then subtract the indirect costs from gross profit to get operating profit. Indirect costs are what we tend to call 'overheads': costs incurred in running the business even though they have no direct link to the product and/or service produced.

So, let's go back to our company. Let's say for every dollar earned it spends 90 cents paying its direct costs and another 5 cents paying its indirect costs. That leaves 5 cents in the dollar. That means its operating margin is 5%. Put another way, operating margin is the ratio of operating profit to turnover. Operating profit is a company's trading profit before tax and interest. So, a company with an operating profit of $20 million and a turnover of $200 million has an operating margin of 10%. In most cases, the higher

> **Revenue** is the amount of money a company gets for selling its goods and/or services.

the margin the better. Analysts often calculate margins by omitting capital profits and losses and any other exceptional matters from the operating profit equation.

Net margin: the percentage of each revenue dollar remaining after deducting *all* the costs that went into producing the good or services involved.

By 'all the costs' we mean that there are other costs besides indirect costs, for example income taxes and corporate debt. This time we're going to subtract these cost as well as direct and indirect costs from revenue. We then convert the amount we have left in cents (our net profit) to a percentage and we have our net margin.

But what are we looking for in these figures? Simple: high margins. High margins indicate a good profit and, importantly, a healthy growing business. But a word to the wise …

Keep an eye on tax rates too when you're sizing profitability. Tax rates can affect a company's profits, which is important since not all companies in the same industry will be paying the same tax rates. For instance, a company may have losses carried forward or other temporary issues, which means it will be paying lower tax which in turn means that the taxman isn't cutting so deeply into profits. However, these will vanish in the future so you may well expect an eventual drop in profits. So check whether or not your company is paying a low tax rate.

Note: gross profit tells us how much money we'd have left from every dollar; gross margin tells us what percentage we'd have left of every dollar. Since there are 100 cents in a dollar, and since per cent means 'in every hundred' (Oxford English Dictionary), the figures for gross profits and gross margin are exactly the same (the same goes for operating profit/operating margin, and net profit/net margin).

Margins are key to understanding the financial structure of a company you plan to invest in. They tie up price to sales ratios with price to earnings ratios. This enables you to see the wood from the trees, for example to place less emphasis on increased sales figures where margins are falling. Net profit increases will emerge only when margins are maintained or widened.

> Analysts often calculate margins by **omitting** capital profits and losses and any other exceptional matters from the operating profit equation.

HOT TIP

Go for high margins (high profits), but check that this figure isn't artificially high because the company is paying lower taxes.

Margins are key to understanding the financial structure of a company you plan to invest in.

Nevertheless, it's important to bear in mind one or two notes of caution when relying too heavily on margins.

1 The higher the margin, the greater the likelihood of competition. The best high-margin companies are those with unique products. This may take the form of a desirable brand and/or a tightly worded patent.

2 But low margins make for a riskier investment. The slightest sales dip can mean disaster. On the upside, however, even a small increase in sales can mean a dramatic increase in margin.

3 It can be difficult for a company used to low margins to break the trend once the market gets used to it. For this reason you should be sceptical about any claims for massive growth from such companies.

4 A major leap in margins can often be put down to a new product or service. Make sure you are abreast of the latest developments by scouring the press for snippets of information such as that found in company press releases.

5 The same applies for changes in management structure as for new products – check the press for the latest news.

Exercises

1 Gross margin is:
   a the percentage of each revenue dollar remaining after deducting the *direct* costs that went into producing the good or services involved;
   b the percentage of each revenue dollar remaining after deducting *all* the costs that went into producing the good or services involved;
   c the percentage of each revenue dollar remaining after deducting the direct and *indirect* costs that went into producing the good or services involved;
   d none of the above.

2 Net margin is:
   a the percentage of each revenue dollar remaining after deducting the *direct* costs that went into producing the good or services involved;
   b the percentage of each revenue dollar remaining after deducting *all* the costs that went into producing the good or services involved;
   c the percentage of each revenue dollar remaining after deducting the direct and *indirect* costs that went into producing the good or services involved;
   d none of the above.

3 Which of the following is false?

   a High margins can lead to increased competition.

   b Lower margins can lead to reduced risk.

   c Lower margins can be the result of higher taxes.

   d Lower margins can be the result of changes in management.

Answers

1 a, 2 b, 3 b.

What you have learned

Revenue is the amount of money a company gets for selling its product. To discover how much profit it has made, it has to first deduct its direct costs. This leaves its **gross profit** – the amount left from every dollar earned.

The company then deducts its indirect costs. This leaves its **operating profit**.

It then deducts all its remaining costs, for instance its income taxes and corporate debt. This leaves its **net profits** – the final amount left from every dollar earning.

Gross margin, **operating margin** and **net margin** show each of these figures as a percentage. Through them we get an idea not just of how profitable a company has been, but in what ways it has been profitable.

Exercises

1 What is the difference between gross profit and gross margin?

2 What is the difference between gross margin and operating margin?

3 Which indicates that the company is in better health: a high margin or a low margin?

Well, that's the mammoth key ratios and statistics section dealt with. As you've probably noticed, we started by looking at sources of information that gave us just the basic facts, like what the recent stock price is or how much stock is traded in a day (average daily volume). But since then we've moved on to sources of information that are more subtle – sources, in fact, that seem to tell us about stock in an indirect way, such what money a company is using to pay its bills (cash flow) or how effectively its managers are using the money given to them by shareholders (return on equity).

We're slowly **building** up a company picture in much the same way that an artist actually paints a picture.

We're slowly building up a company picture in much the same way that an artist actually paints a picture, starting with a basic outline, filling in the background colours, then finally adding the small details. The next module continues this trend towards a fuller and more detailed picture.

Picking stocks based on what **the experts** think

Recommendations

You know how there's always a scene in a detective or spy movie where the hero announces, 'Someone's been here before us!'? Well, in our case another team has been following the same trail as us. They've been sizing up the same clues and they've come to their own conclusions. They're called professional securities analysts, and they've put their conclusions on the recommendation table (Table 10.1).

The vertical columns cover consecutive time periods (working backwards from the present); each horizontal stratum represents different recommendations on the stock: strong buy, buy, hold, underperform, sell. These terms are universally held – sometimes you might see 'neutral' for 'hold', but you can always assume that the advisers in question are ranking stock in a five-step, descending sequence.

TABLE 10.1 Analysts' recommendations

	As of 5/5/2002	As of 4 weeks ago
1 Strong buy	6	5
2 Buy	8	7
3 Hold	7	7
4 Underperform	0	0
5 Sell	0	0
Mean rating	2.0	2.1

> This is the experts' view, but don't treat it as gospel – use it as a **barometer** of opinion with which to compare your own findings.

What use is this table to us? This is the experts' view, but don't treat it as gospel – use it as a barometer of opinion with which to compare your own findings. Note also that advisers rarely give underperform or sell recommendations; they cluster near the top.

The last line of the table is mean rating – the weighted average of all the individual ratings. The best score is 1.0 (that's if every analyst says 'strong buy'); the worst would be 5.0. In reality, given the top-range bias, most averages fall between 1.0 and 3.0. So what are we looking for? Hopefully companies with low number scores, particularly in relation to other companies – it's in making the latter comparison that mean rating proves really useful.

Have a look across the columns to see whether the stock is getting higher ratings or improving its mean rating score. A gradual increase in a lesser known company might show that it has caught Wall Street's attention. On the other hand, some traders like to hunt for stocks that have fallen out of favour, so they're looking for a deteriorating mean rating. A stock that was deteriorating but that has levelled out in its mean rating could be due for a revival in fortune.

Bear in mind that even though these are opinions, and may be wrong, the fact that they are offered by experts means that they do influence investors – an element of self-fulfilling prophecy.

HOT TIP

Listen to what the analysts say, but don't jump just because they say so.

What you have learned

Recommendations tables show us what professional securities analysts think we should do with stock. These recommendations are shown through five ratings – strong buy, buy, hold, underperform and sell – which in turn are shown for a given period so that we can see whether they have been revised.

Mean rating gives the average of all the ratings, ranging from 1.0 to 5.0. The lower the rating, the better the score, i.e. the more strongly you are advised to buy.

Exercises

1 Whose advice does the recommendations table show?
2 The figures on this particular table indicate that we should purchase stock. Has this urging grown stronger or weaker over the past month?
3 Which is better: a higher mean rating or a lower one?

Performance

If recommendations tell you what the experts think, performance shows you how the stock is competing relative to the major indices and the industry it is in – a look at the bigger picture.

Performance often appears on sites in the form of graphs so you can get an instant feel for a company, but Market Guide also offers a price performance table, as seen in Table 10.2.

The table shows the stock's percentage price movements over each of five measurement periods: 4 weeks, 13 weeks, 26 weeks, 52 weeks and the year to date. Across the page are four columns. Let's examine each one in turn.

TABLE 10.2 Price performance

Period	Actual (%)	S&P 500 (%)
4-week	5.2	−1.1
13-week	8	7
26-week	7	7
52-week	0	0
YTD	0	0

(Note: rank is a percentile that ranges from 0 to 99, with 99 = best)

- Actual (%): this shows the stock's overall performance, so large percentage changes are going to catch your eye.
- S&P 500 (%): this is a comparison of the stock's price activity with that of the S&P 500 index. The percentage shows the degree to which the stock's performance differed from that of the index.

> Performance often appears on sites in the form of **graphs** so you can get an instant feel for a company.

- Rank in industry: this shows how the stock performed relative to the average performance for a company in the same industry. The number shows what percentage of companies in the same industry the stock outperformed (so if it says 71, as it does here, our company outperformed 71% of its rivals). Sometimes this is referred to as the 'percentile' rank.
- Industry rank: this reveals how the industry the company is in performed compared with the other industries covered at Market Guide. The figure shows what percentage of the industries it outperformed; in this case 64%.

How does this table help us? Recommendations tell us what the experts think – it's opinion based – but performance gives us a simple 'just the facts' look at how well a company is competing. Since it shows the company in the context of the market and the industry, it doesn't really tell us much about its internal workings in the way that valuation ratios, net income or cash flow do. It's really there to place the company in a wider context.

What are we looking for? Again, you've guessed it: growth. That means we're looking for companies that lead the market in terms of performance.

HOT TIP

Look for growth in all four categories if possible.

Exercises

1 Which one of the following is the industry rank?

  a This shows the stock's overall performance, so large percentage changes are going to catch your eye. This is a comparison of the stock's price activity with that of the S&P 500 index.

  b The percentage shows the degree to which the stock's performance differed from that of the index.

  c This reveals how the industry the company is in performed compared with the other industries covered at Market Guide. The figure shows what percentage of the industries it outperformed.

  d This shows how the stock performed relative to the average performance for a company in the same industry. The number shows what percentage of companies in the same industy it outperformed.

2 Which one of the following is the percentile rank?

   a This shows the stock's overall performance, so large percentage changes are going to catch your eye. This is a comparison of the stock's price activity with that of the S&P 500 index.

   b The percentage shows the degree to which the stock's performance differed from that of the index.

   c This reveals how the industry the company is in performed compared with the other industries covered at Market Guide. The figure shows what percentage of the industries it outperformed.

   d This shows how the stock performed relative to the average performance for a company in the same industry. The number shows what percentage of companies in the same industry it outperformed.

Answers

1 c, 2 d.

What you have learned

Performance figures judge the company's performance in four contexts: **actual** shows how well it is performing overall; **S&P 500** shows how well it is performing in relation to the S&P 500 index; **rank in industry** shows how well it is performing against its business rivals; and **industry rank** shows how well its industry is performing against other industries. These figures place the company in the bigger picture.

Exercises

1 Which of these figures gives us the biggest overview – actual S&P 500, rank in industry or industry rank?

2 What is the difference between rank in industry and industry rank?

Institutional ownership

Institutional ownership can be seen as a sister table to recommendations. Both give us the experts' opinion of the stock's value: recommendations shows us directly, by the extent to which professional securities analysts think we should buy, hold or sell stocks; institutional ownership shows us

> If an institution is buying into a small company, it could be that it has spotted a **potential** for growth.

indirectly, by the extent to which financial institutions, such as pension funds, mutual funds and insurance companies, have themselves purchased stocks in a company.

% shares owned	69.77	
# of institutions	1,556	
Total shares held (mil.)	944,064	
3 monthly net purchases (mil.)		118,945
3 monthly shares purchased (mil.)		192,377
3 monthly shares sold (mil.)	73,432	

Institutional ownership: the amount of a company's stock held by financial institutions.

Institutional ownership tables tell us what percentage of stock has been bought by financial institutions, how many different institutions own that stock, and how many shares this adds up to.

So why should we care? What do financial institutions know that other traders don't? Probably quite a bit. First off, they have a lot of money, a lot of expertise at their fingertips and they don't like to gamble, so if they've bought stock in a company we ought to take a closer look. Second, there's the size of the company to take into account. If an institution is buying into a small company, it could be that it has spotted a potential for growth. Institutions can bring the glare of the spotlight with them, so other traders and institutions will take notice and the company stock may well rise. Of course, if the institutional ownership is high it may be too late to take advantage of that stock rise. And there's the rub: yes, institutional ownership shows that the company has potential, but we only know that because said institution has already bought up shares which means the company is no longer quite the bargain for us.

Of course, institutions don't rush these things – they may have more money than us but they're no less cautious, which gives us an advantage. Ideally it's good to look for a company that is between 5% and 20% owned by institutions. That indicates that there is more than a passing interest in the company, but that institutional interest has yet to mushroom (if, of course, it does – *nothing* is certain).

HOT TIP

Check the '% shares owned' entry and look for 5–20%.

Exercises

1 What is an 'institution'?

2 When an institution buys shares in a company, what is the likely effect on growth – will it improve or decline?

What you have learned

Institutional ownership tables refer to financial institutions. They show us what percentage of the company's shares are held by institutions, how many different institutions hold those shares, and what the total amount of those shares is. From the level of institutional interest, we can get a clue to the growth potential of the company.

Insider trading

Investment securities analysts have a shrewd idea as to whether a company is worth investing in, and financial institutions are no slouches either. But there's one source that has the edge on them: the company itself.

Net insider trades	–6
# Buy transactions	0
# Sell transactions	6
Net shares purchased (mil.)	–0.405
# Shares purchased (mil.)	0.000
# Shares sold (mil.)	0.405

Insider trading: the level of buying and selling of shares by the company's executive and senior officers.

Obviously, the company isn't going to share its deepest hopes and fears with us. But the amount of shares its executives are buying or selling can give us a clue to future developments. Buying can indicate that the company has good prospects – after all, its employees are reducing the diversification of their personal assets by making these purchases. Holding too can be a good sign, for the same reasons.

But then insiders could be buying stock because it's going cheap after a slump – an act of loyalty or perhaps an attempt to jump-start the stock price and reverse a down-

> Buying can indicate that the company has good **prospects** – after all, its employees are reducing the diversification of their personal assets by making these purchases.

> **Insider trading can be ambiguous**. It helps if you have some other information, be it from performance or recommendations, to put it in context and clarify it.

turn. Then there is also the chance that they've got an over-optimistic view of the company's future. Equally, selling generally hints that troubles are ahead. But often it may simply indicate that employees want to convert part of their compensations (their stock options) into ready cash, a decision that has little to do with the health of the company.

The upshot of this? Insider trading can be ambiguous. It helps if you have some other information, be it from performance or recommendations, to put it in context and clarify it. Treat it the same way you treat analyst recommendations: as a useful second opinion rather than gospel truth.

HOT TIP

Check up on this by all means, but take it with a pinch of salt.

Exercises

1 Define insider trading.

2 When might a high level of purchasing be a bad sign?

What you have learned

Insider trading shows us the extent to which the company's own officers are buying and selling shares. Buying generally indicates a healthy future for the company, while selling generally indicates that hard times are ahead – but this isn't always the case.

Earnings estimates

A company issues announcements of its earnings every quarter. These earnings are a prime source of information for traders, much more than being just a gauge of the company's profits. In fact, analysts issue predictions of what these announcements will say. These predictions – or rather, the disparity between them and the actual figures announced – can be as revealing about the stock as the company's own statistics.

If an earnings announcement has just been made, a site like Market Guide will include it in its snapshot report. If it does, our information is 'straight off the presses'. If not, our main source of information remains the company's earnings estimate report (Table 10.3, p. 136). As you can see, it takes the form of a large table – a bit daunting perhaps, but as you look closer you will see that it's broken up into sections.

Expected earnings announcements: the date on which a company issues an official statement detailing its earnings.

Just the **anticipation** of an earnings announcement can affect stock, causing price activity.

Earnings announcements can affect stock in two ways: by what they say about earnings, and by the anticipation generated within the financial community over what they *might* say. Just the anticipation of an earnings announcement can affect stock, causing price activity. Fortunately, the company compares the data it is preparing with analysts' projections. If there is a marked discrepancy, it will issue a written statement and conference call beforehand to tell the financial community that the announcement proper is likely to differ from expectations.

Sometimes a pre-announcement statement can itself be pre-empted by large share price movements, especially if accompanied by above-average trading volume – a sign to sharp-eyed traders of changing expectations. Such traders pay particular attention to stock in the week before release. As should we. When the announcement does appear, it comes in the form of a written statement. If earnings meet or exceed expectations, there can be a sell-off followed by an upward trend in stock price as the news spreads throughout the financial community. If earnings fail to meet expectation, stock price generally falls. The next step is for the company to discuss its results with analysts from the brokerage houses that follow the company. This can affect the opinion of those financial institutions that have bought stock in the company, which again can affect stock price.

Stock **price** can also be influenced if the company issues a 'flash' report announcing earnings for the last quarter. This is less comprehensive than a standard earnings announcement and is issued because the company wants to release its figures early rather than wait for the official date. If the earnings estimates table includes such a report, it means that the information on it is much fresher – and worthy of greater attention.

Earnings per share estimates: a brokerage house's estimates of a company's earnings.

The estimates are broken up into six columns across the page: number of estimates, mean estimate, high estimate, low estimate, standard deviation and projected price to earnings ratios. The wider the range of estimates, the

TABLE 10.3 Earnings estimate report

Expected earnings announcements	Release date
Quarter ending 06/01	17/07/2001
Quarter ending 09/01	18/10/2001

Earnings per share (EPS) estimates

	# of ests.	Mean est.	High est.	Low est.	Std. est.	Proj. est.
Quarter ending 06/01	12	0.38	0.38	0.37	0.01	0.56
Quarter ending 09/01	12	0.38	0.40	0.37	0.01	0.46
Year ending 12/01	23	1.41	1.45	1.39	0.02	1.79
Year ending 12/02	16	1.58	1.61	1.52	0.02	1.83
Long term growth rate	18	13.58	22.70	10.00	2.98	26.47

Analyst recommendations and revisions

	As of 22/04/2001	As of 4 weeks ago
1 Strong buy	6	5
2 Buy	8	7
3 Hold	7	7
4 Underperform	0	0
5 Sell	0	0
Mean rating	2.0	2.1

Quarterly earnings surprise
Estimated vs actual EPS

	Estimate	Actual	Difference	% Surprise
March 2001	0.29	0.30	0.01	3.30
December 2000	0.32	0.33	0.01	3.10
September 2000	0.34	0.35	0.01	2.94
June 2000	0.33	0.33	0.00	0.00
March 2000	0.26	0.24	−0.02	7.70

Historical mean EPS trend

	As of 22/04/01	As of 4 weeks ago	As of 12 weeks ago
Quarter ending 06/01	0.38	0.37	0.37
Quarter ending 09/01	0.38	0.38	NA
Year ending 12/01	1.41	1.41	1.41
Year ending 12/02	1.58	1.58	1.57

greater the disagreement among analysts; the closer the range of estimates, the closer the agreement.

That seems fairly straightforward, but unfortunately there's no good and bad here. True, uncertainty tends to indicate greater stock volatility. But certainty can backfire too if the earnings announced fall short of estimates – the shock will be greater and stock will suffer accordingly. The only solution is to hedge your bets. Think of your whole portfolio, your total holdings. Just as it's shrewd to keep a selection of large and micro cap companies in your portfolio, so it pays to diversify between companies with wide-ranging estimates and those with close estimates. That way if an earnings shock does take place, you won't experience a sudden plummet in the price of your holdings.

> The only solution is to **hedge** your bets. Think of your whole portfolio, your total holdings.

Here are a few tips:

- Note the number of analysts – a large number indicates that the estimates are fairly confident, but a small number may indicate that the company is a relatively undiscovered one, with stock that may perform well as more investors become aware of it.

- A clue to stock overvaluation can be found by looking at the projected price to earnings ratios column. If you divide this number by the consensus growth rate you will get a PEG ratio. A PEG ratio above 1.0 (i.e. above the growth rate) can signify stock overvaluation – handy at least for comparing 'overvalued' stocks against each other.

  Analyst recommendations and revisions: advice given by professional securities analysts with regard to the purchase, holding or sale of stock.

We've been here before. This is what the experts think we should do with the stock. If we're looking at the same company as we were before, then (if the information is up to date) we're looking at the same table of recommendations. Given that these are the experts, we could just trust their judgement and stop reading here. But even if we do that, it helps to learn more about the earnings estimates so that we at least understand their decisions. And experts aren't infallible …

  Earnings surprise: a percentage measure of the degree to which earnings estimates differed from actual earnings.

To wit, the experts got it wrong. Actually, this *used* to be a sign that the analysts had got it wrong. But since companies increasingly help analysts in their estimates, it's now taken to be a sign that the company got it wrong. If the actual earnings fall short of expectations, this sends out worrying signals about the competence of management, thereby driving share prices down. If the announced earnings turn out to be higher, it still means the company got it wrong. But this doesn't seem to have the same detrimental effect. Why? Because it's good news – the company is doing better than we expected. The mere fact that it only seems to be doing better because the management got its sums wrong and fed us a false expectation seems to get lost in the euphoria.

So which is better, an over-estimate or an under-estimate? A simple response is that an under-estimate *should* lead to a price rise while an over-estimate causes a price drop. But there are other factors.

1 In an over-estimate, it helps to gauge the size of the shortfall by looking at the range indicated by the company. A company that indicates a $.1–.11 range and comes in 1c shy is better than a company that indicates a $.1–.10 range and comes in 1c shy. It's still the same amount of money but in the latter the percentage is greater.

2 Look at the vigour with which management offers its guidance. Check price charts and make sure the surprises that occurred in the past were seen to be significant by the market.

3 Sometimes a negative surprise can be a sign of problems outside, not inside, the company. For instance, a computer manufacturer might experience a loss of earnings because the firm that supplies it with semi-conductors has been put out of action by an earthquake (something similar happened to Apple in 1999). Suddenly the company can't make so many computers. As production drops, so do sales, and the stock price plummets. At which point we start buying. Why? Because the source of the problem doesn't lie with the company. Therefore, when the company finds a new supplier of semi-conductors, there's every reason to expect that normal service will be resumed and the stock price will bounce back (making us a tidy profit in the process). Indeed this is exactly what happened to Apple.

FIGURE 10.1   Apple

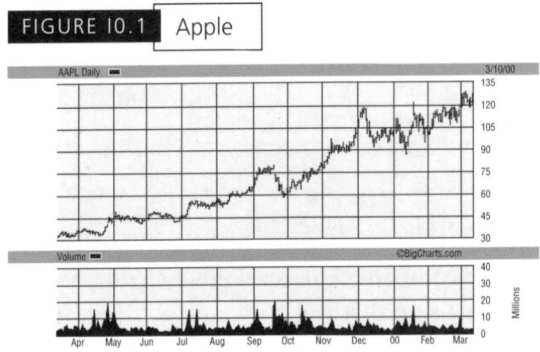

4 And if an over-estimate can be good news, so an under-estimate can actually be bad. A company may find its stock price inflated after a series of earnings announcements exceed the estimates given. As we've discussed, the company isn't actually doing better – the management's simply got its sums wrong. This fact will soon become apparent and the stock price will experience a sudden drop.

Estimates trend: the direction, accuracy and favourability of recent earnings estimates.

Before we look at this table, we should examine the reasons why estimates are revised – and this could take a while! There are four basic reasons.

1 *Changing expectations about the economic environment.* Ergo, the influence economists have on the revision of earnings per share estimates. If they raise their expectations about the performance of the economy, analysts are likely to follow suit and raise their estimates of corporate earnings per share. If economists lower their expectations of the economy (i.e. economic activity is slowing down), analysts will follow with lower estimates. (Other factors come into play too: there might be an upward revision of earnings per share if the company's business becomes more cyclical.)

Similarly, changes in specific aspects of the economy can lead to an EPS revision for certain companies, e.g. changing interest rates forecasts would affect the EPS for companies in the financial sector; revised expectations for commodity prices would affect the EPS for food processing companies and restaurants.

2 *Changing expectations about a company's markets.* Ergo, the influence the changing nature of the market has on the revision of EPS estimates. Take the example of TV broadcasting: in the 1970s, analysts focused on the factors that were likely to influence the demand for commercial advertising (which commercial TV companies rely on for their income). In the 1990s their calculations have been muddied by the fact that other kinds of companies have cut into the broadcasters' market, such as cable and internet companies, making broadcasters work harder to secure viewers. The value of a TV show as a vehicle for advertising is now in greater doubt. And this doubt can lead to greater EPS revision, even if there are no changes in economic expectations (i.e. no revisions from the economists to rock the boat).

> If economists lower their **expectations** of the economy (i.e. economic activity is slowing down), analysts will follow with lower estimates.

The market is susceptible to other factors too, for example the political climate surrounding healthcare needs to be accounted for in estimates for those stocks. In the case of healthcare and broadcasting, the change in the market has been gradual. But changes can also affect quarter-to-quarter analyst expectations – the effects of e-commerce on the traditional retail market demand close and regular scrutiny.

3 *Changes unique to individual companies.* Ergo, changes in a company's business strategies, and its success rate in implementing those strategies. This can often cause analysts to revise earnings estimates.

4 *Changes in the analysts' assessment methods.* The above three are important, but the biggest cause of revised earnings estimates is the corporate earnings announcement (or, if there is one, the pre-announcement). Analysts can never be sure that their estimates are on target, even with company executives guiding. And while those executives may be experts on the working of their own company, they don't have a crystal ball to show them where the market is heading. Interim reports and pre-announcements help both executives and analysts to make a closer assessment of how the economy and various markets are performing, which in turn gives them greater accuracy in predicting how much money companies will make.

The upshot is that estimate revisions are a fact of life. You cannot put together a portfolio that is immune to earnings surprises. The best you can do is look for companies that are likely to have favourable surprises, and avoid those likely to have major negative surprises. And this is where the estimates trend table (Table 10.3) helps us.

Take a look at the way those figures have changed across the time periods given. If the estimates have been increasing (i.e. an upward trend), this means that analysts have been surprised for the better. If there's a downwards trend, it means that the surprises have been negative.

Always bear in mind that this information shows us what happened in the past. There's no guarantee that the future will hold the same outcome. And if surprises do come, there's no guarantee that the stock will be affected in the same way. The longer a trend is in place, the more aggressively the stock will respond when that trend is reversed. For example, a company that has been enjoying a trend of favourable earnings surprises is more likely to be unsettled by a negative surprise than a company which has got used to receiving such bad news.

> You cannot put together a portfolio that is **immune** to earnings surprises.

Exercises

1 A clue to stock overvaluation can be found by looking at the projected price to earnings ratios column. If you divide this number by the consensus growth rate you will get a PEG ratio. We would regard a stock as overvalued if the PEG is:
- **a** less than one;
- **b** between 0.5 and 0.7;
- **c** above two;
- **d** a negative figure.

2 The EPS estimate is:
- **a** the date on which a company issues an official statement detailing its earnings;
- **b** a brokerage house's estimates of a company's earnings;
- **c** advice given by professional securities analysts with regard to the purchase, holding or sale of stock;
- **d** a percentage measure of the degree to which earnings estimates differed from actual earnings;
- **e** none of the above.

3 The earnings surprise is:
- **a** the date on which a company issues an official statement detailing its earnings;
- **b** a brokerage house's estimates of a company's earnings;
- **c** advice given by professional securities analysts with regard to the purchase, holding or sale of stock;
- **d** a percentage measure of the degree to which earnings estimates differed from actual earnings;
- **e** none of the above.

4 Which one of the following is implausible?
- **a** Negative earnings surprise can be a sign of problems outside, not inside, the company.
- **b** A company may find its stock price inflated after a series of earnings announcements exceed the estimates given.

c A negative surprise should lead to a price fall.
   d A positive surprise can lead to a price fall.
   e None of the above.
   f All of the above.
5 Estimates can be revised because of:
   a changing expectations about a company's markets;
   b changes unique to individual companies;
   c changes in the analysts' assessment methods;
   d changing expectations about the economic environment;
   e all of the above;
   f none of the above.

Answers
1 c, 2 b, 3 d, 4 e, 5 e.

Notes

_____

_____

_____

_____

_____

_____

_____

_____

_____

_____

_____

_____

_____

_____

_____

_____

_____

_____

_____

What you have learned

Companies issue details of their earnings for the past quarter in written reports called **earnings announcements**. Analysts following the company also issue predictions of what these announcements will contain – **earnings estimates**.

Earnings surprise is a measure of the difference between what the analysts estimated and what the company announced. **Estimates trend** shows the accuracy of these estimates over a given period and whether the surprises have been favourable (the announced earnings were more than had been estimated) or negative (the announced earnings were less than had been estimated). By looking at past trends we can gauge the likelihood of a future upward or downward trend in stock.

Exercises

1 What are earnings announcements and who is responsible for them?

2 What are earnings estimates and who is responsible for them?

3 Why would a pre-announcement take place?

4 Define earnings surprise.

5 Name two reasons for an earnings surprise.

6 What would be a favourable surprise, and why?

7 What would be a negative surprise, and why?

Fundamentals – web guides and tests

Web guides

Hoover's

www.hoovers.com

Covers the kind of information we have looked at in this section. It some-times syndicates its proprietary company profiles to other financial portals. Mainly for subscription users.

Insider Trader

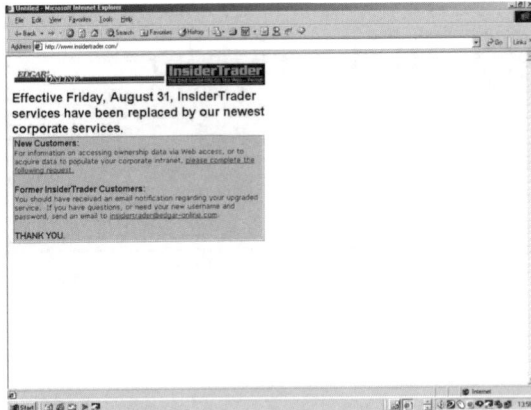

www.insidertrader.com

Like it says on the tin: the perfect source for information about insider trading. It collects under one roof the key insider buying and selling of corporate executives.

Market Guide

www.marketguide.com

Our model for this section. A comprehensive and accessible source of information. Our old friend. What you want to look at here is the earnings table you will find from the home page of any company in which you are investing.

Multex Investor Network

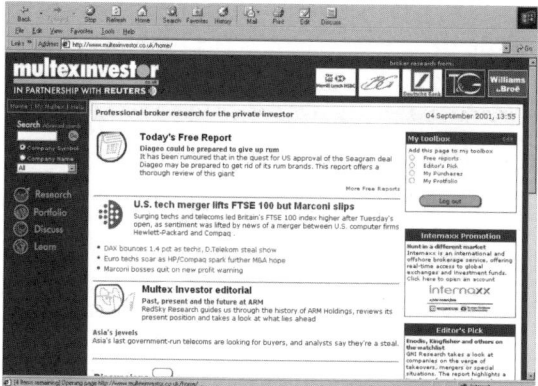

www.multexinvestor.com

Has a multitude of broker research reports, ranging from the free to the very expensive. The free ones are best for an active trader, but long-term investors may want to spend out for a report in order to back up their trading decisions.

Stockpoint

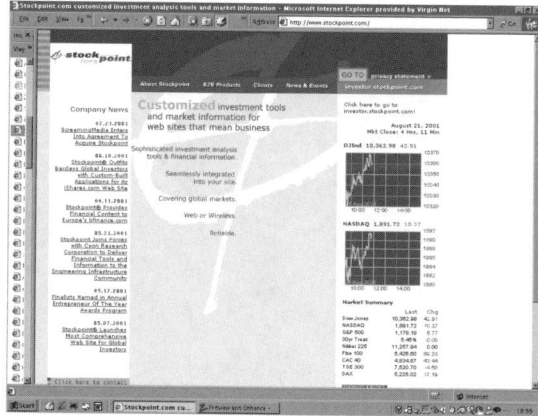

www.stockpoint.co.uk

The data can be a bit sketchy, but it's a good source for the kind of fundamental information we've covered in this section.

Thomson Research

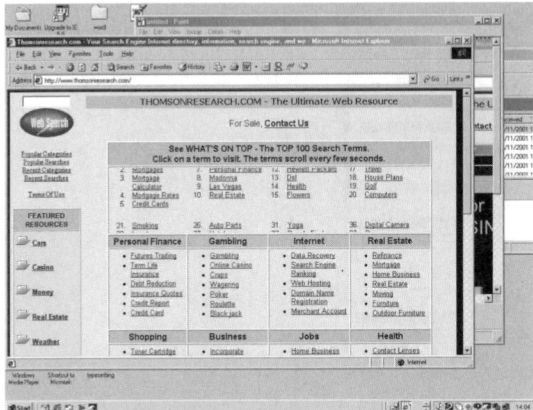

www.thomsonresearch.com

For the serious trader only – it's costly! But you're paying for quality, the information being second only to something from Goldman Sachs. Look for 'Trading'.

The following sites focus on earnings information.

Earnings Whispers

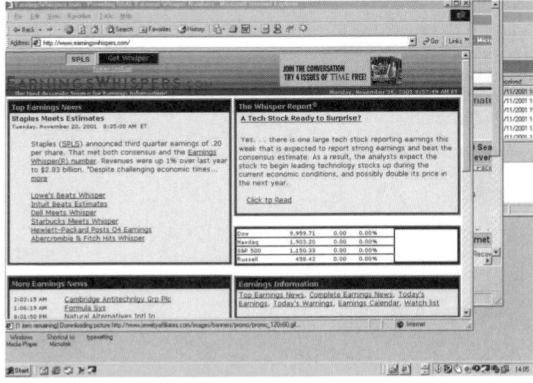

www.earningswhispers.com

Some people argue that it's not the published expected earnings that matter, it's the 'whisper numbers' or real figures Wall Street is examining. Some think this is why stock prices fall in apparently better-than-expected earnings –

because the figure did not meet Wall Street's expectations. This site deals with those whisper numbers and tells you why they can be important.

First Call

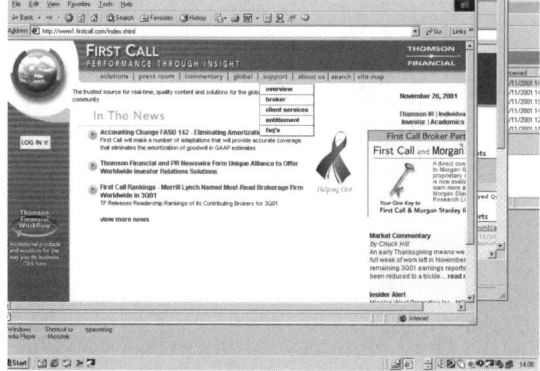

www.firstcall.com

This site is aimed at the 'heavy duty' earnings investor. The most useful part for us is the consensus change link.

Hemmington Scott

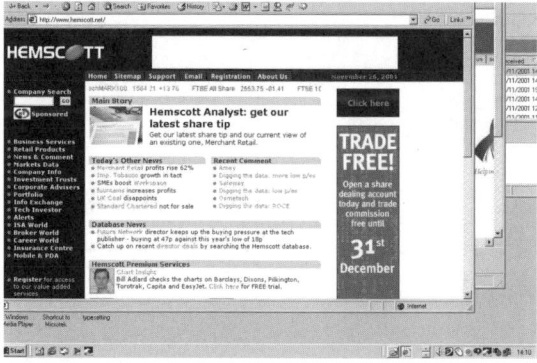

www.hemmscott.co.uk

Another heavyweight, this company syndicates financial information to most online sites, so come here if you want to drink from the source. The key link for us is its earnings and dividends link, though there's a wealth of other information on offer too.

Yahoo! Finance UK

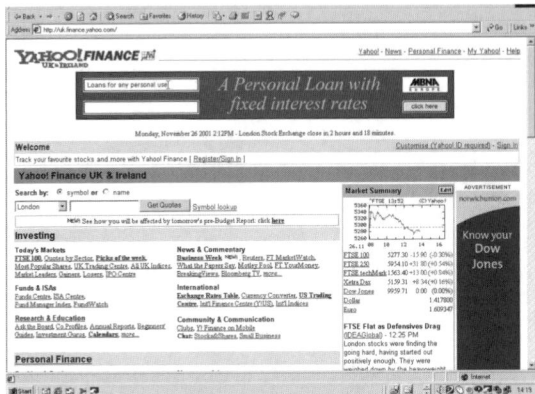

www.uk.finance.yahoo.com

This one just gets better and better. Think of it as your financial 7-Eleven – the place you pop into for the latest essentials.

Zacks Investment Research

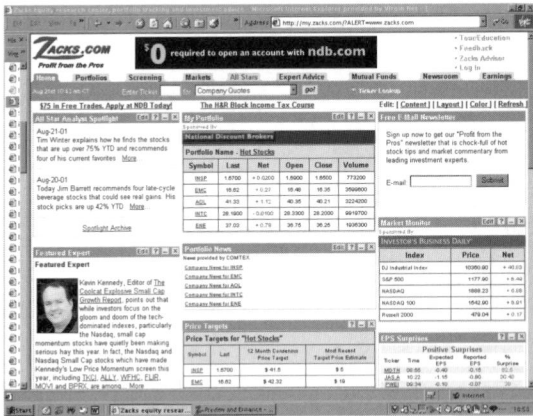

www.zacks.com

One of the most respected companies on the web. The free services show us what we need for earnings data, particularly when it comes to free earnings surprise information. Further information (such as e-mail portfolio earnings updates) comes at the cost of a subscription, but it's best to take advantage of the one-month free trial first.

Summary

Remember we said we were shopping for stock? It helps to make a shopping list before you actually go to the shops – a rough idea of what kinds of goods you want to buy and what your price range is – but we're not always sure what we're looking for. Often we're browsing and don't know what we want until we've had a good look at the goods on offer. So it goes when looking at fundamental information about companies. It helps to have a rough idea of what we want, but we're also looking at these figures to give us trading ideas.

> It helps to have a rough idea of what we want, but we're also looking at these **figures** to give us trading ideas.

In this section we have learned how to read this information and how to act on it. It's given us an insight into how professional investors do their research and what they look for, and we've gained a greater practical knowledge of how the markets work and how companies function – invaluable whether we want to become traders or enter the business world in another capacity.

However, it's important to stay focused. Remember that we're looking for growth – that's our criterion as traders. And a lot of this information is collected over long periods and may take a while to be reflected in stock prices – it's aimed at the long-term investor. We're also looking for a broad, varied portfolio. You may momentarily regret this if one of your investments soars – 'Why didn't I sink it all into this company?!' – but, conversely, if that stock drops, the rest of your holdings will give you a certain amount of stability.

Self-assessment test

Define:
1 operating margin;
2 price to book ratio (what problems are associated with it?);
3 price to cash flow ratio;
4 return on equity;
5 dividend yield (is a high or a low value desirable?);
6 price to earnings ratio (P/E);
7 capital spending;
8 price-earnings growth (PEG).

Suggested answers

1 Operating margin is the ratio of operating profits to turnover – the percentage of each revenue dollar remaining after deducting the direct and *indirect* costs that went into producing the good or services involved.

We subtract the direct costs from revenue to get gross profit and then subtract the indirect costs from gross profit to get operating profit. Indirect costs are what we tend to call 'overheads', incurred in running the business even though they have no direct link to the product and/or service produced. Operating profit is a company's trading profit before tax and interest. Analysts often calculate margins by omitting capital profits and losses and any other exceptional matters from the operating profit equation. The higher the margin the better.

2 Price to book ratio is the share price of a company divided by net asset value per share. Another way of saying this is to divide capitalization by net assets. It is the value of stock compared to the value of the assets it owns (clear of debt).

There are problems with PBVs. They are very subjective.

a It doesn't apply to a services company because the assets don't generate the revenue.

b Assets are valued on the books at the prices the company paid for them, minus cumulative depreciation/amortization charges, but depreciation is hard to measure and simple accountancy formulae will not properly reflect real-world differences in depreciation.

c The indeterminacy of the notion of 'value'. Patents and other intangibles such as copyrights and brands can only be given a value when placed up for auction to test the market. Yet another complication is that companies tend to deal with intangibles in a variety of ways. They can write them off entirely or in part and do so over a period or straight away. Some even revalue their intangibles in their balance sheets.

3 Price to cash flow ratio is the value of stock relative to the level of cash flow. Cash flow represents the amount of money a company generates in a year. It is not the profits (i.e. revenues after expenses) generated in a year. It is the amount of money generated by the company as it went about its business; in short, how much cash it had to hand to pay its expenses.

A company with high cash flow has plenty of money circulating to pay its expenses. A company with low cash flow may have to borrow money or sell assets to meet its costs.

So what are we looking for in a price to cash flow ratio? Ideally a company with a low ratio relative to that of other companies. But we also want to see a cash flow that is rising from year to year.

4 Return on equity is how well a company has managed the equity (capital) given to it by the shareholders. Equity is that portion of the company's assets that would be distributed to the shareholders if the company were liquidated and all its assets were sold at values reflected on its balance sheets. In short, what the company itself – and therefore the shareholders – owns (as opposed to, say, money loaned from a bank).

> A company with low cash flow may have to **borrow** money or sell assets to meet its costs.

5 Yield is the annual dividend rate expressed as a percentage of the price of the stock. This tells you how much income you can expect per $ or £ investment in this stock, which means you can compare it with similar stock.

As with annual dividend, the desired value (high or low) of the yield depends on a number of things. A low value may be indicative of a company reinvesting profits and therefore a sign of organic growth. However, high-yield portfolios often outperform the market on a total return basis. This is because they are often less favoured companies. The more favoured companies are subject to the whims of mass-market attention. This drives up the prices of growth shares to exorbitant levels.

Another reason why high-yielding shares can perform well is that dividends have, historically, accounted for 40–50% of the total return on the Dow. This means a higher annual payout represents a considerable cumulative benefit. But it's a bad idea to seek out high-yield shares just because they seem high yield. High yield may just reflect market fears that the dividend rate may be cut. It's best to avoid companies that are very poorly covered.

6 Price to earnings ratio is the multiple you're paying for each dollar of earnings of the company. It tells you whether you're being overcharged for your shares. You divide the price of the stock by the annual share earnings.

It can be particularly helpful when comparing companies in the same industry – companies which don't seem to be much different to one another. But … a company with a high P/E ratio may be just the ticket because it's going through a period of rapid growth, hence you appear to be being 'overcharged' for your share. Likewise, a company may have a low P/E ratio because it's having difficulties with competition, a cyclical downturn or a lawsuit, i.e. it's being 'forced' to sell cheap. Rules of thumb can be dangerous.

It tends to be the case that an attractive stock is one whose P/E ratio is lower than its long-term compound earnings per share growth rate.

7 Capital spending is the money spent on purchasing and/or expanding company assets.

> It's best to **avoid** companies that are very poorly covered.

The capital spending entry shows you how much a company is spending on assets relative to the rest of the industry. Sometimes an increase will match that of the industry, indicating, say, that a new technology has become an essential purchase (e.g. the need for every company to have its own website).

If the amount is less than the industry, it could be that the company is saving up for a spending increase in the future. If the increase is greater than the industry, the company may already be putting that project into action and, having made that investment, won't have to spend so much over the following years, thereby freeing up the amount of cash the company has to do business with.

It's useful to compare capital spending with sales. This will give you an indication as to whether past capital expenditure has resulted in increased sales as planned – an indication in turn that a company will or won't continue to grow.

8 Price-earnings growth is the price to earnings ratio of a share divided by the estimated future growth rate in earnings per share. PEG is a more sophisticated method of assessment because it ties in the price to earnings ratio with future earnings growth rate. This gives a much better insight into the true potential value of a company. PEG shows how high the P/E ratio could be and whether the shares are a realistic bargain or an expanding bubble. PEG can also be used defensively and not simply to maximize share potential.

The lower the PEG below average, the less vulnerable. It can be a good idea to regularly assess the PEG average of a growth portfolio to see how defensive it would be in a bearish climate.

Of course, PEG shouldn't be seen in isolation as a litmus test of profitability. Nonetheless, as a single financial statement it gives a quick guide to the relative value of growth shares.

Exercises

1 The market capitalization of about $4 billion characterizes a firm that is:
   a large cap;
   b mid cap;
   c small cap;
   d micro cap.

2 An average daily volume of $1.2 million characterizes a firm that is:
   a macro cap;

b large cap;

c small cap;

d micro cap.

3 What should you look for in the following data respectively: recent price, beta, margins?

   a Ignore, low, low.

   b Low, high, ignore.

   c High, ignore, high.

   d High, ignore, low.

4 The '% shares owned' by the company should be around:

   a 0–5%;

   b 5–20%;

   c 20–30%;

   d 30–40%.

5 What should you look for in the following data respectively: sales, earnings per share, the price to earnings ratio?

   a High, high, high.

   b High, low, high.

   c High, low, low.

   d High, high, low.

6 What should you look for in the following data: capital spending, price to cash flow ratio, price to sales ratio?

   a Strong, low, low.

   b Strong, high, high.

   c Weak, low, low.

   d Strong, low, high.

7 Which of the following is a good reason for going to low dividend-yield shares?

   a Low yield suggests that the company is undervalued as the price is very low relative to the dividend payout.

   b Historically low-yield shares have outperformed the market on a total return basis.

   c Low yield suggests the company is reinvesting profit into the company.

   d Low yield has a higher annual payout and this suggests a higher cumulative benefit.

Answers

1 b Market capitalization level.

    Large cap – greater than $5 billion.

    Mid cap – between $1 billion and $5 billion.

Small cap – between $300 million and $1 billion.
Micro cap – below $300 million.

2 c Average daily volume.
Over 4 mil – macro capitalization
1.6 mil – large capitalization
1. mil – small capitalization
Less than 1 mil – micro capitalization.

3 c Check that the recent price is strong; ignore ADV, ignore beta. Go for high margins (high profits), but check that this figure isn't artificially high because the company is paying lower taxes.

4 b Check the '% shares owned' entry and look for 5–20%.

5 d Look for rising sales, rising EPS and a low price to earnings ratio relative to the EPS.

6 a Go for strong capital spending, low PCF ratio suggesting good value for money, low. In particular, look for high cash flow (represented in part by a low PCF) and high capital spending, low debts, high investments.

7 c Low-yield shares may suggest the company is retaining profits in order to invest in growth and so offering a low dividend payment. The other options – a, b, d – are arguments for high dividend-yield shares. A high dividend yield suggests that the share price may be undervalued. Historically high-yield shares have outperformed the market because of the cumulative benefit of higher dividend payments.

Exercise

Look at the following sets of tables for two firms and evaluate as much as you can of note in the data. What other data would you want to look at?

SET 1

Prev. Close	Shares/Issue (m)	Mkt Cap (m)	Employees	P/S Ratio
306.5000	613.256	1879.630	11,059	26.8

PE Ratio	EPS (Norm)	FRS3 EPS	Annual Div	Div Yield	Div Cover
22.3700	13.700	7.800	2.8000	0.9100	5.1900

Yr high (curr)	Yr low (curr)	Yr high (prev)	Yr low (prev)
1086.00	306.50	1761.50	789.75

year ended 31 December	1998	1999	2000
turnover ($m)	444	609	810
pre tax profit ($m)	57.5	83.6	83.1
norm earn per share (c)	7.68	11.1	13.7
FRS3 earn per share (c)	7.25	10.7	7.80
div per share (c)	1.50	2.17	2.80
intangibles ($m)	28.5	45.6	1,087
fixed assets ($m)	17.8	16.9	28.9
fixed investments ($m)	2.79	2.80	2.80
stocks ($m)	-	1.40	3.90
debtors ($m)	116	145	236
cash, securities ($m)	39.5	31.2	52.2
creditors short ($m)	115	116	180
creditors long ($m)	5.45	4.70	235
prefs, minorities ($m)	-	-	-
low ord cap, reserves ($m)	84.4	122	996
mkt capitalization ($m)	867.45	1980.56	1879.63

SET 2

Prev. Close	Shares/Issue (m)	Mkt Cap (m)	Employees	P/S Ratio
725.0000	5538.763	40156.032	85,847	10.89

PE Ratio	EPS (Norm)	FRS3 EPS	Annual Div	Div Yield	Div Cover
13.6400	53.140	49.100	30.6000	4.2200	1.6200

Yr high (curr)	Yr low (curr)	Yr high (prev)	Yr low (prev)
772.00	610.00	742.50	517.00

year ended 31 December	1998	1999	2000
pre tax profit ($m)	3,015	3,621	3,886
norm earn per share (c)	36.9	47.9	53.1
FRS3 earn per share (c)	38.5	45.3	49.1
div per share (c)	22.2	26.6	30.6
intangibles ($m)	216	231	2,599
fixed assets ($m)	1,634	2,035	3,037
fixed investments ($m)	31,562	36,124	64,005
advances, debtors ($m)	112,236	117,980	126,951
short term assets ($m)	16,323	14,591	14,957
liquid assets, cash ($m)	6,026	5,018	6,433
creditors short ($m)	152,804	128,844	142,135
creditors long ($m)	3,655	32,028	58,048
subordinated loans ($m)	4,021	6,493	7,510
prefs, minorities ($m)	42.0	33.0	552
ord cap, reserves ($m)	7,475	8,581	9,737
mkt capitalization ($m)	46849.78	43464.031	40156.032

Suggested answers

Set 1: the company is a mid cap shown by a market capitalization of about $1.9 billion. Looking at the price data the share price is clearly on a downtrend, with the current price at a 52-week low and well below the price range of the previous year. However, we will have to look at some technicals to fully understand the price trend. Turnover has increased well, but the 'pre-tax profit' or operating margin has remained stagnant over the past two years, which is not particularly good. Furthermore, investment has remained static at $2.8 million. Debts have risen sharply as the rows showing short-term and long-term creditors suggest. A low dividend yield shown by the data is not particularly indicative of reinvestment given the investment trend, but rather reflects poor growth in operating margins. Normal earnings per share have risen since 1998, but when compared with the price to earnings ratio, EPS is too low and/or the P/E too high (we would need to examine P/E ratios for other companies in the same sector to gauge whether the P/E ratio is too high – below 30 seems all right). The price/sales ratio is also quite high compared with the P/E ratio. Cash flow has grown well.

Set 2: in contrast to Set 1 this larger company looks healthier. The price (725) is in the middle of the range defined by the latest and previous year's low and high. We would therefore have to look at the price chart to gain more insight. Operating margin ('pre-tax profit') has grown well over the past three years along with fixed assets and investments. Cash flow has grown since 1999, although it fell in 1998–99, perhaps as a result of financing investment expenditure. The time structure of debts has increased, with long-term creditors (debts) having increased and short-term debts fallen. Market capitalization has also fallen. However, the price-earnings ratio and price to sales ratio are low relative to the EPS which suggests the shares are good value. EPS has increased strongly over the past three years along with the annual dividend – this will represent a high total return on the share. Even though the dividend yield is high, profits have been sufficiently reinvested to finance tangible and intangible investments.

A low dividend yield shown by the data is not particularly **indicative** of reinvestment given the investment trend, but rather reflects poor growth in operating margins.

Of course, we would want to look at information on management effectiveness, performance measures, what activities the company is involved in, earnings estimates, and more data on growth rates and value ratios. Technical analysis and comparing the company with others in the same sector will also be essential.

Making the **trade**

Choosing brokers

Having analyzed and planned the trade, and done all the groundwork and preparation, you are ready for the kill. You obviously need some method of putting theory into practice and actually placing the trade. This is where the broker comes in.

- What are the things I should look for in a broker?
- How do I choose a broker suitable for me?
- Who are the best brokers?

What you will learn

Having worked through these modules you will:

- understand the choices available in selecting brokers;
- appreciate the pitfalls associated with each choice;
- know what to look for in a broker;
- know how to get an account up and running.

Module outline

- Decide whether you want an online broker or an off-line traditional one.
- Examine security issues to do with online accounts.
- Things you ought to look for when deciding on a broker.
- Some sites.

- Some broker ranking tables.
- Further lists of brokers and sites – by the time we've finished you'll think of little else.

On or off?

Online brokers allow you to place your trade orders via the internet. However, while they are a product of the internet and so even the oldest online broker can claim to be only a few years old, the firms that provide the online services tend to be very well-established off-line brokerage firms.

The key benefits of using online brokerage services to execute your trades

- **Cost.** Internet services tend to cost less than comparable off-line ones, with lower costs being passed on in part to consumers, in the form of low commissions and margin rates and competitive rates of interest on credit balances.
- **Convenience.** You can enter an order at any time night or day according to your own timetable. Useful if, like me, you do your analysis late at night.
- **Quick confirmation.** Your trade is usually confirmed electronically, so you need not waste time hanging around on the phone, or call back busy brokers.
- **Total account keeping and monitoring.** Because trades are handled electronically, most online brokers have a facility to permit users to monitor their account and positions on the net. This again is another minor convenience.

The firms that provide the online services tend to be very **well-established** off-line brokerage firms.

If you already have an established relationship with an off-line broker you may not wish to place your orders online. Even if you decide to stay with an off-line broker, many of them have websites that are worth visiting to find out more about the services they provide and the 'free stuff', such as analysis.

Online brokers are worth investigating, if only to compare costs. As a small trader, your costs are relatively large compared with the size of your investments and anything which alters that balance in your favour has to be worth examining.

With these factors in mind, I have listed some online and off-line brokers that meet certain criteria. You are encouraged to visit their sites, see what they offer and compare them. To save you time all broker sites listed in this module have descriptions of key services they provide and particularly what is available for free.

Security: how safe is the process?

The sites

All the major online brokers assure their clients that they have unbreachable security in terms of someone placing rogue trades or transferring money out of your account. Security is usually assured through several procedures.

- The broker will give **audit trails** of all trades and cancellations, which are available for you to inspect.
- In addition to this all firms listed in this book have some form of **insurance protection** (usually Securities Investor Protection Corporation, SIPC), ensuring client funds are either segregated or protected should the firm have financial difficulties. However, as E*Trade points out in its small print: 'Protection does not cover the market risks associated with investing.' Pity!
- Use of **firewalls**. These are like, well, walls of fire that prevent access from the outside through links, etc.
- Use of **account numbers**, **user names** and **passwords**.

The browser

If you are using Internet Explorer 4 or Netscape Navigator 4, you are using a secure browser. Data passing through your browser to and from your broker will be encrypted. You can tell you are in a secure site because:

1 the URL changes from http: to https;

2 a pop-up window informs you that you are about to enter a secure site;

> All the major online brokers assure their clients that they have **unbreachable** security in terms of someone placing rogue trades or transferring money out of your account.

3 in Internet Explorer 4, a lock icon appears in the bottom left-hand corner;

4 in Netscape Navigator 4, an unbroken key icon appears in the bottom left-hand corner of the browser.

You

The most important thing you can do to help yourself is guard your personal identification number (PIN), account number and user name. The PIN is the most important of these.

HOT TIPS

Things to do when placing an online order:

■ Double-check and read the order carefully.

■ If in doubt, check by phone.

■ Be careful when clicking on the Submit order button. Do not send a duplicate order.

What you have learned

When choosing a broker you should think about **convenience**, **costs**, **quick confirmation**, **total account keeping**. For the first three reasons, online brokers are best.

When looking at security requirements, look at differences in sites. Look for **audit trails**, **firewalls**, **insurance protection**, **account numbers** and **password requirements**. Your browser should be fine.

What to look for

At a glance

There are many, many online brokers. It is hard to choose between them. In deciding the online brokerage firms to include in this module I have considered the following criteria, which are based on what any good trader or investor should have in mind when investigating brokers.

1 Competitive commissions.

- Check for what size trade the advertised 'low' commission applies.
- Any maintenance or handling charges (i.e. hidden costs)?
- Commissions sometimes vary on the price of the stock, e.g. extra charges for a stock trading less than 50c.

2 Account details.

- Minimum initial deposit.
- Minimum account balance.
- Interest rates for idle funds.
- Good brokers ought to automatically sweep excess funds to a high interest account.
- Margin and checking accounts:
  - A margin account will allow you to borrow – what are the rates?
  - It would be convenient to be able to write cheques.
  - Is there a cost for wiring funds from the account?
  - *See Module 13 on opening an account.*
- Availability of account data online.
- How often is the account updated? Intra-daily may be important for the day trader.

3 Established on the net; not new, with potential teething problems.

4 Price quotes.

5 Methods of confirming orders (an online screen and an e-mail at least).

6 Emergency back-up.

7 Types of orders accepted.

8 Portfolio monitoring.

- How often is your portfolio updated?
- Is a tax summary available?
- Is an automatic performance measure calculated?
- Is a transaction summary available?

9 News.

10 Research available.

- What is available, is it free, is it online or posted?

11 Customer support.

- Phone, fax, e-mail is ideal.

Other factors – customer service

Of course, price is of primary concern. Online trading is popular partly because it offers discount commissions for investors who do not want to pay a full-fee broker for advice they could have discovered themselves on the internet or for trades where they do not want advice. But even among online brokers, the commissions can vary greatly and comparison is near impossible with each calculating commissions on a different basis – some using the value of your trade, others the number of shares bought, and others the frequency with which you trade.

But there is more to online broker selection than price – if there wasn't, Schwab in the USA, which is one of the most expensive online brokers, would not have the largest market share.

The most important factor in selecting an online broker is customer service. Consider the following.

Reliability   Reliability in service is an essential prerequisite for any online trader. There is no point saving $20 in commission on buying a stock, only to find you can't sell it because your online broker has broken down. Such 'downtime' by online brokers is becoming increasingly frequent in the USA, and only recently even the mighty Schwab had one full hour where trades could not be placed.

> In a survey of US brokers by US clients carried out by TheStreet.Com, DLJ Direct came top in the category of reliability.

Execution   Poor execution, too, can override price as a concern for an online trader. The price at which your trade is 'executed' should be as close as possible to the real-time price quote you see on the screen before you trade. Poor execution can often end up swamping any commission savings.

> In the same TheStreet.Com survey, Schwab came above DLJ Direct, which in turn narrowly beat E*Trade on the issue of execution prices.

There is more to online broker **selection** than price.

Design   Site design is an important consideration for me. There is nothing worse when you are trying to find a quote, do some research, or quickly place a trade than to find navigation around the site as difficult as up the Amazon (the river, not the site). I want my online broker to be easy and intuitive to use. There is only one way to see what suits you and that is to visit the sites themselves.

I am sorry to report I find the purely UK online brokers, unlike US brokers with UK sites, rather off-putting.

Free pickings   Online trading is about more than placing a trade through an online broker instead of phoning a traditional broker. Trading online profitably still requires research to arrive at stock picks and the internet is an excellent resource to offer this. I always check to see what research the online broker offers. Do they provide free portfolio monitoring, charting, news from major wires, research from renowned institutions, commentary, or is it just a website appended to a traditional brokerage?

> Trading online profitably still requires **research** to arrive at stock picks and the internet is an excellent resource to offer this.

HOT TIPS

Look for headings, llike the following, on the broker websites to make your task easier. Good brokers will present what they have well and you will be able to decipher whether you are getting quality.

- **Trading**, where you can place a trade for stocks, options or mutual funds.
- **Portfolio or account**, where you'll find information about your account, such as balances and holdings.
- **Markets**, where you can check the latest market indices, headlines and reports.
- **Quotes**, where you'll find real-time quotes for stocks and options, as well as model portfolios.
- **Research and news**, where you'll find authoritative research on the markets, companies and mutual funds. There should also be a good charting facility.
- **Community or chat**, where you can discuss or argue at length about what's hot and what's not.
- **Customer service**, where you can open new accounts, message the broker online, withdraw cash, etc.

What you have learned

When you consider different brokers there are many possible things to look at.

- **Competitive commissions** are an obvious starting point – look at the structure of possible costs, e.g. the size of trades that receive 'low' commissions, **how commissions vary**, handling charges and other **hidden costs**. Evaluate what **free pickings** there are, e.g. free research, portfolio monitoring. Of course, you do not have to do your research at your broker's website if there is better free research elsewhere, but then you will have to trade off other benefits of your broker against the inconvenience of doing research elsewhere.

- **Account details** include the minimum required initial funds, account balance, the interest rate for idle funds, **types of accounts available** (see below).

- Data, price **quotes**: are they **real-time**, **delayed**, do they cover financial derivatives as well as stocks?

- The speed at which you can get to **research**, is it free, what's the quality like? Assess the quality of the news items on the site.

- Methods of **confirmation**.

- Look at facilities for **portfolio monitoring**. The website should have a preview tutorial for potential members.

- What **emergency** back-up does the site have – telephone, fax?

- The **design** of the site is of course important given the time you'll be spending surfing.

- **Reliability**, **execution speed** will be important to you – see the ranking.

The sites

Broker watch

In this section we take a run through sites which rate and rank brokers according to different criteria such as performance, speed, commissions, etc.

Gomez ***

www.gomez.com

An excellent site covering rankings of many different things, not just brokers. A clear and easy-to-navigate site that is up to date.

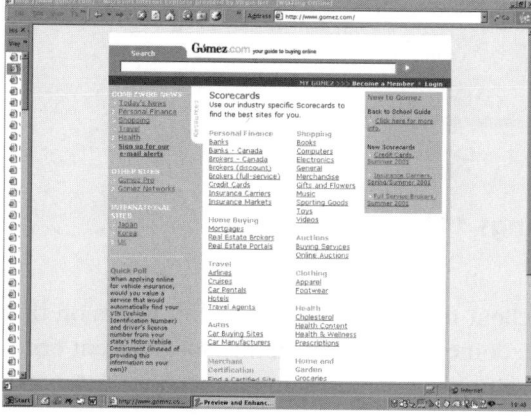

Internet Investing **

www.internetinvesting.com

internetnews.com

Gives quite a detailed list of commission rates for all major online brokers, but has a semi-professional feel to it.

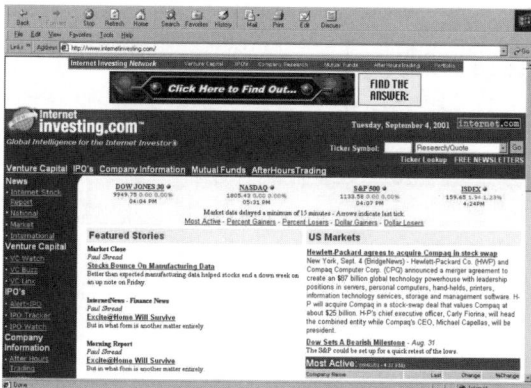

Keynote Web Brokerage Index *

www.keynote.com

Most useful for its rankings of speed of access. Design not too bad either.

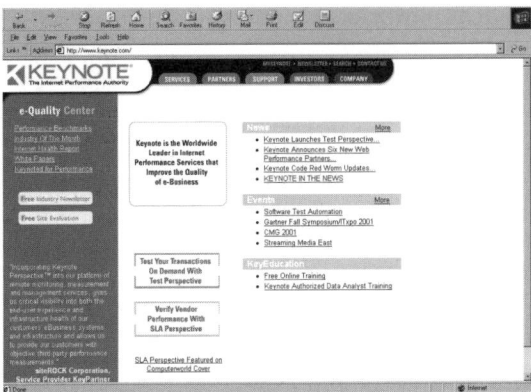

Smart Money Brokers Ratings ***

www.smartmoney.com

An excellent site (and an excellent magazine). I could spend hours on this one playing on the broker speedometer! Lots of rankings for different criteria. A lesson in how to present info.

Brokers

To help you gauge the sites, I have provided a rough-and-ready rating, based on general impressions of the services from inspecting the sites and the charges they inflict.

Ameritrade ✶✶✶

www.ameritrade.com

Ameritrade
PO Box 2209
Omaha, NE 68103 2209
Tel: 1 800 454 9272

A very good site. The home page is a lesson in simplicity coupled with professionalism. Research is not as good as others but then again the broker is one of the cheapest around. The site is quick, easy to navigate, well designed and less cluttered than other sites.

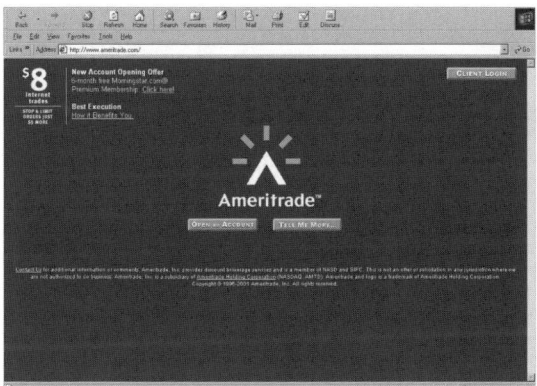

CSFB Direct (now sold to TDW)***

www.csfbdirect.com

Formerly DLJ Direct, the brokerage was taken over by CSFB and has now been sold to TD Waterhouse.

The site is very nice and well organized. It gives you reasons to open an account and makes it easy to find commission rates. DLJ realizes it has to offer added value through research and does so. The only thing is, it is not the cheapest.

Charles Schwab***

www.schwab.com

Charles Schwab
101 Montgomery Street
San Francisco, CA 94104
Tel: 415 627 7000/ 1 800 435 4000

Charles Schwab is not the cheapest broker, and it doesn't care because it is the largest. Very experienced at what it does, and has an enormous number of positive press comments. If you are a little concerned about trading on the net then a broker such as Schwab provides some added security in that you are dealing with an old hand in internet broking. I wish it would use its size to do more strategic alliances and offer its clients even more free stuff.

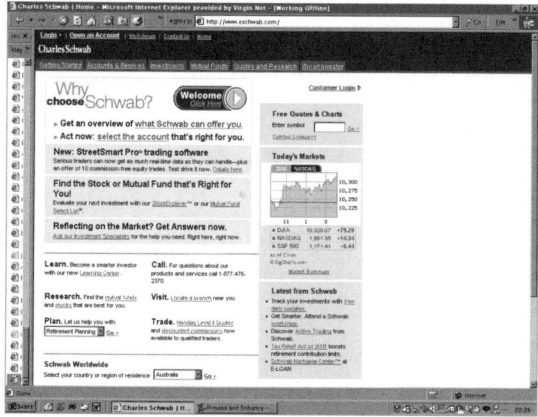

Charles Schwab Europe***

www.schwab-europe.com

Charles Schwab
Cannon House
24 The Priory
Queensway
Birmingham B4 6BS
UK
Tel: +44 121 200 7788

An increasingly impressive site, with free research, easy navigation, and good design. There is a phone brokerage service for those not quite ready to jump onto the cybertrain. Site also offers UK investors the opportunity to buy US securities.

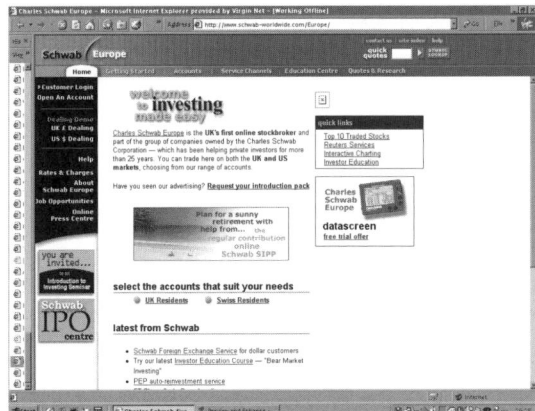

Datek***

www.datek.com

Datek
50 Broad Street, 6th Floor
New York, NY 10004
Tel: 212 514 753

Datek is not only cheap, but I do keep on hearing good things about it from chat boards, e-mails and press comments. Either it has a very good CIA-like undercover publicity machine or it is, in fact, very good. The site also has a reassuring number of positive press reviews. I always find that comforting when considering a site marketing itself on the basis of having a very low cost base.

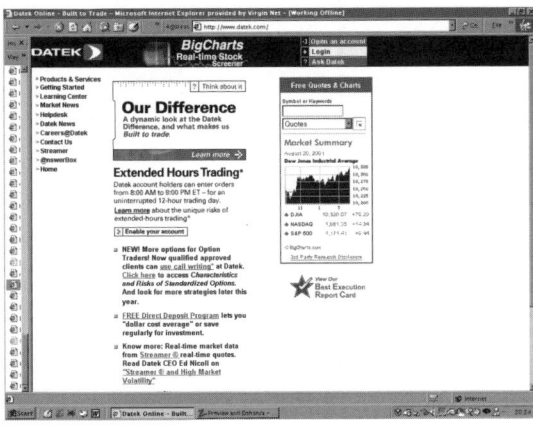

Discover **

www.discoverbrokerage.com

Owned by Morgan Stanley, but the site does not come in as having the cheapest commission, or the best design, or the most research. It sort of does a bit of everything without excelling at any one. However, given who owns it, it provides the security you may want in an online broker.

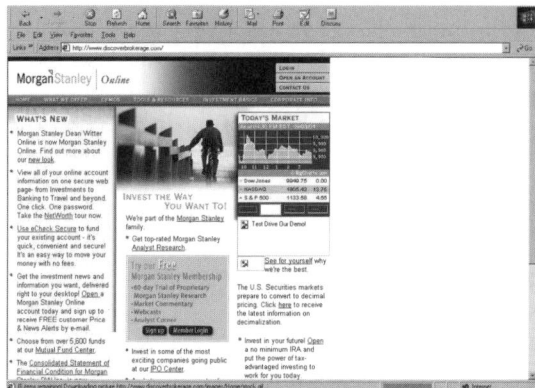

E*Trade ***

www.etrade.com

E*Trade Securities
4 Embarcadero Pl
2400 Geng Road
Palo Alto, CA 94303
Tel: 1 800 786 2575

A site with a lot of features, some free before you register, others for account holders. The site is easy to navigate and the information is simple to find. There are also message boards and financial services available. On the Gomez rankings it has been the Number 1 overall broker for some time. As a broker, it has a lot of awards and positive reviews, making it a must-consider choice.

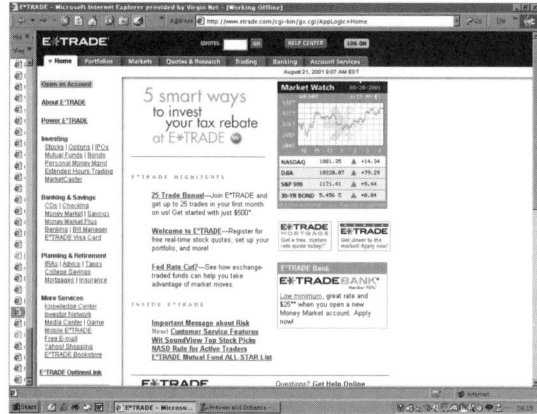

E*Trade UK ***

www.etrade.co.uk

The UK version of the US site is among the very best of all the sites open to UK investors. The charting section is especially good. The site offers portfolios, message boards (which could be better organized but are one of the most active in the UK for stock chat), news and research. Well designed and organized. Did I mention the commissions are among the UK's cheapest?

IMIWeb ***

www.imiweb.co.uk

A relatively new entrant, part of Italy's second largest bank. Offers very clear cost structure. UK trades £10. European trades £15. No other costs. Their live chat with customer services is very innovative too. Useful if you like good service and cheap online trading with the option to trade abroad. Who doesn't?

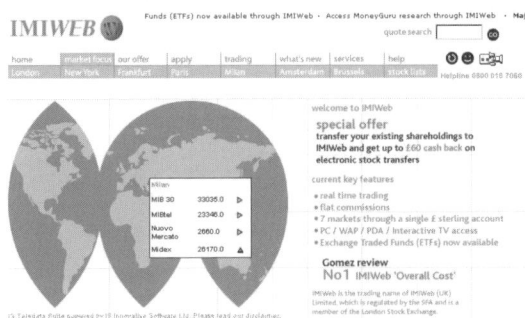

Merrill Lynch HSBC ***

www.mlhsbc.com

Excellent research provided by both Merrill Lynch and HSBC. The site is fast and slick.

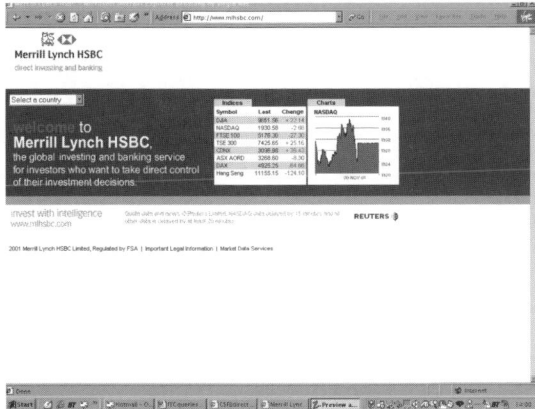

Pathburner.com **

www.pathburner.com

'Now there is no disadvantage to trading online' as the company offers advice from professional brokers at execution-only prices. If you are looking for good tools and advice or professional management of your funds use this. If you want no advice and dirt cheap trades then obviously look elsewhere.

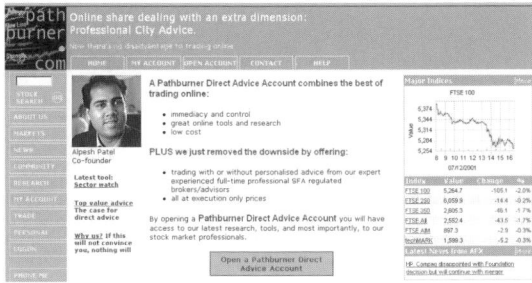

ScoTTrade **

www.scottrade.com

The site seems to be extremely slow. It is supposed to be cheap, however, and I liked the design and layout.

Broker ranking tables

I have compiled a number of broker ranking tables to give you a varied and perhaps balanced view of some of the brokers already mentioned, as well as some new ones (Table 12.1).

TABLE 12.1 What some of the brokers offer

Broker	One-step online account activation	Time from 'set up account' to 'first trade'	Online and immediate fund a/c by debit card	Firm real-time price for trade	Limit 'good for the day' option	Immediate reinvestment of nominee sales proceeds	Certified sales without prior nominee registration	Free comprehensive online and interactive education
Abbey National	No – telephone to get account dealing number	Within 15 minutes (during business hours only)	No – must set up DDM	Yes	No	No	Yes	No
Barclays	No – paper application process by post	10 days	No – must set up a DDM	Yes	Yes	Yes	Yes	No
Charles Schwab	No – paper application by post	1 week	By phone only – not immediate	Yes – limit required	Yes	No	No	No – 2 courses only on tax and investing fundamentals
Com Direct	No – paper application by post	3 days	No	Yes	Yes – shortly	Yes	No	No
DLJ	No – must wait for e-mail to activate account	24 hours	By phone only – not immediate	Yes	No	Yes	No	No
Egg	No	1 week	No – Egg savings account only	Yes	No	Yes – 10 minutes	No	No
E*Trade	No – paper application by post	5 days	No	No	No	Yes	No	No
Fastrad£	No – paper application by post	3–4 days	No	No	Yes	Yes	No	No

TABLE 12.1 Continued

Hargreaves Lansdown	No – paper application by post	1 week	No	Yes	No	Yes	No	No
iDealing	No – paper application by post	7–8 days	No	Yes	No	Yes	No	No
NatWest	No	5 – 10 days	No	No	Yes	No	Yes	No
Selftrade	No – paper application by post	3 days	No – online, not immediate	Yes	No	Yes	No	No
Sharepeople	No – paper application by post	1 week	No	Yes	No	Yes	Yes	No
Stockacademy	Yes – online and immediate	Approx. 10 minutes (any time)	Yes – online and immediate	Yes	Yes	Yes	Yes	Yes – 19 courses for 3 levels of investor experience
Stocktrade	No – paper application by post	10–15 days	No	Yes	No	Yes	No	No
TD Waterhouse	No	1 week	No	Yes	No	Yes	Yes	No

Source: information compiled through websites and customer service teams of cited companies. Information correct as at 31/07/00.

Broker rankings for Europeans from EuropeanInvestor.com

The excellent BlueSky rankings to be found on www.europeaninvestor.com help European and US residents to choose the best brokers for trading European stocks. Table 12.2 shows some findings from a site that has to be essential visiting. BlueSky ranked the sites from more than 700 brokers in Europe.

TABLE 12.2 BlueSky ratings for brokers trading European stocks

Germany: top rated broker sites (updated June 2001)

Broker name	Residency requirements	Mutual fund offer	Offers options or warrants	Offers IPOs	Basic fees	BlueSky usability rating 100% scale	BlueSky e-mail+phone service rating 100% scale	BlueSky overall rating 100% scale
Comdirect Bank	Residents and non-residents can apply	Yes	Warrants and options	Yes	link	78.8%	81.4%	**88.5%**
DAB Bank	Residents and non-residents can apply; only US residents are excluded	Yes	Warrants	Yes	link	67.6%	80.3%	**82.5%**
maxblue	Both residents and non-residents can apply	Yes	Warrants	Yes	link	75.2%	62.8%	**75.6%**

UK: top rated broker sites (updated June 2001)

Broker name	Residency requirements	Mutual fund offer	Offers options or warrants	Offers IPOs	Basic fees	BlueSky usability rating 100% scale	BlueSky e-mail+phone service rating 100% scale	BlueSky overall rating 100% scale
E*Trade	Uk residents only, must have UK bank account	Yes	Warrants	Yes	link	72.9%	76.1%	**74.5%**

TABLE 12.2 | Continued

| Charles Schwab | UK, Swiss, German, Belgian, Finnish, Spanish, Norwegian and Luxembourg residents only | $ funds | No | Yes | link | 80.0% | 65.9% | **71.7%** |
| Merrill Lynch HSBC | UK residents only | No | No | No | link | 87.0% | 84.9% | **67.2%** |

✚ Switzerland: top rated broker sites (updated June 2001)

Broker name	Residency requirements	Mutual fund offer	Offers options or warrants	Offers IPOs	Basic fees	BlueSky usability rating 100% scale	BlueSky e-mail+phone service rating 100% scale	BlueSky overall rating 100% scale
UBS	Residents and non-residents can apply; certain countries excluded	Yes	Warrants	No	link	83.5%	48.4%	**75.9%**
Credit Suisse	Residents and non-residents can apply; certain countries excluded	Yes	Options and warrants	Yes	link	81.1%	59.8%	**67.1%**
Swissquote	Residents and non-residents can apply; certain countries excluded	Yes	Warrants	Yes	link	67.0%	51.6%	**61.1%**

▬ Spain: top rated broker sites (updated June 2001)

Broker name	Residency requirements	Mutual fund offer	Offers options or warrants	Offers IPOs	Basic fees	BlueSky usability rating 100% scale	BlueSky e-mail+phone service rating 100% scale	BlueSky overall rating 100% scale
eBankinter	Residents and non-residents can apply	Yes	No	Yes	link	74.7%	75.4%	**79.5%**
Patagon	Residents and non-residents can apply	Yes	Yes	Yes	link	72.9%	58.1%	**78.5%**

TABLE 12.2   Continued

Banesto	Residents and non-residents can apply	Yes	Yes	Yes	*link*	65.8%	72.2%	**73.6%**

Italy: top rated broker sites (updated June 2001)

Broker name	Residency requirements	Mutual fund offer	Offers options or warrants	Offers IPOs	Basic fees	BlueSky usability rating 100% scale	BlueSky e-mail+phone service rating 100% scale	BlueSky overall rating 100% scale
IMI Web Trader	Only Italian residents and citizens can apply	Yes	Warrants and covered warrants	Yes	*link*	70.5%	59.9%	**78.3%**
Banca Sella	Residents and non-residents can apply	Yes	Warrants and options	Yes	*link*	75.8%	55.3%	**71.3%**
121 Internet Banking	Only Italian residents and citizens can apply	Yes	Warrants	Yes	*link*	72.3%	47.2%	**66.3%**

Belgium: top rated broker sites (updated June 2001)

Broker name	Residency requirements	Mutual fund offer	Offers options or warrants	Offers IPOs	Basic fees	BlueSky usability rating 100% scale	BlueSky e-mail+phone service rating 100% scale	BlueSky overall rating 100% scale
eBanking	Non-residents can apply; US residents and non-FATF members are excluded	Yes	Warrants	Yes	*link*	68.2%	55.6%	**65.4%**
VMS-Keytrade	Belgium residents and non-residents	Yes	Warrants	Yes	*link*	60.5%	71.1%	**64.9%**
OneTwo Trade	Belgium residents and non-residents	Yes	Warrants	Yes	*link*	64.7%	30.5%	**59.0%**

TABLE 12.2 | Continued

France: top rated broker sites (updated June 2001)

Broker name	Residency requirements	Mutual fund offer	Offers options or warrants	Offers IPOs	Basic fees	BlueSky usability rating 100% scale	BlueSky e-mail+phone service rating 100% scale	BlueSky overall rating 100% scale
Selftrade	Residents and non-residents can apply	Yes	Warrants	Yes	link	74.1%	60.7%	**70.7%**
Fimatex	Residents and non-residents can apply	Yes	Warrants and options	Yes	link	64.7%	54.7%	**70.3%**
CPR Online	Residents and non-residents can apply	Yes	Warrants	Yes	link	67.6%	60.9%	**63.4%**

Brokers' tables from Cyberinvest.com

Tables 12.3–12.5 are very useful, examining some more brokers, using different criteria. Some of the regions examined include Japan, China, Latin America, Africa and Australia.

TABLE 12.3 | The Americas

	Language	Quotes	Forex rates	Market update	News & articles on region	Economic outlook	Of interest	Int'l links	Cost
CANADA									
Bank of Canada	English/ French		✓				Financial Statistics	✓	Free
Bank of Montreal	English/ French	✓		✓	✓	✓	Online Investing		Free
Bay-Street.com	English	✓	✓	✓	✓	✓	Canadian Top Volume Leaders Bond	✓	Free

TABLE 12.3 Continued

Name	Language						Description		Cost
Canada Investment and Savings	English/French						Interest rates and bond calculators	✓	Free
Canada NewsWire	French/English			✓	✓			✓	Free
Canada Trust	English	✓	✓	✓			Economic reports, RSP Toolkit, RIFs, Mutual Funds, Global Asset Allocation Fund		Free
Canoe Money	English	& Charts		Charts & Industry Groups	✓		Mutual Fund Search, Link to The Financial Post	✓	Free
Dept. of Finance	English/French				✓	✓		✓	Free
Dept.of Foreign Affairs & Int'l Trade	English/French				✓		Market info on Europe, Asia-Pacific, US, Latin America, Africa-MidEast	✓	Free
GLOBEfund	English	Fund Charts		Related to Mutual Funds			'Canada's National Mutual Fund Site'	✓	Free
The Globe and Mail	English		✓		✓		'Report on Business'	✓	Free
Ontario Ministry of Finance	English/French				✓	✓		✓	Free
Report on Business Magazine	English				✓				Free
MEXICO									
InfoSel	Spanish				✓				Free
Mexican Consulate	English/Spanish				✓	✓		✓	Free
US/Mexico Chamber of Commerce	English				✓	✓	White Papers on NAFTA	Mexican gov't Links	Free

▶

TABLE 12.3 Continued

CENTRAL & SOUTH AMERICA

	Language	Quotes	Forex rates	Market update	News & articles on region	Economic outlook	Of interest	Int'l links	Cost
Argentina's Ministry of Economy	English/ Spanish			✓		✓			Free
Brazil Financial Wire	English	✓	✓	✓					Free
The Wall Street Journal Americas	Spanish/ Portuguese			✓	✓				Free
Venezuela Analitica	Spanish			✓	✓				Free

TABLE 12.4 Asia, Australia

	Language	Quotes	Forex rates	Market update	News & articles on region	Economic outlook	Of interest	Int'l links	Cost
ASIA									
APEC (Asia-Pacific Economic Cooperation)	English					✓			Free
Asia Business Connection	English							Business Links	Free
Asia, Inc. Online	English		✓	✓	✓	✓		✓	Free
AsiaOne	English	Singapore & Kuala Lumpur	✓	✓	✓	✓		✓	Free
Business Times (Singapore) Online	English		✓	✓	✓	✓		✓	Free
CNBC Asia Business News	English			✓	✓		Personalized News	✓	Free
Far Eastern Economic Review	English				✓	✓		✓	Free

TABLE 12.4 Continued

Interactive Investor International	English & some Chinese	Incl. Hong Kong stocks	Coming	Hang Seng Tracker et al	✓		6,000 funds incl. Hong Kong approved funds	✓	Free
ThaiStocks.com	English			✓	✓		Articles & Stock Picks	✓	Free & $
CHINA & JAPAN									
China.com	Chinese				Portal site				Free
China Business Net	English	✓	✓		✓			✓	Free
China News Digest	English				✓				Free
Inside China Today	English				✓			✓	Free
Japan: Ni-Ka Online	English/ French						Japan-Canada Trade	Japanese Gov't Links	Free
Japan: The Nikkei Weekly	English/ French		✓	✓	✓	✓		✓	$
Yahoo! Finance: Japan	Japanese	✓	✓	✓	✓			✓	Free
AUSTRALIA									
The Australian Financial Review	English	✓	✓	✓	✓				Free
The Australian News Network	English			✓	✓				Free
The Australian Online	English	✓		✓	✓		Shareholder Scorecard covers Australia & New Zealand		Free
Macquarie Online	English			✓	✓				Free
Westpac	English		✓		✓			✓	Free
Wilson HTM	English	✓		✓	✓		Reports on selected Australian companies	✓	Free

| TABLE 12.5 | Europe, Africa and the Middle East |

	Language	Quotes	Forex rates	Market update	News & articles on region	Economic outlook	Of interest	Int'l links	Cost
ENGLAND									
The Bank of England	English				✓				Free
FT.Com (Financial Times)	English	✓	✓	✓	✓	✓			Free
HM Treasury	English				✓	✓			Free
The Times of London	English		✓	✓				Media Links	Free
UK-iNvest.com	English		✓	✓	✓				
WESTERN & CENTRAL EUROPE									
Central Europe Online	English	✓	✓	Covers the Czech Republic, Hungary, Poland, Romania, Slovakia, Slovenia				✓	Free
Europe Online	English & language of each country			Portal to 25 European countries and the UK					Free
FirstInvest.com	French			A leading investment site in France					Free
Institute of Finance & Banking, Univ of Goettingen	German/ English			Links to worldwide banking & finance sites, and currency converters					Free
Scandinavia OnTheNet	English		✓		✓			Links to Danish Sites	Free
Spain: La Gaceta de los Negocios	Spanish			✓	✓	Spain/Latin America			Free
Switzerland: SwissInvest.com	English	✓		✓	✓	✓	Business reports on Swiss companies	✓	Free

TABLE 12.5 Continued

RUSSIA & EASTERN EUROPE

Interfax	English		✓	✓	✓	✓	Emphasis on emerging markets	✓	Free
Russia Today	English	✓			✓		Guide to the Russian Stock Market	✓	Free
Russian Embassy	English				✓	✓			Free
Rye, Man & Gor Securities	English	✓	✓	✓	✓	✓	Russian Brokerage firm		Free
SKATE	English	✓		✓	Corporate Action Watch		Specializes in emerging markets	✓	Free

AFRICA & MIDDLE EAST

Africa: Africa News Online	English				✓	✓		✓	Free
Africa: Africa Online	English			✓	✓	✓	Chat groups; Africa forums	✓	Free
Africa: Mbendi	English	Company profiles, country profiles, info on stock exchanges							Free
MidEast: Arabia Online	English & Arabic	Portal to the MidEast: Emirates, Jordan, Kuwait, Lebanon, Oman, Palestine, Qatar, Saudi, Syria and Yemen							Free
Israel: Globes Arena	English/ Hebrew	✓	✓	✓	✓	✓	S&P Reports		Free
Israel: S&P Israel	English	✓		✓	✓	✓	Reports on Israeli companies	✓	Free

More and more lists of brokers

Here are some other brokers and their websites if you want more addresses. They're in alphabetical order. Have fun.

Online brokers (North America)

Canada		
	Bank of Montreal Investorline	www.investorline.com
	E*Trade Canada	www.canada.etrade.com
	Investnet	www.investnet.com
	Waterhouse Securities	www.waterhouse.com

USA		
	AB Watley	www.abwatley.com
	Accutrade	www.accutrade.com
	Ameritrade	www.ameritrade.com
	Amex Financial Direct	www.americanexpress.com
	Brown & Co.	www.brownco.com
	Charles Schwab	www.schwab.com
	Computel Securities	www.rapidtrade.com
	Datek Online	www.datek.com
	E*Trade	www.etrade.com
	Empire Financial Group	www.empirenow.com
	Farsight	www.farsight.com
	Freedom Investments	www.freedominvestments.com
	Intltrader	www.intltrader.com
	JB Oxford	www.jboxford.com
	National Discount Brokers	www.ndb.com
	Net Investor	www.netinvestor.com
	Pacific Brokerage	www.traderpbs.com
	Protrade	www.protrade.com
	Prudential Securities Inc.	www.prusec.com
	Quick and Reilly Quickway Net	www.quick-reilly.com
	Savoy Discount Brokerage	www.savoystock.com
	Scottrade	www.scottrade.com
	Scottsdale Securities	www.discountbroker.com
	Siebert	www.msiebert.com
	Swifttrade	www.swifttrade.com
	Tradewell Discount Investing	www.tradewell.com
	Wall Street Access	www.wsaccess.com
	Wall Street Electronica	www.wallstreete.com
	Waterhouse	www.waterhouse.com
	Wyse Compu-trade	www.compu-trade.com

Online brokers (Europe)

Belgium	Banque Cera	www.cera.be
	Banque Commerciale de Bruxelles	www.bcb.be
	Bolero (KBC)	www.bolero.be
	Cortalstreet	www.cortal.be
	DMRJ	www.dmrj.com
	Keytrade	www.keytrade.com
	Leleux	www.leleux.be
	One Two Trade (ING)	www.12trade.be
	Société de Bourse Gestrabel	www.gestrabel.be
France	ABAX	www.abax.tm.fr
	ABS (Actions Bourse Système)	www.absysteme.com
	Barclays-Bourse	www.barclays bourse.direct.com
	Bourse Direct	www.boursedirect.com
	Capitol	www.capitol.fr
	Cortal	www.cortal.fr
	Courcoux Online	www.courcoux-bouvet.fr
	CPR-E*Trade	www.cpr-etrade.com
	Directfinance	www.directfinance.com
	Euraxfin/Consors	www.euraxfin.com
	Ferri	www.ferri.fr
	Fimafex	www.fimafex.fr
	I-Bourse	www.i-bourse.fr
	NFMDA	www.nfmda.fr
	Portzamparc	www.portzamparc.fr
	Self-trade	www.selftrade.fr
	Wargny	www.wargny.fr
Germany	1822 Direkt	www.1822direkt.com
	Bank24	www.bank24.de
	Comdirect Bank	www.comdirect.de
	Conservative Concept	www.conservative-concept.de
	Consors	www.consors.de
	Deutsche Bank	www.deutsche-bank.de
	Direkt Anlage Bank	www.diraba.de
	Dresdner Bank Investmentgruppe	www.dit.de
Italy	Cedborsa	www.cedborsa.it
	Connect	www.connect.sella.it

	Directa	www.directa.it
	Fin-Eco Online	www.online.fineco.it
	Mediosim	www.mediosim.it
Luxembourg	Ebanking.com by Fortis	www.ebanking.com
	Eurotrade (Stockholm Trading)	www.eurotrade.lu
	Robeco Bank Luxembourg	www.robecobank.lu
	VMS-Keytrade	www.vms-keytrade.lu
Netherlands	Alex	www.alex.nl
Norway	K-Bank	www.kreditkassen.no
	Net Fonds	www.netfonds.no
Spain	Ciberbroker	www.ciberbroker.es
Sweden	Aktiedirekt	www.aktiedirekt.com
	Aktiespar Online	www.aktiespar.com
	Avanza	www.avanza.se
	E-Sider	www.esider.com
	E*Trade	www.etrade.se
	H&Q Online	www.hq.se
	Matteus Online	www.matteus.se
	Net Trade	www.nettradeswedbank.se
	Nord Net	www.nordnet.nu
	Skandia Banken	www.skandiabanken.se
	Swiss Netbanking	www.swissnetbanking.com
	Teletrade	www.teletrade.se
UK	Barclays	www.barclays-stockbrokers.co.uk
	Charles Schwab Europe	www.schwab-europe.com
	Currency Management Corporation	www.forex-cmc.co.uk
	DLJ Direct	www.dljdirect.co.uk
	E*Trade UK (Holdings) Ltd	www.etrade.co.uk
	Killick&Co	www.killik.co.uk
	Stocktrade	www.stocktrade.co.uk
	Xest	www.xest.com

Exercise

Write down as many headings as you can about what you value in a broker and why they are important to you. Having done that, check the section on 'what to look for'. How extensive were you?

Now rank these criteria depending on which you feel is the most important virtue of a broker. Use this ranking when choosing your broker from the various websites listed above.

Summary

With security no longer a significant issue, a major benefit of online brokers is the lower cost and greater convenience. However, with such fierce competition it is most important to shop around for one that meets your particular needs.

- Determine which security, option, fund etc. you want to trade in.
- Whittle down a list of the relevant brokers to those that are the biggest and most popular.
- Prioritize the criteria that you feel a broker should fulfil (see the 'what to look for' section above).
- Score the brokers on your short-list and then rank them.
- When choosing a broker you should think about **convenience**, **costs**, **quick confirmation**, **total account keeping** – for the first three reasons online brokers are best.
- Consider **competitive commissions** and pricing structure, **hidden costs**, **free pickings**, e.g. free research, portfolio monitoring. **Account details** include the minimum required initial funds, account balance, the interest rate for idle funds, **types of accounts available** (cash, margin, short).
- Look at data, price **quotes**: are they **real-time**, **delayed**, do they cover financial derivatives as well as stocks?
- Assess **emergency back-up**.
- The **design** of the site is of course important given the time you'll be spending surfing.

> When choosing a broker you should think about **convenience**, **costs**, **quick confirmation**, **total account keeping** – for the first three reasons online brokers are best.

Opening an
account

Questions, questions ...
and more questions

What is the fastest way to open an account?

Filling out an online application for an individual or joint account is currently the fastest way to open an account.

What is the best way to check the status of my new account?

You can check the status of your new account on the homepage of the broker's website.

Surf time ...

It is time to get on the net. Check out the websites of the following popular brokers (you can look at the listing in the previous module for more good brokers).

www.etrade.com
www.schwab.com
www.ameritrade.com
www.datek.com

Now, find information about the commission rates for these brokers and other service fees, and what unique offers they have. Try to find what makes their product distinct from that of the other brokers – check out the research, news, charting, reports, market round-up, chat, etc. Is it free?

For each site give a mark out of 10 in terms of the following criteria:

- layout/design – does it present its products well? Is it mundane or colourful?
- ease of use – how quickly can you navigate and get the information you need?
- value – how much value does the site add? Would you use it even if you did not hold an account? Think about quality.

Now rank the sites overall.

You should think methodically whenever you make further decisions about which broker you want to apply to. Do the same exercise for any other potential brokers. Prioritize the different things you look for in a broker and then determine which broker performs the best.

Getting going: opening an account and all that jazz

- OK, how do I go about opening an account then?
- What do all those terms mean anyway?
- What's the good hardware to have? Have I got it?
- What about the software that gives me the edge?

Setting up

Can I open an account? Sure you can, but it can depend on which country you're a resident in. For example, a US citizen may not be able to open an account with a UK online broker. But don't worry, the e-broker's account opening process will make all that clear.

Also, you'll almost always need to be over 18 and have a bank account. Most brokers allow you to set up an account online in minutes. There are usually no set-up charges and no requirement for a minimum balance either. But note that some brokers don't yet allow a joint account.

What sort of account do I need? These are the different types.

1 *Cash account.* The simplest form of account. A minimum opening balance is commonly required. You can trade only if you have the cash in your account. No credit is given and you'll have to maintain a balance

(sometimes termed the 'equity balance') to keep your account alive. This needn't always be as much as the opening balance though. Some brokers may charge you if you don't trade for a certain period.

2 *Margin account.* Essentially a credit facility enabling you to trade without necessarily having all the cash in your account. A proportion of the price is usually needed, but the rest comes from a loan – with interest. The loan will be from the broker or one of its affiliates so it might not always be at the most competitive rate.

Margin trading is when a broker lends an investor money with which to trade, using the cash and stocks the trader has with the broker as collateral. If you have $10,000 in your account, your broker may lend you a further $10,000 on margin. Imagine you bought Intel shares without using margin, and they rose 50%. You would of course have a 50% return on your $10,000. But using the margin you would increase returns by leveraging your capital. If you used your margin, you would have the same 50% return but this time on $20,000. That represents a 100% return on your initial $10,000.

A margin account lets you make a secured loan against your own portfolio. The advantage …

- is that you do not have to sell any of your portfolio to obtain the cash. Furthermore, you have no repayment schedule. You are free to repay the loan at any time, unless your collateral falls below the required amount. While most investors use the borrowed cash to buy additional securities, you can use it for any purpose. However, the wholly owned securities in your portfolio are collateral for the loan. You will also need a margin account if you are engaging in short sales.

But…

- Margin trading adds risk to an already risky environment. If Intel shares had fallen 50% in the boxed example and you did not trade on margin you would have lost $5000. If you used margin, you would have lost all your initial capital of $10,000. In consequence, you have an amplified loss.
- Under broker margin rules, if your stocks fall sharply you may be required to provide additional cash, otherwise the broker may sell them without any notification and potentially at a substantial loss to the investor.

Margin trading is only really **for the more experienced** trader and not the beginner as the risk is that you lose your money a lot quicker.

Not all brokers offer a margin facility. Those that do will do all the calculations for you in terms of how much you can borrow to invest.

3 *Short account.* A short sale involves selling securities that you don't actually own with the intent of buying them back at a lower price. It takes quite a sophisticated kind of broker to offer this facility – many brokers won't have it.

How do I set it up? Typically, you can be up and running in minutes by completing a simple online registration form on the broker's site. Have your bank details to hand and follow the on-screen instructions.

Three simple steps

The procedures for opening an account are explained on the particular broker's website as part of the procedure. But, generally this is how it goes:

1 Fill out an online application. Submit the application electronically or print and mail your signed application and initial deposit. You must be at least 18 years old to open and trade.

2 Return your completed application forms to activate your account. When your account becomes activated, the broker will send your account number, usually by e-mail.

3 Fund your account. There may be a minimum balance so check first. The fastest way to activate your account is to include a cheque with your printed and signed application forms. You cannot usually place a trade until your initial funding is reflected in your account portfolio. The broker will send a notification any time funds are deposited to your account.

Once the account is set up, passwords and account numbers confirmed, access login will require an account number and password or PIN (see Fig 13.1).

Do I need special hardware or software? No. Anyone with an internet connection can trade online. Having said that, make sure you read the next chapter, just in case you have an unusual system.

> Anyone with an internet **connection** can trade online.

You should try to ensure you have the latest Microsoft Internet Explorer (www.microsoft.com) or Netscape Navigator (www.netscape.com). These days most internet service providers give a secure connection. If in doubt verify with your ISP's customer support people. One of the advantages of an online broker is that you don't have to access your account from the same PC – you can trade anywhere, any time. Just go to the broker's website and log in with your user name and password which you would have been given when you opened the account (Fig 13.1). There I go, getting carried away again.

FIGURE 13.1 Typical login screen

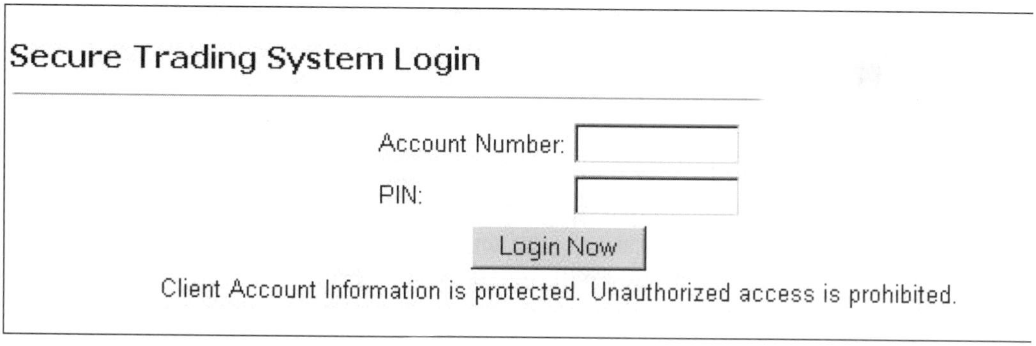

Secure Trading System Login

Account Number: [   ]

PIN: [   ]

[Login Now]

Client Account Information is protected. Unauthorized access is prohibited.

Exercises

1 What are the differences between a cash, margin and short account?
2 What do they involve?

See below for answers.

What you have learned

- To open a trading account you will need to have a bank account.
- Opening an account really is not that difficult. Go to the broker's website (see below) and follow the instructions. ▶

- Remember it is in the interests of the e-brokers to make it as easy as possible for you. It can be fiddly, but take your time and you'll be fine. Trust me. Or just call up their customer services number as you go through the form. A simple **cash account** requires a minimum opening balance and you can trade only if you have the cash in your account. No credit is given and you will have to maintain a balance.
- **Margin accounts** offer a credit facility enabling you to trade without necessarily having all the cash in your account. A proportion of the price is usually needed, but the rest comes from a loan from the broker. You do not have to sell any of your portfolio to obtain the cash. But margin trading adds further risk – under broker margin rules, if your stocks fall sharply you may be required to provide additional cash, otherwise the broker may sell them without any notification and potentially at a substantial loss to the investor.
- A **short** sale involves selling securities that you don't actually own with the intent of buying them back at a lower price. It takes quite a sophisticated kind of broker to offer this facility.

Placing your first trade

What should I know before I begin investing?   Before placing your first trade, I recommend placing a practice trade in the trading demo section of the broker site. Because the trading demo mirrors the real thing, you can simulate an actual trade without spending a cent.

When can I place my first trade?   If you applied for your account online and received an instant approval, you may be able to trade immediately, depending on your broker. Of course, payment for this trade must be received. If you applied by mail or your online application was not approved immediately, you may be eligible to place your first trade within one business day of receipt of your application. As soon as you receive a welcome message with your account number, you can access your account online.

Remember ... payment for purchase transactions is due by the trade settlement date. You should not wait until you receive your confirmation in the mail to send your payment. Similarly, if you sell securities, you must deliver the certificates by the settlement date. Some accounts will require a deposit of funds or securities before trades can be placed. These accounts are referred to as cash-on-hand accounts. If you have a cash-on-hand account, you will be notified.

> Remember ...
> **payment** for purchase transactions is due by the trade settlement date. You should not wait until you receive your confirmation in the mail to send your payment.

How do I start trading? Once you've opened an account and logged in you'll need to put money into your account before you can start trading. Now you just have to decide what to buy.

What are the stages for placing a trade online? Brokers vary, but typically you'll need to give the following information.

Once you've opened an account and logged in you'll need to put **money** into your account before you can start trading.

1 Account number and PIN – your PIN will often be sent separately under plain cover, like a credit card PIN.

2 Your ID – the name you registered in. (Sometimes called user name, etc. – you get the idea.)

3 Action required – buy, sell, sell short, buy to cover, etc.

4 Order size – number of shares.

5 Type of order – market price, limit, stop, stop limit (see Table 13.1).

6 Price – if order is a limit, stop or stop limit.

7 Duration – how long offer is to continue (e.g. good for the day offers lapse at close of the day's trading).

Do I have to place orders on-screen? It makes sense to use the on-screen facility if you're keen to maximize the efficiency of online trading (see Fig 13.2, p. 214), but there may be times when this isn't so desirable. Brokers acknowledge this and often offer different methods of placing orders. In addition to on-screen ordering you'll commonly be able to place orders by touch-tone telephone, by fax or even – for those big, complex orders – by speaking directly to a broker. However, if it isn't placed online, it usually costs a little more.

What sort of stocks can I buy? Most brokers will let you buy the stocks on just about all, except perhaps the more esoteric, exchanges of the country you are in. In the US that means NYSE, Nasdaq stocks of course, and usually more. In other words, don't worry, you'll have loads to choose from.

Can I trade mutual funds? It depends on your broker. Check this out as a feature when deciding on your broker.

Can I open a margin or options account? Again, it depends. If you can, you need to fill out the margin and options section on the application. The broker will review this information, and if appropriate will extend margin or option privileges to the account.

FIGURE 13.2 An order screen

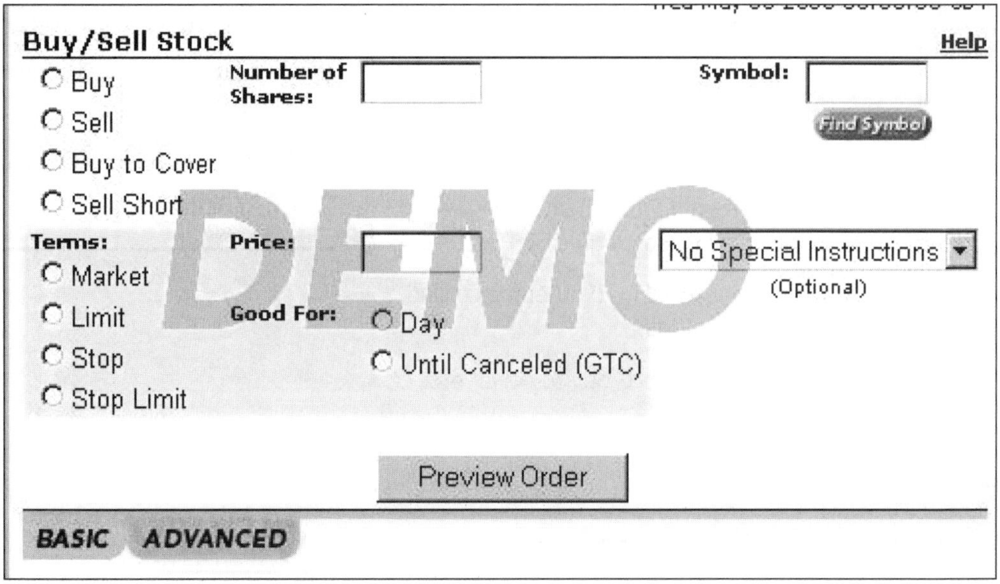

Buy/Sell Stock   Help

- ○ Buy   **Number of Shares:** [   ]   **Symbol:** [   ]
- ○ Sell   *Find Symbol*
- ○ Buy to Cover
- ○ Sell Short

Terms: **Price:** [   ]   [No Special Instructions ▼]
- ○ Market   (Optional)
- ○ Limit   **Good For:** ○ Day
- ○ Stop   ○ Until Canceled (GTC)
- ○ Stop Limit

                         [Preview Order]

BASIC ADVANCED

Can I trade OTC bulletin boards, pink sheets or penny stocks? It depends on your broker. You may be able to buy and sell over-the-counter bulletin board (OTCBB), pink sheets and penny stocks via the internet, interactive voice recognition (IVR) telephone system or with a broker. OTCBB securities usually represent shares of new or small companies, which are traded by dealers via manual procedures. But note that investing in OTCBB securities can be very risky and you may lose all or part of your investment in a short period of time.

In consequence, the trading rules for OTCBB securities differ significantly from listed or Nasdaq securities. For example, only limit orders to buy, and limit or market orders to sell will be accepted for the regular market sessions. Quotes for OTCBB securities are not guaranteed as the securities trade on a manual basis, and frequently 'real-time' quote information, or even firm quotes, may not be available. You should also be aware that frequent symbol changes, additions and de-listings occur in the OTCBB market. Take the time to carefully research the company and examine your investment objectives.

> Take the time to carefully **research** the company and examine your investment objectives.

What price do I trade at? You trade at the real-time price, that is, the price offered in the market place. But bear in mind that many of the research tools provided to you by your broker will be delayed by 15 minutes. So you're buying at the true price but using slightly old analysis. If the research is delayed it will tell you nearby.

How long does it all take?   How long do you want it to take? Assuming you have money in your account and know what you want to buy, you can commence trading right away. If the stock market is open and you want to buy at market price, your order will be executed immediately. See 'When can I trade' below for information about after-hours trading.

However, during busy periods you may not be able to access the broker's site, or if you do, your order may not reach them through the internet immediately. In other words, there can sometimes be delays. With most major reputable brokers, this should not happen.

Is there any advice about what to buy?   At the end of the day it's your call – you have to make a decision what to buy. But most brokers offer research and analytical tools to help you make an informed decision (see Fig 13.3, p. 216). Typically, a brokerage site will enable you to view a graph of the price and other trading history of a particular stock. You should also be able to get news updates about a specific company and compare its performance against similar companies. Also, by reading this coursebook, you'll be better able to understand what all those tools can do for you and make more informed decisions.

How easy is it to sell?   This will vary according to the particular broker you've registered with. Generally, you'll simply have to log on in the prescribed way – entering your ID and password is typically what's called for – then click onto the trading page and select the shares you wish to sell. There will usually be clear, step-by-step instructions on the screen. Figure 13.4 (p. 217) shows a typical market overview screen that will allow you to navigate your account easily.

What's a nominee account?   Sometimes you'll find that your broker refers to a nominee account. This is simply a means of facilitating the rapid processing of each trade. The broker holds your shares in a pooled nominee account. You remain beneficially entitled to your shares (i.e. you still 'own' them) but the nominee account allows the broker to process your trade immediately, rather than waiting for the formal legal certificates to be completed. Practically all online accounts are nominee accounts.

> Sometimes you'll find that your broker refers to a **nominee** account. This is simply a means of facilitating the rapid processing of each trade.

News Headlines

››

INTERVIEW-Vietnam, China, can't hold back Internet-AOL
Reuters, 04/24/2000 07:18

INTERVIEW-Vietnam, China, can't hold back Internet-AOL
Reuters, 04/24/2000 07:18

RESEARCH ALERT - TMP Worldwide reinstated
Reuters, 04/24/2000 07:13

Edgix Appoints Mike Young to Lead Global Network Operations; Edgix Strengthens Management Team with Seasoned Executive from UUNet
Business Wire, 04/24/2000 06:48

NYSE INDICATION LAST 60 2/8 BID 56 ASK 59
Reuters, 04/24/2000 06:42

Be Free and Webs Unlimited Announce Channel Cash; First Affiliate Marketing Add-In for Microsoft FrontPage 2000
Business Wire, 04/24/2000 06:26

ARAX				
Last: **57 3/8**	Change: **-2³/₈** ↓	Open: **57 9/16**	High: **61 3/8**	Low: **55 13/16**	Volume: **8,692,3**
		Yield: **n/a**	P/E Ratio: **139.94**	52 Wk Range: **38 15/32 to 95 13/1**

1-Year Historical Chart

Daily ▬

Volume ▬ ©BigCharts.com

FIGURE 13.4 Typical market overview screen

Market Snapshot — Refresh

Symbol	Last	Change	View
DJIA	10434.92	-6.98	Summary
S&P 500	1244.94	-0.92	Summary
NASDAQ	2254.98	-7.53	Most Actives
AMEX	899.33	3.25	Most Actives
NYSE	624.73	1.73	Most Actives

my Account

View:

- Balances
- Positions
- Electronic Statements

- Transactions
- Review Orders

Can I access my account any time? Yes, most brokers permit access round the clock, seven days a week, all year (Fig 13.5).

What about evenings and weekends? Although you can access your account and place trades any time, trades will be executed only when the stock exchange is open. Beware: trades placed outside opening times will be executed at the price when the market next opens – this may vary from the price at the time you place the trade. For this reason, you'll find that

FIGURE 13.5 Check the status of your account 24/7

Balances — Help

	Current Balances	Start of Day Balances
Buying Power	2,797.44	2,797.44
Available Funds	1,398.72	1,398.72
Cash Balance	0.00	0.00
Margin Balance	-182.53	-182.53
Equity Balance	2,350.27	2,350.27
Equity Percentage	93.00%	93.00%
- Long Value	2,532.80	2,532.80
- Short Value	0.00	0.00
Total Maintenance Requirement	801.87	801.87
Liquidation Value	2,353.27	2,353.27

Start of Day - Account balances are based on the previous market close.
Current - Account balances are adjusted by the most recent activity. Open orders are not included in this calculation.
Balance amounts are subject to change.

brokers will usually ask you to set a limit order for every out-of-hours trade placed.

Exercises

1 List the stages/information necessary for placing a trade online.

2 What is a nominee account?

3 Assess the pros and cons of placing a trade outside stock market opening hours.

Answers

1 a Account number and PIN.
   b Your ID (user name, etc.).
   c Action required – buy, sell, sell short, buy to cover, etc.
   d Order size – number of shares.
   e Type of order – market price, limit, stop, stop limit.
   f Price – if order is a limit, stop or stop limit.
   g Duration – how long offer is to continue (e.g. good for the day offers lapse at close of the day's trading).

2 A nominee account is a means of facilitating the processing of each trade. The broker holds your shares in a pooled nominee account. You remain entitled to your shares, but the nominee account allows the broker to process your trade immediately, rather than waiting for the formal legal certificates to be completed. It's like the system used by banks to process your money and hold it for you – it keeps administrative costs down without undermining your ownership of the shares.

3 Trades placed outside opening times will allow more flexibility in your trading. You may not have time in the day to get on the net and execute a trade. However, the trade will be executed at the price when the market next opens, and this may vary from the price at the time you place the trade. The share price tends to jump at the start of trading on each day as expectations have changed overnight and trading expectations have not settled at a consensus. For this reason, you'll find that brokers will usually ask you to set a limit order for every out-of-hours trade placed.

What you have learned

The best way to understand what the process of placing a trade involves is to use the **trading demo** on the broker's site (check out the websites below and start surfing). Setting up and starting to trade on a nominee account is very quick if you **send funds with your application**.

You do not have to place your orders on-screen, rather you can phone or fax.

You can trade after closing and almost all broker sites act as a one-stop-shop, providing trade in most shares and derivatives, extensive research, news, chat, etc; you can spend all day and night in front of a computer screen…tragic thought.

Types of orders

So I just place my order and go? Not quite. After you have decided whether you plan to buy or sell a stock, the typical order ticket will give you a few more choices. You can choose between a market order, a limit order, a stop order and a stop limit order. Each of these choices has its own implications, as seen in Table 13.1. It sounds complicated, but most people start with market orders, then, as they become more confident, move to the others. Soon you'll be talking stop limit order placement like an old pro.

TABLE 13.1 The different types of orders

	Market	Limit	Stop	Stop limit
Description of fill	Filled at best price available when order reaches the market.	May be filled when the stock trades at the limit price you set.	Will be filled at best price available in the market after the stock trades at your stop price.	Will be filled at the stop price, if possible, after the order is activated.

A market order is an instruction to buy or sell a stock at the best market price available at the moment.

For example, you may want to buy 100 shares of XYZ stock. If the current market for XYZ is 50 bid and 50 1/8 ask, you may or may not get the stock at 50 1/8.

Market orders will definitely be filled, but you cannot be sure of the price. Prices will vary with current conditions, and these conditions are not always reflected on your computer screen. The actual price at which your order is filled may be better or worse than you expected.

A limit order lets you place a price restriction on your transaction. You indicate that you are only willing to buy or sell a stock at a certain price or better. Your order is not filled unless the stock trades at that level. Placing a limit order is not a guarantee that your trade will be executed at your limit price. It does, however, eliminate the risk that your order will be filled at a price worse than you expected.

For example, if you want to buy CrazyGuy stock at $80 a share once again, and the market price is 80 bid and 80 1/8 offer, your order cannot be filled immediately. If somebody comes to sell the stock at $80, then your order will be filled if it is next in line for execution. If more buyers enter the pit and drive up the stock price, your order will not be filled.

A stop order is an order to buy or sell a stock at the market price once the price reaches or passes through a specified point, called the 'stop price'. This type of order is generally used by people who own a stock and want to make sure they sell out if the stock price starts to drop. The stop price placed on a sell stop order must be below the current bid price of the security.

For example, if you buy 100 shares of Maniac Driver at $50 a share and you want to protect yourself from a potential loss, you might place a stop order. If you placed a stop order at $45 a share, the moment Maniac Driver traded at $45, your order would become live and the broker or specialist would sell it to the highest bidder. Stop orders in volatile issues will not guarantee an execution at or near the stop price. Once triggered, they are competing with other incoming market orders.

Stop orders can be placed for buy orders as well. The stop price specified for a buy order must be above the current asking price.

A stop limit order performs like a stop order with one major exception. Once the order is activated (by the stock trading at or 'through' the stop price), it does not become a market order. Instead, it becomes a limit order with a limit price equal to the former stop price.

For example, you place a stop limit order to sell stock with a stop price of $45 a share. As with the stop order, once the stock trades at $45, your order is triggered. However, the broker canot sell it below $45 a share no matter what happens.

The advantage of this order is that you set a minimum price at which your order can be filled. The disadvantage is that your order may not be filled in certain fast market conditions. In this case, if the stock keeps moving down, you will keep losing money.

Fill or kill (FOK) is an instruction to either fill the entire order at the limit price given or better, or cancel it.

How do I know if my trade has gone through? You should always receive on-screen confirmation of executed trades in your secure area. Trades placed with a limit attached, either in or out of market hours, will also appear on the screen as pending. On top of online confirmation, you should receive a formal contract (often by e-mail).

What if I make a mistake when placing an order? It's not in anybody's interests to let you make an erroneous trade. Online brokers usually require you to confirm the details of your trade at least once and more often than not, twice. But there's only so much an automated brokerage system can do to protect you, so make a mistake twice and you will have entered into a contract on that basis – so be careful.

| Exercises

1 What is a stop order?

2 What is a limit order?

3 What does FOK mean?

For answers see below.

It's not in anybody's interests to let you make an **erroneous** trade.

What you have learned

Trades are simple to make. You will get on-screen confirmation of your trade and be asked to confirm your choice.

A number of orders are possible:

- A **market order** is an instruction to buy or sell a stock at the best market price available at the moment.

- A **limit order** lets you place a price restriction on your transaction. You indicate that you are only willing to buy or sell a stock at a certain price or better. Your order is not filled unless the stock trades at that level. This is not a guarantee that your trade will be executed at your limit price but does eliminate the risk that your order will be filled at a price worse than you expected.

- A **stop order** is an order to buy or sell a stock at the market price once the price reaches or passes through a specified point, called the 'stop price,' generally used if you want to make sure you sell out if the stock price starts to drop.

- A **stop limit order** performs like a stop order with one major exception. Once the order is activated, it does not become a market order. Instead, it becomes a limit order with a limit price equal to the former stop price.

FOK (fill or kill) means that you want to either fill the entire order at the limit price given or better, or cancel the order.

Using your account

How do I get money into my account? The standard ways of transferring money are just as applicable to online trading accounts: debit card payment, bank transfer and cheques. But note you can only use a debit card or direct debit once the transaction has been confirmed. Your broker may not offer all of these. But one thing is for sure – they want your money, so they *will* have lots of easy explanations on how to transfer money into the account.

> One thing is for sure – they want your money, so they *will* have lots of easy **explanations** on how to transfer money into the account.

How do I extract money from my account? You can get money out of your account at any time up to the cleared funds balance in your cash account. Just nominate a destination bank, usually the one given when you registered with the broker. Many brokers don't charge for transfers, but give yourself three working days at least for the transfer to be effected.

How can I close my account? Not usually a problem. Ensure that you notify the broker in writing – remembering to keep a copy of the letter. Your remaining shares will be transferred to your nominated broker or to you in paper form. The latter will often attract a handling fee.

Can I keep track of what my stocks are worth? Simple – your broker will provide a means of clicking straight into your portfolio so that you can keep tabs on your holdings. To view your up-to-the-minute share dealings some sites require you to re-enter your password and ID.

Can I move my existing holdings of shares into my account? Your broker will have an online explanation of how to do this. Usually it is the broker to whom you are transferring who will try to do most of the work for you once you give them your details online and confirm you want to transfer to them.

How do I withdraw my shares from my account? You can withdraw shares from your account by making a request to your broker. This can be online or in person via your broker's customer services team if you need a little more assistance. Again, transfer in paper form will usually attract a fee.

How will dividend payments be handled? You will receive any dividends accruing to your shares straight into your cash account. All tax vouchers relating to dividend receipt will be collected by your broker and forwarded to you annually for the tax year.

What if I am a foreign resident? Many e-brokers service foreign accounts. However, due to the fact that overseas mail delivery is not conducive to meeting a three-day settlement, they often require funds or securities to be in the account prior to placing orders.

Charges

What will I be charged per trade?

Online brokerages are not always known for the clarity of their pricing schedules. A good way of selecting an online broker is to choose one with a simple pricing structure. A good broker might, for example, keep things to a simple charge of, say, $10 per trade plus a quarterly management fee.

Some brokers are more competitive, such as Ameritrade at $8 per online trade. But note that you may be charged more for touchtone or direct broker access trades. Brokers will typically charge you an additional fee for limit, stop and stop limit orders.

Interest rates

How will interest rates be calculated?

When your money is sitting in your nominee account you'd expect it to be accruing interest, wouldn't you? Every broker will differ slightly, but rates are always similar in my experience except for special offers.

What you have learned

- You can **transfer cash** in and out of your account within a couple of days by using standard means.
- **Transferring holdings** will take longer than cash but can always be done by following the procedure made clear by your broker.
- **Dividends** will accrue straight into your cash account.
- It is important that you decipher the **broker's pricing schedule**. Make note of the interest rate you receive for idle funds and compare brokers.
- Your broker will provide a monitor for keeping track of how much your stocks are worth.

Exercises

1 How would you close your account?
2 What happens to your dividends?
3 What is a stop limit order?
4 What is a market order?
5 What are the risks associated with margin trading?
6 What website security features should you be looking for when choosing an online broker?

Some suggested answers

1 **Closing your account**: ensure that you notify the broker in writing and keep a copy of your letter. Your remaining shares will be transferred to your nominated broker or to you in paper form. The latter will often attract a handling fee.

2 You will receive any **dividends** accruing to your shares straight into your cash account. All tax vouchers relating to dividend receipt will be collected by your broker and forwarded to you annually for the tax year.

3 **A stop limit order** is like a stop order (buy/sell a stock once price passes through a certain stop price) except, once the order is activated (by the stock trading at or 'through' the stop price), it does not become a market order. Instead it becomes a limit order with a limit price equal to the former stop price.

4 **A market order** is an instruction to buy or sell a stock at the best market price available at the moment.

5 **Margin trading** adds further risk as you have an amplified potential loss.

Under broker margin rules, if your stocks fall sharply you may be required to provide additional cash, otherwise the broker may sell them without any notification and potentially at a substantial loss to the investor.

6 **Site security**: the broker will give audit trails of all trades and cancellations, which are available for you to inspect, some form of insurance protection (usually Securities Investor Protection Corporation, SIPC), ensuring client funds are either segregated or protected should the firm have financial difficulties, the use of firewalls that prevent access from the outside through links, etc., and the use of account numbers, user names and passwords.

Summary

- Opening an account really is not that difficult. Go to the broker's website and follow the instructions.
- The best way to understand what the process of placing a trade involves is using the **trading demo** on the broker's site.
- **You can trade after closing** and almost all broker sites act as a one-stop-shop, providing trade in most shares and derivatives, extensive research, news, chat, etc. You can spend all day and night in front of a computer screen...tragic thought.
- Trades are simple to make – you will get on-screen confirmation of your trade and you will be asked to confirm your choice.
- A number of orders are possible: **market order**, **limit order**, **stop order**, **stop limit order**.
- **Transferring cash** in and out of your account can be done within a couple of days by using standard means.

It's easy...or maybe not.

Planning trades

You can't just go out there and wildly speculate.

BILL LIPSCHULTZ,
FORMER GLOBAL HEAD OF FOREIGN EXCHANGE, SALOMON BROTHERS

What you will learn

- A trading plan is probably the most important part of any trade. It is also the most neglected.
- We examine your trading strategy in brief and what planning a trade ought to involve.
- Then you will be able to use this in an actual trade and produce an actual trading tactic.
- To avoid the many pitfalls of trading we also examine keeping a journal, diversification, your tolerance to risk and risk management, and the types of traders that fail.
- We will devise a template for you to use when analyzing investment decisions, and a transactions record at the end of the module.

Module outline

- Learn to produce and use a trading strategy and trading tactics as part of a trading plan.
- See how to keep a journal as part of profitable trading.
- Examine the types of traders that fail.

The unfortunate answer is that nothing works and everything works.

- Find yourself (i.e. your tolerance to risk).
- Manage risk, understand proper diversification (risk-tolerance test).
- Share analysis template and transaction template (photocopy and fill out for record keeping and assessment purposes).

What works? Building a trading strategy

So, having examined both fundamental and technical analysis in broad outline together with some common resources followers of those techniques use, you may well be tempted to ask what works. Does looking for analysts' upgrades of stock performances work? Does an examination of stock momentum work?

The unfortunate answer is that nothing works and everything works. Nothing works, because if it did it would be consistently profitable and the puzzle of the markets would be solved. Everything works in that all the individual techniques are successful part of the time – that is why people follow them.

DIY trading strategy

So where do we go from here? The best advice to give you is:

1 **Read a lot more** about fundamental and technical analysis from the recommended reading.

2 **Develop a trading strategy**.

A trading strategy is a set of rules which must be met before you enter a trade, as opposed to trading tactics, which are the actual specific plans for what to do once you enter a trade (Fig 14.1).

HOT TIP

Every individual's trading strategy will vary and likely be unique, based on their own perspectives.

This is a very simple guide to building a trading strategy to give you some idea of how it ought to be done. As you actually do it you will begin to realize the complexities and your plan will doubtless become more sophisticated.

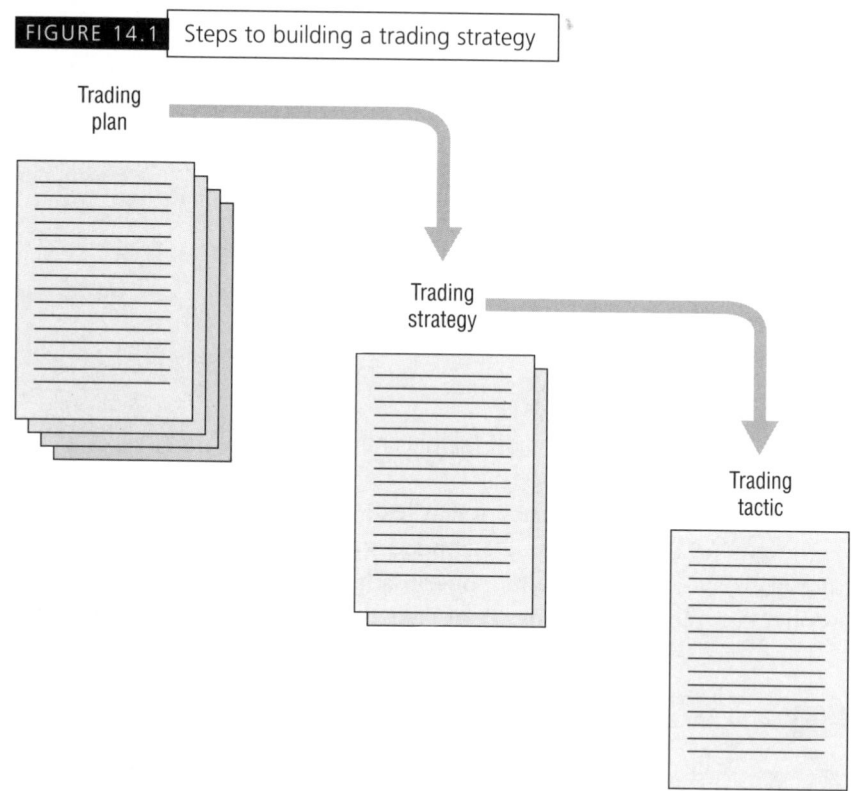

FIGURE 14.1 Steps to building a trading strategy

Trading plan

Trading strategy

Trading tactic

Select some indicators   Having examined what fundamental and technical analysts commonly look for, and having done some reading about those subjects, choose some indicators you think may be potentially indicative of a rising market.

Hypothesize!   Choose some rules you consider worth testing, bearing in mind the period of time you want to be in and out of the market for each trade. Choose a target price for exit, a stop-loss figure and other circumstances for exit.

Example   A fundamental analyst of company stocks may choose to buy a stock only if the following rules are met:

- P/E ratio less than 8;
- analyst recommendations all being buy or higher;
- profit margin of 10% or higher;
- dividend yield of 13% or higher;

> Choose a target price for exit, a stop-loss figure and other **circumstances** for exit.

- target price: rise of 15%;
- stop loss: drop of 10% or below the 9-week low;
- exit if one of these fundamental factors changes adversely.

A technical analyst may choose stock purchase rules based on:

- MACD crossover;
- stochastic crossover;
- a bounce off a trendline;
- target price: rise of 15%;
- stop loss: drop of 10%;
- exit if one of the above technical factors changes adversely (Fig 14.2).

Important   There is a tendency when testing trading rules to 'overfit' the rules (i.e. amend them) to the data at hand so the results are good for those data only. To avoid this, do some 'out-of-sample testing', i.e. test the same rules on a completely different set of data. But beware: it may be that your

FIGURE 14.2   A technical approach

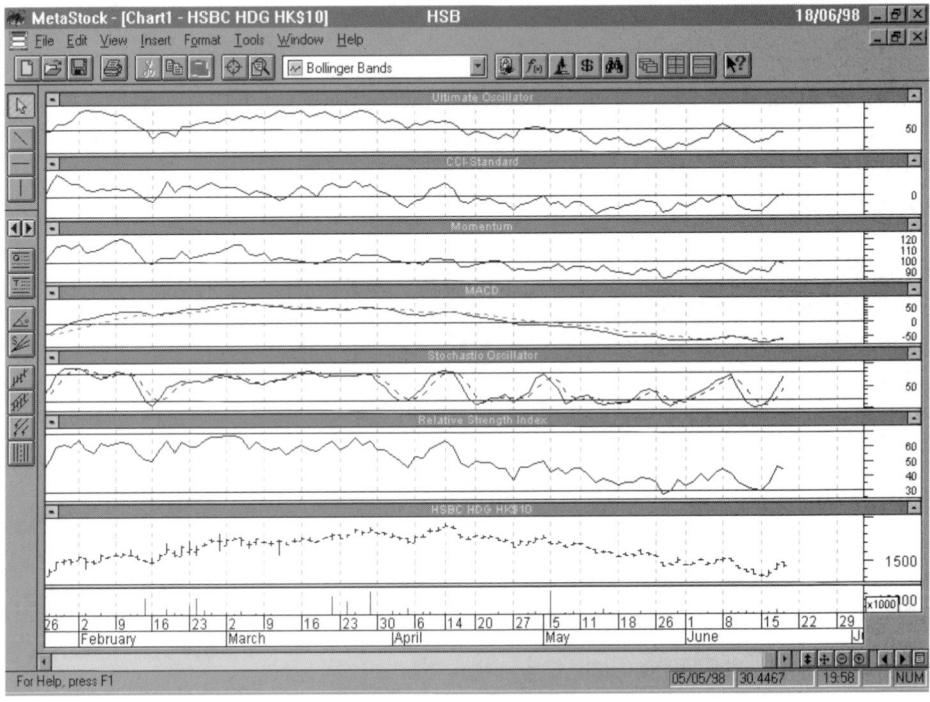

trading rules do genuinely only work with that one company, both historically and in the future, and you may be throwing away a good system by out-of-sample testing. To avoid this, do some paper trades on the same stock as well.

Test Now test the rules. Select some stocks and obtain their historical price charts (see skeleton plans for sites). Next see what would have happened had you used your trading strategy. What would a notional $20,000 have been at the end of one year, after dealing costs? Is the return better than bank rates of return? Did you beat the Dow or a typical mutual fund?

The preponderance of evidence rule When testing and developing look for a balance of probability. Examine many different indicators, e.g. news stories on your product, analysts' views, market momentum. When there is a preponderance of evidence suggesting price movement, make a paper trade. Keep doing this until you are comfortable that what you are doing works. If it does not, find out what aspects do not work, e.g. the technical indicators are always wrong, and either amend or ditch that particular indicator – be ruthless.

Always paper trade with different methods of selecting trades. For instance, you may try to combine stock filters with technical indicators and plot the results together with other systems, and go for what appears to make sense and is profitable. When you find a trading strategy you are fairly happy with, you are ready to trade.

Action plan 1 – The plan, the strategy, the tactic

1 Decide whether you need or want to find out more about fundamental and technical analysis.

2 Surf sites which provide analysis for your product choice.

3 Choose the site(s) which you like the best for fundamental and/or technical analysis.

4 Develop a trading strategy using the guidelines provided in this chapter, then test it to satisfaction (if need be, return to Step 2 in this programme of action).

> When testing and developing look for a balance of **probability**.

> Always paper trade with **different** methods of selecting trades.

How to back test well

1 I tend to test one indicator at a time and add more and more and see how that affects results.

2 Look at a chart and identify areas in which your indicators should produce signals and then find indicators that tend to.

3 Are the results very volatile, e.g. large losses and profits (even though overall profitable)? Can you handle such losses along the way?

4 Do not just test bull markets, test bear and sideways or find a different set of indicators for each type of market (Fig 14.3).

FIGURE 14.3 Looking to buy

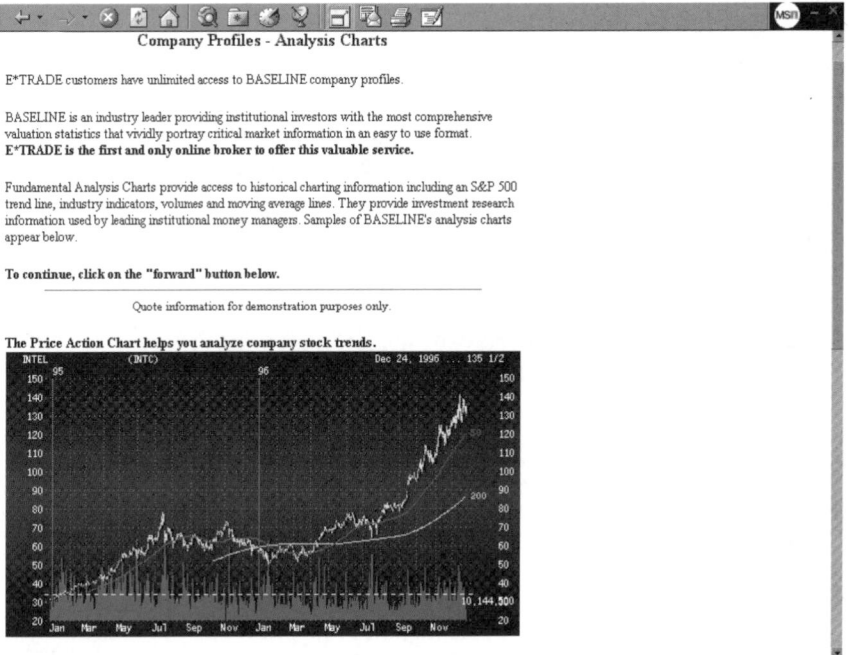

Risk–reward As a rule of thumb your upside target should be a greater percentage than your stop-loss.

Action Plan 2 – Creating a trading tactic

1 Using the trading rules contained in your trading strategy, go through the relevant stocks, etc.

2 Select the best possibilities for price moves. Remember the preponderance of evidence rule.

3 For each possibility list the pros and cons (see Table 14.1). Select the best of the best to trade.

4 Set an upside target. What do you expect the price to reach and in what time frame? You may want to attach a rough probability of this occurring.

5 Set a stop-loss – a point at which you will exit the trade: either a specific price level or a percentage.

6 Set a point at which you will sell irrespective of 4 and 5 in this list, i.e. you may get negative news on the company and decide to sell even though the stop-loss has not been reached.

TABLE 14.1   Part of a simple trading tactic

Pros	Cons
MACD crossover occurred	Sector undergone long bull run
Stochastic crossover	
SAR upward	
Trendline bounce	
All analysts buy or strong buy	
Sector strong	

HOT TIP

The mind of a trader
Stick to your plan. Do not start hoping for price moves or denying losses. Try to keep objective. Do not get attached to a position: each day is a clean slate. To learn more about trading plans and trading like a professional you might consider reading my book *The Mind of a Trader* (FT Pitman Publishing, 1998).

Exercises

1 What is a trading strategy?

2 Outline the process necessary in order to create a trading plan.

3 What is overfitting? What is significant about it?

4 Look at and follow action plan 1. For example, you may decide that you want to concentrate on technicals such as MACDs, stochastics, trendlines and stop-losses with a few fundamentals, e.g. P/E and PEG ratios, in which case you would look at www.bigcharts.com, www.tradingcharts.com, www.etrade.com, etc. Develop a trading strategy keeping in mind the issues you have outlined for questions 2 and 3.

5 Now follow action plan 2.

What you have learned

A **trading strategy** is a set of rules which must be met before you enter a trade, as opposed to trading tactics, which are the actual specific plans for what to do once you enter a trade.

Choose some indicators you think may be potentially indicative of a rising market (or a falling one). Choose a target price for exit, a stop-loss figure and other circumstances for exit, i.e. **hypothesize**.

Beware of overfitting – there is a tendency when testing trading rules to 'overfit' the rules (i.e. amend them) to the data at hand so the results are good for those data only. To avoid this, do some 'out-of-sample testing' and do some paper trades on the same stock as well.

Test by selecting some stocks and obtain their historical price charts. Next see what would have happened had you used your trading strategy. What would a notional $20,000 have been at the end of one year, after dealing costs?

When there is a **preponderance of evidence** suggesting price movement, make a paper trade. Keep doing this until you are comfortable that what you are doing works. If it does not, pinpoint which aspects do not work and amend.

Test one indicator at a time. Look at a chart and identify areas in which your indicators should produce signals. Are the results very volatile? Test bull, bear and sideways markets.

Notes

_____

_____

_____

_____

_____

_____

_____

_____

_____

_____

_____

_____

_____

_____

_____

_____

_____

Journal keeping

I am regularly asked by traders what they can do to improve their trading. One of the easiest and simplest steps is to keep a journal. Imagine all that information and experience you collect as you trade.

- Without a journal you are throwing away so much of it.
- Without a journal you are in serious danger of repeating your mistakes.
- Keeping a journal is a money and risk management technique. By identifying possible trading problems, you can start to resolve them. So, make journal keeping a goal.

> I am regularly asked by traders what they can do to **improve** their trading. One of the easiest and simplest steps is to keep a journal.

What to record

1 A **copy of your goals**. Note your progress in achieving them.

2 The **anatomy of every trade**. Write down, from the moment you started analyzing a stock to the moment after you sold it, how you felt at each key moment about every activity you undertook. You may want to compare that with what you know about how you should have reacted, in light of what you have read in this book. For example, how did you feel as you approached your stop-loss?

3 **What feels good and what feels uncomfortable** about what you are doing.

Remember to keep your notes clear and well presented. You will have to return to them at a later date.

Seven traders

There are many types of trader. An awareness of the varieties when looking at your trading plan allows you to avoid the pitfalls.

Disciplined   This is the ideal type of trader. You take losses and profits with ease. You focus on your system and follow it with discipline. Trading is usually a relaxed activity. You appreciate that a loss does not make for a loser.

Doubter   You find it difficult to execute at signals. You doubt your own abilities. You need to develop self-confidence. Perhaps you should paper trade.

Blamer   All losses are someone else's fault. You blame bad fills, your broker for picking up the phone too slowly, your system for not being perfect. You need to regain your objectivity and self-responsibility.

Victim   Here you blame yourself. You feel the market is out to get you. You start becoming superstitious in your trading.

Optimist   You start thinking, 'It's only money, I'll make it back later.' You think all losses will bounce back to a profit or that you will start trading properly tomorrow.

> Trading is usually a **relaxed** activity. You appreciate that a loss does not make for a loser.

Gambler You are in it for the thrill. Money is a side issue. Risk and reward analysis hardly figure in your trades; you want to be a player; you want the buzz and excitement.

Timid You enter a trade but panic at the sight of a profit and take it far too soon. Fear rules your trading.

> You are in it for the **thrill**. Money is a side issue.

What you have learned

Keeping a **journal** is a risk management technique. Without a journal you are in serious danger of repeating your mistakes. By identifying possible trading problems, you can start to resolve them. So, make journal keeping a goal.

There are many types of traders. Above all **be disciplined**, take profits and losses with ease. Focus on your system.

Notes

How much risk can you tolerate?

You might need to pursue an aggressive investment strategy but you might also have a conservative stomach. Greater volatility is double-edged; the potential upside is bigger, but the potential downside is bigger. The issue is, where do your preferences lie?

Conservative risk-takers are likely to define risk as potential loss of their principal. Concerned more about safety than anything else, they're more willing to accept a lower rate of return in exchange for a lower degree of risk. This may mean that they choose fixed-income investment tools such as bonds and even a higher percentage of money in their portfolio.

More aggressive risk-takers are less willing to tie up too much money over long periods in low-yielding fixed investments, preferring the bigger potential returns the riskier stock market may offer. Of course, your degree of risk tolerance can change over time as you approach certain goals. For example, investors tend to hold on too long to falling stock (risk loving on downturn) and can sell too quickly on the upside.

HOT TIP

Assessing and reassessing your investing personality regularly is crucial. Find yourself.

Important Because each of your financial goals may be weighted differently, you may want to consider your total portfolio as a collection of several goal-specific portfolios when making the evaluation. It is also important to consider your age, the time horizon for each of your specific goals, and your income and asset base.

Exercise – risk tolerance

An investor's risk tolerance in making investment decisions can depend on investment goals as well as the investor's personality. The following exercise will measure your reaction to market risk, weight the relative importance of your goals and uncover your personal investment preferences. Give yourself the points in the brackets for your answer.

1 The degree to which the value of an investment moves up and down is referred to as 'volatility'. In general, more volatile investments tend to grow faster than more stable investments – they have a larger potential upside. However, volatile investments are more risky, since there is no guarantee the 'upturns' will be larger than the 'downturns'. How much volatility are you willing to accept?

a Slight. I do not want to lose money, even if it means my returns are small. (1)

b Some. I am willing to accept the occasional loss as long as my money is in sound, high-quality investments that can be expected to grow over time. (3)

c Considerable. I am willing to take substantial risk in pursuit of significantly higher returns. (5)

> Your degree of risk **tolerance** can change over time as you approach certain goals.

TOTAL POINTS_____

2 Suppose your investment portfolio contains a significant portion of large company stocks in addition to several other assets. Large company stocks have averaged a compound annual return of 11% over the past 72 years. However, if large company stocks had lost 18% of their value in the past year, what would you do?

a Sell the large company stock portion of my investment portfolio and realize the loss. (1)

b Sell some, but not all, of the large company stock portion. (2)

c Continue to hold the large company stock portion of my investment portfolio, following a consistent long-term strategy. (3)

d Buy more large company stocks. (4)

TOTAL POINTS_____

3 Please provide your response to the following statement: *Given my investment time horizon, I am willing to accept significant fluctuations in the value of my investments to achieve potentially higher long-term returns.*

a Strongly disagree. (0)

b Disagree. (1)

c Agree. (2)

d Strongly agree. (5)

TOTAL POINTS_____

4 Which of the following statements is most true about your risk tolerance and the way you wish to invest to achieve your goal(s)? My investment should…

a be completely safe; I do not wish to run the risk of losing any principal at any time. (1)

b generate regular income that I can spend. (2)

c generate some current income and also grow in value over time. (3)

d grow over time, but I would also like to generate some current income. (4)

e grow substantially in value over time. I do not need to generate current income. (5)

TOTAL POINTS_____

5 An investor must be prepared to expose his/her investments to increased chances for loss in attempting to achieve higher expected returns. The following statements represent possible outcomes for three hypothetical portfolios at the end of one year. Which investment portfolio would you be most comfortable holding?

a Portfolio A has a likely return of 6%, and there is a 10% chance for loss at the end of the year. (2)

b Portfolio B has a likely return of 10%, and there is an 18% chance for loss at the end of the year. (3)

c Portfolio C has a likely return of 14%, and there is a 25% chance for loss at the end of the year. (4)

TOTAL POINTS_____

6 I understand the value of my portfolio will fluctuate over time. However, the maximum loss in any one-year period that I am prepared to accept is:

a 0%   (1)

b –5%   (2)

c –10%   (3)

d –20%   (4)

e –30%+   (5)

TOTAL POINTS_____

7 Investments in which the principal is '100% safe' sometimes earn less than the inflation rate. This means that, while no money is lost, there is a loss of purchasing power. With respect to your goal(s), which of the following is most true?

a My money should be '100% safe', even if it means my returns do not keep up with inflation. (0)

b It is important that the value of my investments keeps pace with inflation. I am willing to risk an occasional loss in principal so that my investments may grow at about the same rate as inflation over time. (3)

c It is important that my investments grow faster than inflation. I am willing to accept a fair amount of risk to try to achieve this. (5)

TOTAL POINTS_____

8 Which statement best describes your main concern when selecting an investment?

a The potential for loss. (1)

b Mostly the potential for loss, but also the potential for gain. (2)

c Mostly the potential for gain, but I am still concerned about the potential for loss. (3)

d The potential for gain. (4)

TOTAL POINTS_____

9 Consider the following two investments, A and B. Investment A provides an average annual return of 7% with minimal risk of loss of principal. Investment B provides an average annual return of 10% but carries a potential loss of principal of 20% or more in any one year. If I could choose between Investment A and Investment B to meet my goal(s), I would invest my money:

a 100% in A and 0% in B. (1)

b 75% in A and 25% in B. (2)

c 50% in A and 50% in B. (3)

d 25% in A and 75% in B. (4)

e 0% in A and 100% in B. (5)

TOTAL POINTS_____

If you tended to go for the former options in the above questions then you are quite averse to risk in your tolerance. So, if you scored between:

- 8 and 20 you tend to be particularly risk-averse;
- 21 and 35 you tend to be neutral towards risk and volatility;
- 36 and 50 you like market volatility – regarding it as the best opportunity to make money.

Types of risk

Does investing online lessen the risk of losing money? Only to the extent that it puts all the tools and resources in your hands to conveniently make your own investing decisions. When you're online, you can easily scan the market indicators and track price movements. This will reduce the risk of error in judgement.

Interest rate risk

When the cost of borrowing money goes up, it erodes the value of certain investments since it reduces the relative return on the investments. This is especially vigorous for long-term fixed securities like bonds. For example, if you bought a bond with the 'fantastic' rate of 8% and five years later interest rates move above 8%, you will have a lower relative return compared to, say, savings accounts.

Investor psychology

Overreaction to fluctuating interest rates and inflation fears by panicky investors prompts a market sell-off that affects the value of investments, even among those who kept their heads. Herding behaviour can create exceptionally volatile markets.

Market conditions

Stock prices can soar to such highs per dollar invested that the market and your individual investments become more vulnerable in the event of a decline. This is also referred to as market indices.

Liquidity

A liquidity risk is the inability to convert an investment quickly and easily to cash, which is purely liquid, without incurring a significant loss in the value of the investment.

Notes

_____

_____

_____

_____

_____

_____

_____

_____

_____

_____

_____

_____

_____

_____

_____

_____

_____

_____

_____

_____

How to manage risk

There are some simple yet wily strategies that can help mitigate the effects of most risk.

Asset allocation   Basically, don't put all your eggs in one basket. Rather, you must diversify.

- Spread your investment among different investment products – stocks, bonds, mutual funds and risk-free cash equivalents – to lessen the chance that a poor showing by one will jeopardize the overall performance.

- Choosing stocks that are not perfectly correlated will give similar results. For example, stocks from different sectors will move imperfectly, i.e. they will not drop together but neither will they rise perfectly together. The weight you give to each sector should be re-evaluated and shifted on a regular basis depending on how your perceptions to your aversion to risk change. This is called hedging risk.

- Although no strategy can guarantee success, history has shown that a balanced portfolio is less vulnerable to economic shock.

Dollar cost averaging   Dollar cost averaging is a very effective investment tool. Say you have $20,000 to invest. If a security you're interested in is trading at $2 a share in January, your $20,000 will buy you 10,000 shares. But with a dollar cost averaging strategy, you instead buy $1,000 worth every month for ten months. Using dollar cost averaging you do not expose your whole $20,000 in one go, but rather stagger the investment along the fluctuating cycle of the share price.

> Although no strategy can guarantee success, history has shown that a balanced portfolio is less **vulnerable** to economic shock.

Exercises

1 Why do your preferences to risk matter?
2 What is interest rate risk?
3 What is liquidity risk?
4 How could one manage risk?

What you have learned

Greater volatility in the market means that prices will fluctuate with a higher variance – that means that potential profits on an upturn are higher but potential losses on a downturn are greater. **The rewards of well-timed trades increase with market volatility but so increase the punishment for poor timing**.

What is important is how you value volatility. Do you have the stomach to ride the rollercoaster? An investor's **risk tolerance** in making investment decisions can depend on investment goals, age, the investor's personality, etc.

There are a number of types of risk. **Interest rate risk** is associated with fluctuating interest rates and so with changes in relative rates of return. Changes in the market indices and **herding behaviour** can make stock prices particularly vulnerable. **Liquidity risk** is the inability to convert an investment quickly and easily to cash.

Asset allocation is a crucial investment tool: **diversify** your principal in different types of investment, different stocks, and invest gradually (dollar cost averaging).

Notes

Ten-step trading analysis form for shares

Reassessment will allow you to avoid mistakes and improve. The more thoroughly you examine your decision-making processes, the better placed you are to improve them. What you should do is record your thoughts and predictions, then, at a later date, revisit them to see if and why you were wrong or right.

I suggest you photocopy the following template form and fill it in when you are considering a trade. In the process you will clarify your thinking, improve your decisions and record keeping (taxes, portfolio tracking, etc.), and learn from your mistakes. Look back on this module, especially the sections on risk for questions 6, 7 and 8. As you progress you may actually want to create your own template, tailoring it to your own needs and types of investments, e.g. derivatives and options strategies.

Furthermore, periodically check the transactions you decided not to do to see if you made the right choice and why. You should examine the forms you have filled out on a regular basis to see how well you did. Put them in order, from best to worst, and see if you can discover any patterns or systematic tendencies, e.g. you may regularly go too long.

Having finished the template, show it to an investor you know for a second opinion.

1 Date_____

2 General company information and share price. What does the company do? (Keep this concise)

_____

_____

_____

_____

_____

_____

_____

_____

Current share price_____

52-week high_____

52-week low_____

3 Fundamental data on the company. (What you include will depend on your trading strategy but below are some suggestions and space for you to add extra data – try not to overload the section. Keep your recordings concise/sharp.

P/E ratio (compared with rest of industry)

_____

_____

PEG ratio

_____

Price to cash flow ratio

_____

Analyst recommendations

_____

_____

_____

Dividend yield

_____

_____

Profit margin

_____

_____

Etc.

_____

_____

_____

_____

_____

_____

_____

_____

_____

4 Technical analysis

MACD crossover

_____

_____

Stochastic crossover

_____

_____

Trend characteristics

_____

_____

_____

_____

Target price

_____

_____

Stop loss

_____

_____

Etc.

_____

_____

_____

_____

_____

_____

_____

5 Does this purchase make sense given the **rest of your portfolio**? What about your **overall strategy**?

6 What is the **downside risk** of this investment? What could go wrong? What is your tolerance to this? Think about such things as interest rate risk, investor psychology, market conditions.

7 What is the **upside potential**? (Consider optimistic and pessimistic scenarios.)

8 What **news** or **trends** should you watch that might affect the stock? How likely are they, and what would the effect be? Look at the nature of the sector the company is in, the **state of the economy** and related sectors.

9 a **If buying the share**:

When will you sell this investment?

_____

_____

Will it be sold after a certain time or certain profit level?

_____

_____

_____

How much are you buying and why that amount? What percentage of your portfolio does this represent?

b **If selling the share**:

Look at the analysis form you filled out when you bought the stock to see what you thought then. Do the circumstances match your 'sell plan' that you made?

_____

_____

_____

_____

c **If you decide not to buy or have decided to sell**:

Under what circumstances in the future would you reconsider buying?

_____

_____

_____

_____

10 Action (buy / not buy / sell / not sell)

_____

If you decided to buy or sell:

The Transaction Record

If you have decided to go ahead with the transaction, you will need to have a record of the following information.

Company name _____

Symbol_____

Exchange_____

No. of shares_____

Date bought _____

Share price _____

Total cost_____

Reason bought _____

_____

_____

Plan of when/why to sell _____

_____

_____

_____

_____

Date sold _____

Proceeds _____

Reason sold_____

_____

_____

_____

_____

_____

Under what conditions would you buy again? _____

_____

_____

_____

_____

_____

_____

_____

_____

_____

Gains/losses_____

_____

_____

_____

Short/long-term investment (for tax purposes) _____

_____

_____

_____

_____

_____

_____

_____

_____

_____

Monitoring

Keep your eyes and ears open.

It takes a lot of patience and energy and motivation.

BERNARD OPPETIT,
GLOBAL HEAD OF EQUITY DERIVATIVES,
BANQUE PARIBAS, DISCUSSING TRADE

What you will learn

Having executed your position after analyzing numerous possibilities, monitoring your open positions and positions you may open is a key part of any trader's time. In this chapter we examine what you monitor, when and why, and how it fits into the overall trading approach.

Module outline

- Understand the importance of portfolio monitoring.
- Examine how the internet can assist in the task.
- Add to a professional approach.

Monitoring what?

Traders monitor:

> Monitoring your open positions and positions you may open is a **key** part of any trader's time.

- what they own in anticipation of the time when they will want to sell according to their trading plan;
- other products they may buy but for which as yet all the factors they look for are not quite aligned, e.g. the price may not be high or low enough as yet;
- the price of the product;
- in the case of an open position, all the fundamental and technical factors which led to the decision to buy and are contained in the trading tactic;
- in the case of a potential position, all the fundamental and technical factors the trader usually examines as part of the trading strategy before entering a position.

In other words, monitoring involves a constant reanalysis and revaluation of a position to see what has changed (Fig 15.1). Having examined fundamentals, state what they are. And then if looking to exit in one month, say, monitor every two days.

FIGURE 15.1 To have or not to have a Big Mac

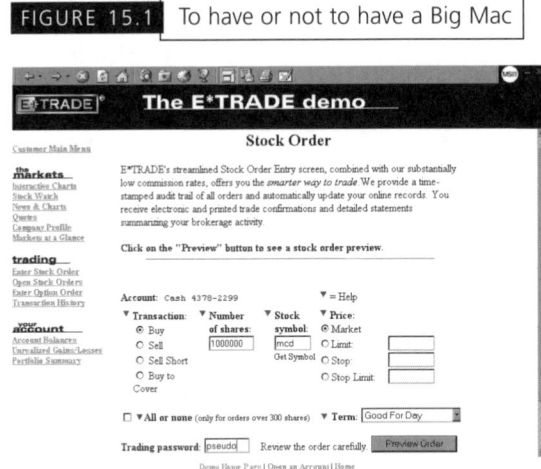

Monitoring when?

How often you monitor mainly depends on two things:

1 Your trading strategy time frame: are you looking to enter and exit in a short, medium or long period of time? Table 15.1 should help.

2 How close is the position to your stop or target? The closer it is, the more regularly you need to monitor.

TABLE 15.1	Suggested monitoring time frame

Period expecting to enter and exit	Monitor
24–96 hours	Constantly – hourly
1–2 weeks	Twice during day monitor price; end of day monitor everything else
1 month	End of day monitor price; every 2 days monitor everything else
3–9 months	3–4 days monitor price; every week monitor everything else
9+ months	Monitor situation every 3/4+ weeks

How the internet helps

Numerous sites have portfolio monitors or trackers. These usually relate only to stocks. Figure 15.2 shows a typical portfolio. These are helpful in that you can see all the detail for your stock in one place. Most update the price and volume of your stock.

What to look for when seeking an online portfolio tracker

- Does it recalculate the value of your total holdings?
- How many stocks can you list in one portfolio?

FIGURE 15.2	Online portfolio monitor

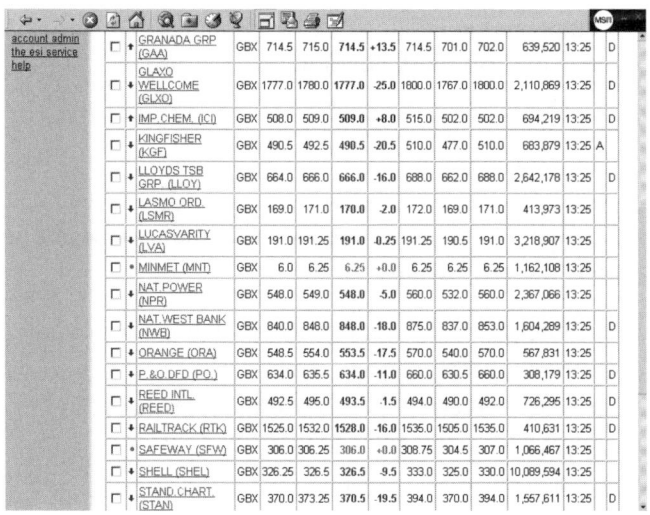

- How many portfolios can you have at one site?
- How often is the portfolio updated?
- Does the portfolio tracker alert you about news, earnings or other related items which may affect your stock?
- Does it monitor and alert you to a change in the technicals of your stock?

The sites

ClearStation **

www.clearstation.com
A good, if occasionally fiddly, portfolio. The site goes offline a bit too often to be totally reliable.

E*Trade ***

www.etrade.co.uk
This one has all the features you would expect. Could do with more graphics though.

Interactive Investor International ***

www.iii.co.uk
It's free, it's easy and it allows UK, US and other country stocks on the portfolio.

MoneyNet ***

www.moneynet.com
This Reuters site adds graphical depictions of your profits and losses and makes things more interesting than most e-brokers.

Summary

We have now examined what a professional approach to trading requires in terms of monitoring open and potential positions.

- With both the trading strategy and the trading tactic in hand, monitor both the open and the potential positions.
- Frequency of monitoring depends on how close the target or stop is and generally on how quickly we expect to enter and exit.
- Portfolio monitors can help reduce the workload.

Notes

Stay sharp –
educate thyself

> The exciting part of being a trader is being involved.
>
> JON NAJARIAN, PRESIDENT AND CEO,
> MERCURY TRADING

What you will learn

So, you're ready to trade… But let's hold on a minute. No matter what you are interested in, whether it is Nasdaq futures or OJ, we need to get learned! Therefore, we will now examine sources of further information which many traders use to supplement their analysis and which add to an overall professional and thorough approach.

I will not include questions in this part of the course because much of the information here is not technical. Rather, I will present you with a number of methods by which you can learn.

Module outline

- Educate yourself. Search for trading info the old skool way – search engines, yippee! yahoo! et cetera. Know how and when to use them.
- Understand why and how to use market commentary and online magazines.
- Learn how to choose newsgroups and newsletters.
- Look at some popular web-based discussion forums.
- Join the chat community.

- Read electronic magazines.
- See how to incorporate these into an action plan.

Trawl the net: search engines

> If you meet a trader who is very, very successful, and he truly, honestly believes it is because he is smarter and faster and more insightful and more aggressive than all of his peers, I don't believe him. I truly don't.
>
> BILL LIPSCHULTZ, FORMER GLOBAL HEAD OF FOREIGN EXCHANGE,
> SALOMON BROTHERS

We are going to examine one of the most used methods of finding information on the internet: the search engines. A search engine (Fig 16.1) is simply a site that 'searches' other sites depending on keywords entered by a user.

Search engine fortunes

Search engines were created in the early days of the popular internet by Silicon Valley students who decided to collect listings of sites. Several years later they had floated their companies (use of the engine being free, but advertising bringing in revenue) and had become multimillionaires.

FIGURE 16.1 Example of a search engine

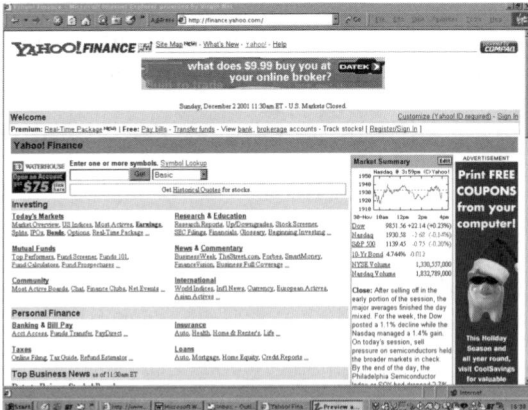

Some things to know:

- Since pages on the internet change quickly, a search engine is unlikely to be up to the minute, and some results returned may be outdated.

- Just because an engine does not find a site does not mean it does not exist.
- Because of the different way each engine works they will return different results.
- Results are ranked according to closeness of match to your request, and not of course according to best available site in terms of content.
- If you are not satisfied with the results, try a different engine.

> A search engine is simply a site that 'searches' other sites depending on **keywords** entered by a user.

How to search

Very simply, type in the keyword and press enter. If you want to be technical, most search engines will have options which allow you to specify whether the engine is to provide results that contain the keywords as a phrase or any one of the key words.

Advanced searching

- To search for sites that are country related, go to the search engine's home page and look for the link to the appropriate country, usually at the foot of the page, or try typing **domain:*country code***. For example, in the search box for Alta Vista **domain:de** lists websites which display the domain **de** (Germany).
- The asterisk (*) can often be used as a 'wild card', i.e. trad* would look for 'trader', 'trade', 'traditional', etc.
- In the keyword box of the search engine, if you enter two words be careful as to what you are looking for:

Keyword	Result
Dow Jones	All sites containing somewhere in them the words Dow or Jones or both, not necessarily together
Dow AND Jones	All sites containing somewhere in them the words Dow Jones, not necessarily together
Dow OR Jones	All sites containing somewhere in them the words Dow or Jones or both, not necessarily together
'Dow Jones'	All sites containing somewhere in them the words Dow Jones together
+Dow –Jones	All sites containing the word Dow but not those containing the word Jones

> Different search engines will all have their own language to assist **searches**, but in most cases the pure and simple keywords will do.

Beyond this different search engines will all have their own language to assist searches, but in most cases the pure and simple keywords will do.

Top search engines

See Table 16.1 for the top search engines and their ratings.

*** Means the search engine lists a very large number of sites, supports complex searches, includes directories and other category-based searching links, and the amount of information displayed can be altered.

** As above but fewer results, and category links may not be as good.

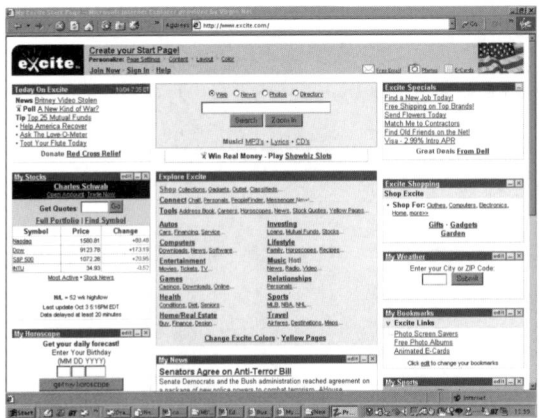

TABLE 16.1   The top search engines

Name	Address (www.word below.com)	Rating
Alta Vista	altavista.digital	*** (Recommended)
Excite	excite	***
Lycos	lycos	***
Yahoo!	yahoo	***
Deja News	dejanews	***
InfoSeek	infoseek	***
WebCrawler	webcrawler	**
MetaCrawler	metacrawler	**

What you have learned

We have seen the **basic operation** of search engines. Today they are sophisticated sites providing a wealth of information beyond merely search facilities. They are worth checking out for that alone.

… before moving on, get connected to the web and check out some of the search engines above. Search for anything, not just trading – you'll find out what the internet is really about (though keep it clean).

Notes

Market news and commentary

Almost all traders, whatever form of analysis they use and whatever product they trade in, whether bonds or shares, will want to examine daily market news and commentary, as these provide a context for all trading.

Market commentary may relate not only to what is happening to the world economy but also to the particular product in question. So, for instance, a futures trader in currencies may want to know what is happening to the US macroeconomy. If you trade UK stocks you may think it safe to ignore market commentary related to US non-farm payrolls, but you will then have missed why, on so many occasions, stocks with little US exposure, such as domestic electricals, are affected each month when the US non-farm payroll data are revealed.

What happens is that the market often uses those data to gauge the likely changes in US interest rates, which in turn affects whether more funds are likely to flow into London or New York. That in turn can affect the share price of companies that have little to do directly with the US. The key rule is that everything is connected to everything else.

This does not mean you have to be an economics whiz to trade, but it does mean that the better informed you are about what the market is examining, the more likely you are to make better trading decisions. In any event, few people would argue that more information can do harm…though don't get bogged down. Here endeth the case for following market news and market commentary.

Let's move on to some criteria for including market news and commentary sites in the skeleton plans.

> This does not mean you have to be an economics whiz to trade, but it does mean that the better **informed** you are about what the market is examining the more likely you are to make better trading decisions.

- The news providers have to be **well known**, widely respected and with ample resources.
- They should offer **quality commentary** on the markets.
- There should be **categorized news**, such as industry, business, commodity, etc. for ease of searching.
- Make sure there are **regular updates** during the day.

News sites

Here are some sites I find particularly useful for keeping abreast of market news. However, broker sites often have such useful market commentary nowadays that you may not need these.

BBC News ***

news.bbc.co.uk

This one is good for world news as well as a general overview of market news. If you are looking at macroeconomic and political considerations, use this site.

Bloomberg ****

www.bloomberg.com

World-beating provider of up-to-the-minute financial news. For market news and general background just focus on the headline stories on the home page. Click on the columns link and there you will see not only the columnists but reports for all world markets – a really convenient way to get the low-down quickly. The news link is self-evident.

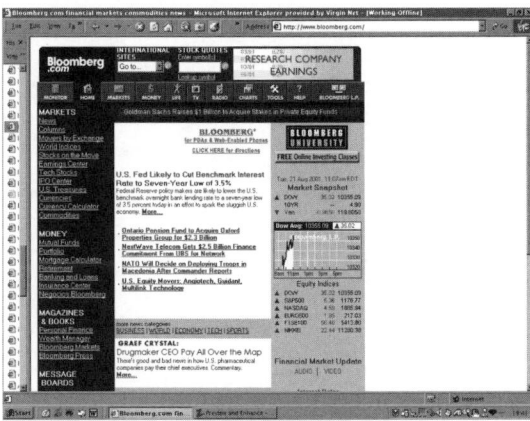

CBS MarketWatch ★★★★

cbs.marketwatch.com

Great value this free site. News is solid. The free tools include personal port-folios, company research, charts, mutual funds and delayed quotes. The front page has all the essential breaking news. There are well-thought-out links to relevant sites.

Also see the following links:

- Investing tools and data.
- Free shop's top ten free offers.
- Headlines.

CNBC ✻✻✻

www.cnbc.com

The most useful things about this one are the news updates and the archived interviews, which can be helpful when researching a company.

The Daily Rocket ✻✻✻✻

www.dailyrocket.com

Packed full of original articles. Download the Investment Monitor – a personal portfolio-management software that delivers investment news, stock data and market analysis to your PC.

Financial Times ★★★

www.ft.com

Use the drop-down menu to get market news for various sectors and regions of the world. That is probably the feature most useful to traders. Other things like the portfolio are OK but you will probably use the one your broker provides.

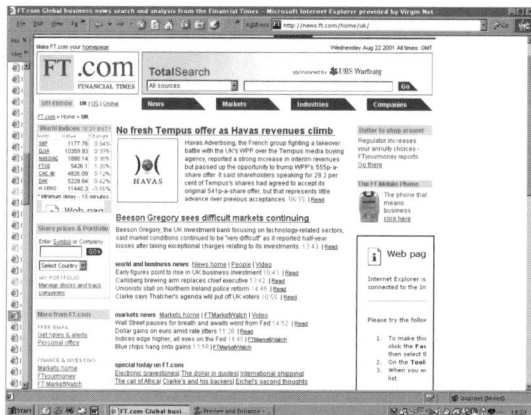

Wall Street Journal ★★★

www.wsj.com

This site is divided into WSJ Europe, US, Asia. Use it for market news and use the columns for a bit more analysis.

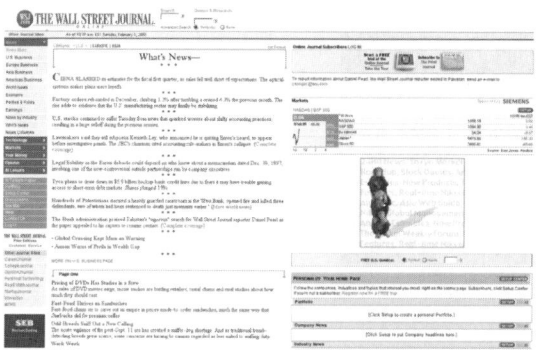

Now, go forth and check out these sites…go on, do it now. Don't miss today's breaking stories – there may be a trade in it. You cannot afford to miss out.

What you have learned

News sites are essential as part of any person's diet (they inform us about the world we live in), and for particularly stressed traders news may even become a substitute for food and drink. Look for reputable sites with quality commentary and up-to-the-second coverage. Keeping abreast of breaking stories in finance will keep you sharp and make your trading far more informed and interesting.

Notes

Recommendation pedlars: gurus and their newsletters

Many traders subscribe to one or more newsletters for the particular product they are interested in.

> My experience is that the hottest person on the floor is just about the worst teacher.
>
> JON NAJARIAN, PRESIDENT AND CEO, MERCURY TRADING

What are they?

Essentially a market newsletter will contain recommendations as to what to buy and sell. The individuals who write them are often termed gurus. I suppose priest, rabbi and imam would also suffice.

Why use them?

A typical newsletter will contain analysis of why a particular stock or other product is recommended. Most traders, if they use newsletters, do so to get a second opinion on their own analysis or to gain ideas. Sometimes a newsletter is a confidence builder for those a little tentative or unsure of their own analysis.

HOT TIP

Using newsletters

Do not merely follow a newsletter: you may as well give your money to the newsletter author. And if you are willing to do that then why not give it to a professional fund manager? Remember, Soros and Buffett do not write newsletters. In other words, the truly successful trade; they do not recommend trades. So I would recommend that you do your own analysis before or after looking at the newsletter you have subscribed to and form an independent view as to the trade.

Product   Make sure the newsletter trades in the same products as you! Seems obvious – it is. But it also means that if you trade stock options, it will almost certainly be better to have a newsletter making stock option recommendations than one making purely stock recommendations.

Strategy   Are the strategies the newsletter recommends ones with which you are comfortable? For instance, the newsletter may specialize in shorting stocks or spread trading. You need to be aware of the type of analysis you believe in and ensure the newsletter follows a similar form. For instance, if you tend to follow earnings surprises and do not care much for technical indicators, it would be perverse for you to subscribe to a newsletter that selected recommendations based on technicals.

Time frame   Ideally, you want a newsletter that selects recommendations on a time frame you like to trade to. An extreme example of a mismatch would be if you prefer to enter and exit trades on a weekly basis and the newsletter is monthly. Its value to you would be limited.

Method of delivery   Are you happy with the mode by which the newsletter is delivered: e-mail, fax or snail mail?

Comprehensible?   The issue here is whether you like the layout and can understand why the guru is recommending a stock. One thing that will ensure a wasted subscription is if you cannot understand the guru's choice. If you do not fully comprehend how he selects his recommendations, you cannot critically analyze them and so are following blindly.

Ideally, you want a newsletter that selects **recommendations** on a time frame you like to trade to.

Pay cash, take your choice

As the table below outlines, there are an enormous number of factors that determine the type of newsletter best suited to your particular needs. Moreover, for every possible demand there seem to be several suppliers. That being so it would be ridiculous and unhelpful to list and review each and every available newsletter. Instead the sites listed are 'umbrella' sites which do precisely that. Furthermore, because they are net sites, they are going to be more up to date.

	My Choice	Newsletter 1	Newsletter 2	Newsletter 3
Product				
Strategy				
Analysis				
Time frame				
Method of delivery				
Comprehensible (score)				
Trial period				
Cost				

The sites

The sites referred to below are 'umbrella' sites. They have in aggregate the following features.

- Search criteria – the facility to search for newsletters by publisher, author, product, strategy.
- Free samples – the facility to view or order many of the newsletters for free for a trial period.
- Track record – a comparison of the newsletters based on their performance.

Hulbert Financial

www.hulbertdigest.com

- **Analysis** of investment approaches of newsletters.
- **Profiles** of strategy and methods used for recommendations.
- **Addresses** of all listed newsletters.
- **Ranking** of past performance of all newsletters.

How to use this site and what for

Hulbert Financial is well known for its ranking of newsletters. It is a comprehensive service; however you will have to pay for it.

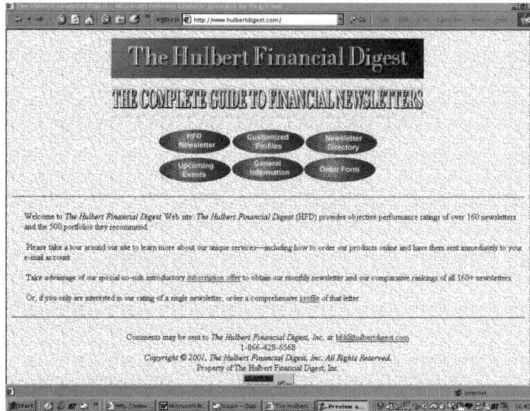

Investools

www.investools.com

- **Search** according to strategy, product, analysis (e.g. charts).
- **Free issues** of some of the listed newsletters.

How to use this site and what for

A wide selection of newsletters here, but no ranking except by a link to Hulbert Financial.

Newsletter Network

www.margin.com

- **Search** the extensive database according to publisher, letter, author.
- **Free** samples.

How to use this site and what for

Similar to Investools, but it may be that the sites do not cover exactly the same newsletters and so it is worth using both sites as search tools.

> **HOT TIP**
>
> **Diamonds in the dirt**
>
> Many prospectors for newsletters kid themselves that if they find some esoteric and little-known newsletter they may find something everyone else has missed and so strike oil. Don't kid yourself – the newsletter writer wouldn't be writing the letter if he was sitting on a potential oil field littered with diamonds.

What you have learned

As you will have guessed I am not a great fan of newsletters. But at least with the resources described in this chapter you have more information about how good they are than ever before. At least your choice will be informed.

Notes

Discussion forums

What are they?

A newsgroup is simply a collection of messages posted by individuals to a news server. Posting is the act of putting your message onto the server. News servers are just big computers that host (i.e. store) lots of newsgroup messages for people to view. You read and post messages using a news reader. A news reader is software much like a browser and the best news is that most browsers include news readers that launch automatically when you want to go to a newsgroup. With Internet Explorer 4, for example, the news reader is bundled with the e-mail reader called Outlook Express. In Netscape Navigator it is called Netscape News.

There are some websites that provide their own news readers and so permit web-based 'newsgrouping' which can be easier for the novice. There are newsgroups on virtually every topic under the sun. Some newsgroups are monitored or moderated, which means someone sifts through them to ensure the content meets certain quality standards and is not generally scurrilous, libellous or outrageously offensive.

There are **newsgroups** on virtually every topic under the sun.

Adding a news server

To add a news server you will need the name of the server and your account name and password.

In Internet Explorer 4 go to Outlook Express and click on **Tools**, then **Accounts** and next on **News**. Follow the on-screen instructions.

In Netscape Navigator:

In the browser click on **Options**, then select Mail and News Preferences and click on **Servers** (you may need to click on **News** first if this tab is available). Next enter the server name in the **News (NNTP) Server** box and follow the instructions.

HOT TIP

Web-based newsgroups
One of the easiest ways to use newsgroups without all the trouble of linking to servers and fiddling with browsers is to go to www.infoseek.com. From there you can search for newsgroups and download the **My Deja News** news reader and subscribe to lots of newsgroups.

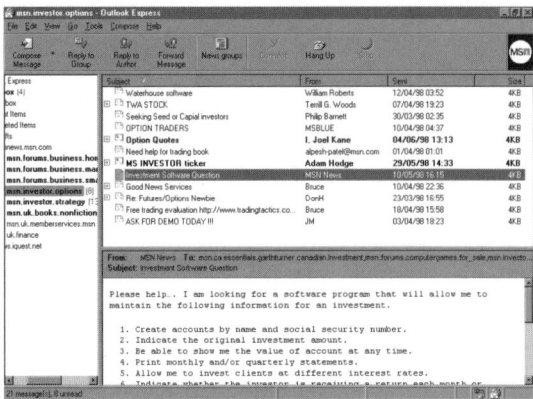

Viewing newsgroups

In your browser simply type in the URL box news:name of newsgroup, e.g. news:misc.invest.

The major problem with newsgroups, which even a short visit will reveal is that:

- they often get used by a small clique of users who are in fact just talking to each other, with outside messages not replied to readily;
- the focus of the clique can be quite narrow;
- the messages can get abusive and personal;
- unregulated groups often get postings from unwelcome 'get rich quick' schemes;
- investors often try to talk up positions they may be holding, so the information can be biased and not credible.

Consequently, for anyone coming to a newsgroup it can be a little like going to a drinks party and trying to join in a conversation with a circle of individuals who have been chatting away for a few hours. My advice would be to use newsgroups only for asking questions, and be wary of the replies even then. In my opinion, they are not a good source of investment advice.

Alternative advice

If you have an investment query, rather than seeking the amateur advice of a newsgroupie you could always go to a website dealing with the area of your query (e.g. bonds, etc.) and seek out e-mail addresses of people on them. Often, the advisers who produce the site provide their e-mail addresses and they can be a useful source of free advice on an issue.

Internet chat rooms seem to be a pretty great way for people to talk with each other to see if they find something they can mesh with.

JON NAJARIAN,
PRESIDENT AND CEO,
MERCURY TRADING

Some newsgroups found using a general internet search are listed in Table 16.2 while Table 16.3 offers some popular web-based discussion forums.

TABLE 16.2 A variety of newsgroups

Name	Content
alt.invest.penny-stocks	Low-priced stocks talk
Misc.invest	Investments
Misc.invest.commodities	Commodities
Misc.invest.emerging	Emerging markets
Misc.invest.forex	Foreign exchange
Misc.invest.funds	Mutual funds
Misc.invest.futures	Futures
Misc.invest.stocks	Stocks
Misc.invest.technical	Technical analysis
uk.finance	UK personal finance

TABLE 16.3 Popular web-based discussion forums

Name and address	Stocks	Mutual funds	Futures	Options	Bonds	Technical analysis	Fundamental analysis
Avid Traders Chat avidinfo.com	✓					✓	
The Financial Center On-Line www.tfc.com/chat	✓	✓	✓	✓	✓	✓	✓
Investors Free Forum www.investorsforum.com	✓	✓	✓	✓	✓	✓	✓
The Motley Fool www.fool.com	✓			✓			
Quicken People & Chat quicken.excite.com/forums	✓	✓					
The Stock Club www.stockclub.com	✓						✓
Yahoo! Finance Message Boards messages.yahoo.com/yahoo/ Business_and_Finance/	✓	✓	✓	✓	✓	✓	✓

One of the best collections of web-based discussion is located within Yahoo! at: **messages.yahoo.com/yahoo/Business_and_Finance/Index.html**

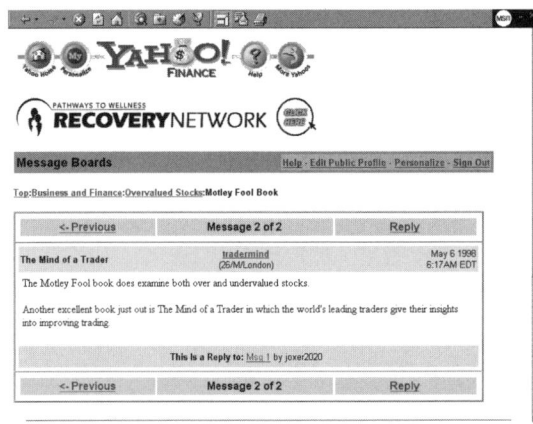

There are newsgroups on:

- brokerages
- market trends
- mutual funds
- options
- overvalued stocks
- short-term trading
- stocks (financial, consumer, energy, healthcare, service, technology, transport, utilities)
- company-specific news, so you can discuss a single stock in splendid isolation.

What you have learned

Although the quality of content can vary widely on newsgroups and web-based discussion groups, they can be a useful source of second opinions. **Remember to always query the motives of those posting messages**. Their opinions carry more weight if they can be verified **independently** (e.g. a news item you may otherwise have missed). Overall the web-based discussion groups are of a higher quality than the newsgroups and my advice would be to choose one or two at the most, otherwise you will not be able to keep abreast of them all.

Notes

_____
_____
_____
_____
_____
_____
_____
_____
_____
_____
_____
_____
_____

Chat rooms and boards

What you need to learn:

- How best to use online chat sites, if at all.
- Which are the key sites online traders use to talk trading?

The aim of this book, as with all good trading books, is to impart not just information but also knowledge and wisdom. The experience of others besides our humble selves is essential to such a task. In trying to maintain a community feel, boards and chat rooms are an essential source of information. A top chat room or board will create a genuine community feel, with intelligent conversation from users of all levels of experience. Unfortunately such chat rooms are rare; if you find one that you like, grab hold of it and don't let go.

With a chat room you can talk real-time by typing and posting and seeing instant replies (if anyone is in the room and deigns to reply). With boards you post a message and wait for a reply at some future time. In this chapter we shall see some of the best ones, what 'best' means, and how to use them.

Why use them?

I can suggest a few reasons...

- To **pose questions** about issues on which you are unsure.
- To **get ideas** about what to trade. Be very wary of using them for this however. A lot of posters put the 'bull' into 'bulletin board'. Be especially concerned if anyone offers insider information – it is usually the last cry of someone stuck in a bad losing position.
- As an educational tool by **learning from the experiences of others**, for instance in which orders to use at what time of day.
- As a **review of online trading sites**. By this I mean many people posting may sum up which are the best brokers or the cheapest sites, etc.
- Just to **'chill' and bond, find some buddies**.

> A top chat room or board will create a genuine **community** feel, with intelligent conversation from users of all levels of experience.

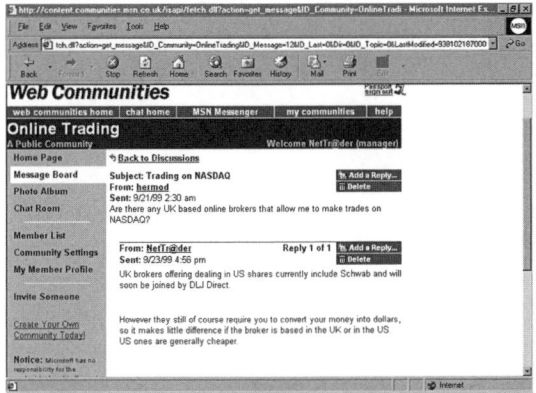

Learn the lingo

They speak a different language in chat rooms. You will need to know the following terms just so you too can appear hip by knowing what the board's coolest in-crowd are talking about. It's a sociological thing.

B4 – Before.

BBL – Be back later.

BCNU – Be seeing you.

BFN – Bye for now.

BRB – Be right back.

BTW – By the way.

CUL8R – See you later.

F2F – Face to face.

FAQ – Frequently asked questions.

FWIW – For what it's worth.

GBH&K – Great big hug and kiss.

HHOK – Ha ha only kidding!

IMHO – In my humble opinion.

IRL – In real life.

J/K – Just kidding.

LOL – Laughing out loud.

NT – No text.

NTR – Not trading related.

OIC – Oh, I see!

OTOH – On the other hand.

OTT – Over the top.

ROTFL – Rolling on the floor laughing.

TIA – Thanks in advance.

TTFN – Ta ta for now.

Before I set you loose, you will also want to know the following:

- Flaming – a nasty or rude response to someone who breaches netiquette, e.g. by posting adverts and thereby treating the board members like buffoons.
- Posting – the act of placing a comment on a board, done by a poster.
- Thread – a line of discussion on a board with one person making a posting and the replies being the threads. Also a thin piece of material used to keep garments together.

What to watch out for on chat and board sites

When considering which chat and board sites to make your regular hang-outs, you should consider the following issues.

Size When it comes to boards, size matters. You obviously want a board with lots of subject matter and members to ensure you get the broadest views and are not sharing the site with a sad lonely broker from Florida.

> Sometimes posters are simply not that good, and postings **degenerate** into slanging matches and challenges to settle matters outside the board.

Quality of postings Some sites simply have poor-quality postings, for several reasons. The site may have been taken over by a few 'bully' posters who cajole, intimidate or poke fun. Sometimes posters are simply not that good, and postings degenerate into slanging matches and challenges to settle matters outside the board. Sometimes you get an invasion of ramping postings; those morons who inform you something is about to sky-rocket because they know a man, who works for this woman, whose husband's mistress's cousin's niece's stepmother's alien dog told her the stock was a good purchase.

Topics   As well as a wide range of topics the boards should be divided into sub-groups so you can get into a relevant topic in enough detail and quickly.

Design and navigability   It can sometimes seem there are millions of messages on billions of topics posted every nanosecond. In fact it is worse. All this makes design and navigation especially important so that you get to read about what you want to know and can post questions or replies.

Price   Ideally you want a free site. Failing that, a free trial period followed by a cheap subscription will have to do.

Investorville ***

www.investorville.com

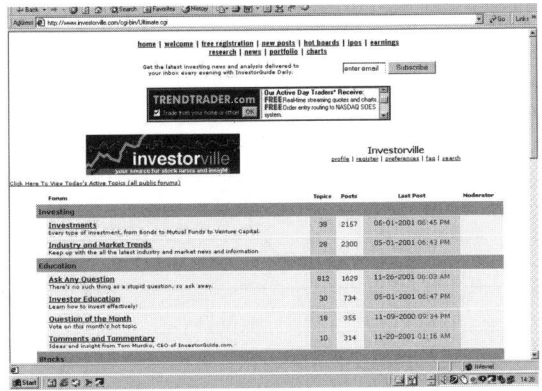

This site reeks of good ideas. It is easily one of the best chat sites on the web. Here's why.

Size   Lots of members and postings – no worries there.

Quality   A very high-quality content. Editing by the mayor of Investorville ensures that adverts and bad postings are deleted. In fact I could not find a poor-quality posting!

Topics   As well as covering topics by stocks, there is also a 'user created' forums section which ensures relevance to the online trader, discussing the issues of most relevance to them. There is an 'ask a question' forum for all those questions which may not be answered elsewhere, and this also ensures there is a welcoming place for the novice. Now, that is my kind of community. An excellent 'overheard' section lists and links to all the best, most perceptive and intelligent postings. Yet another good idea. Another section worth a mention is 'Hot Boards' which lists the most popular boards so you can instantly get a feel for where the most vibrant discussion and latest issues may be being discussed. The 'new posts' section keeps you up to date with the most recent new discussions.

Design and navigability   Very easy to read and navigate. I cannot think how it could be simpler. Yeah, I know I am heaping praise on it, but when I see something I like, I just gotta let ya know. There are no annoying reference codes cluttering threads, as on so many other sites.

Price   Free as air, and twice as sweet.

Marketforum **

www.marketforum.com

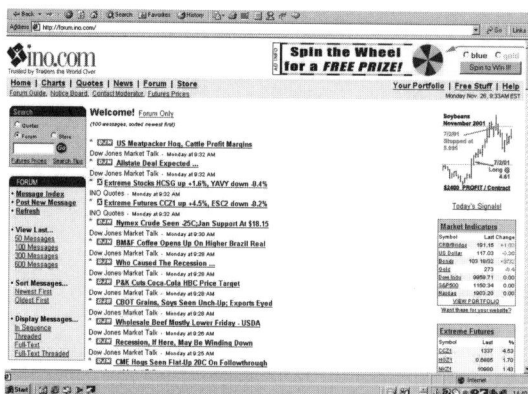

This is a futures and options message board from INO Global Markets. The board is excellent for those who are futures-minded. I hear plans are in the works for discussions with experts.

Size   The site claimed 3,676 messages in the past two days when I did a search under 'online'.

Quality   A very high-quality site with 'serious' talk.

Topics   Topics are restricted to talk about commodities at an intermediate level.

Design and navigability   Not too bad a design, though navigation was a bit difficult – it could have been easier to see a long list of articles than having to search by topic.

Price   Free.

The Silicon Investor ✱✱✱

www.techstocks.com

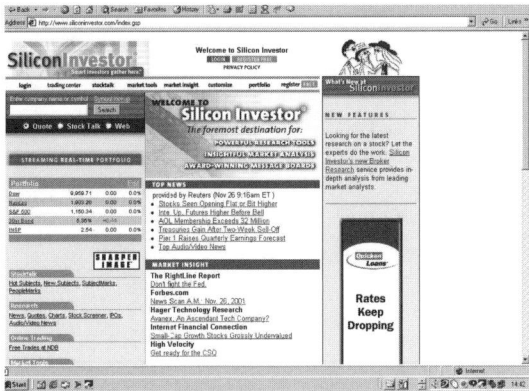

Despite having a name that does not match its web address, this is probably one of the most famous online trading board sites. These are the stats it proudly proclaims to all visitors.

Size   There are 140,000+ messages posted each week, and 580,000 messages posted per month. There are 10,769,922 searchable messages stored in the silicon investor (SI) database, and 29,788 discussion threads have been created by SI members. More than 120,000 people have become active members of Silicon Investor.

Quality of postings   Quite high, not much 'noise'.

Topics   Topics include the following (with sub-topics within):

- Aerospace and defence
- Banking and finance
- Brokerages/investment resources
- Canadian stocks
- Casinos/gaming
- Coffee shop

- Five dollars and under
- Food processing and agriculture
- Futures and commodities
- Gold, mining and natural resources
- Initial public offerings
- International
- Internet financial connection
- Iomega (IOM) and IMP (IMPX)
- Market trends and strategies
- Miscellaneous (biotech/medical)
- Miscellaneous (general)
- Miscellaneous (technology)
- Mutual funds
- Overvalued stocks
- Puts, calls and other options
- Real estate/REITs
- Short-term traders
- Specialty retail
- Transportation
- Web/information stocks
- Welcome to SI
- Year 2000 stocks & discussion

Design and navigability The site's design used to smack of 1970s styling (that is, if the internet had been around then). However, a recent redesign makes this great site better. Message boards are easier to look at. It is relatively simple to find topics, and some help-ful chaps collect the best postings for a particular topic and archive them – I love that idea.

Price Reading is free, posting costs. There is a free trial membership plan for a fortnight and also a subscription fee of $100 for a year and $200 for life (best not take out the latter if you're 101 years old then).

The Stock Club **

www.stockclub.com

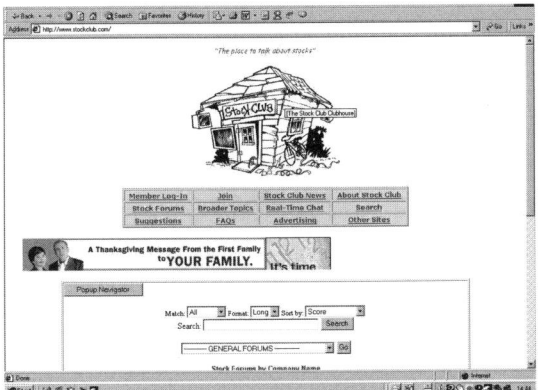

The site offers real-time chat as well as boards. Specializes in stocks alone.

Size   I got the impression there were a few people there, but not as many as on, say, Silicon Investor.

Quality   About average.

Topics   Stocks are covered in alphabetical order and can be searched by industry group which is helpful. But they should have industry-based discussion, too.

Design and navigability   The design and navigability are fine. Not too bad, not too great. Since the site focusses on particular stock talk, there is very little you could do to improve it, although it could have a hot boards section to list those stocks with the most postings.

Price   Free, but you have to become a member even to read, let alone post, messages.

Stock Talk

www.stocktalk.com

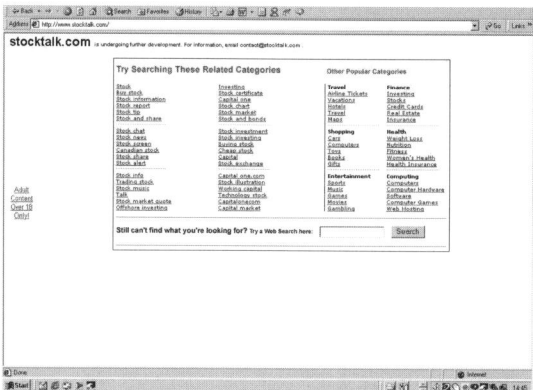

The only reason this site is mentioned is for readers who may have a stock-specific query and cannot find the answer on any other site. It is a last resort.

Size   Lots of room, not enough people. There are supposed to be 7,800.

Quality   An example of a site hijacked by non-traders. Low quality. Postings ramp stocks or ramp porn sites. How sad do they think online traders are?

Topics   As well as stocks the site does have boards for 'hot stocks' and for initial public offerings (IPOs).

Design and navigability   Design is fine, but try to find some information – I dare you.

Price   Price reflects quality.

What you have learned

There are a few very good sites which can be used for some restricted purposes outlined above, such as getting the 'word on the street' from those who have been there, done that. **Do not use them for stock tips – ever.**

Nevertheless, if you are looking for a chat room to call home, remember what to look for:

- **size** – you need to talk to someone;
- **quality** of postings – you need quality chat;
- the range of **topics**;
- the **design** and ease of navigation, and of course…
- **price** – I suggest you look for a site priced at $0 per day. Failing that, a free trial period followed by a cheap subscription will have to do.

Notes

E-zines

> Most of the new traders read the newspapers…so they do not have a plan, they just have a general feeling that due to a situation they read in the paper they want to do this or that. What I try to do is to help them make a plan.
>
> PHIL FLYNN,
VICE PRESIDENT, ALARON TRADING

The sites here deal exclusively with quality online financial magazines. See Table 16.4 for a list of the top e-zines.

TABLE 16.4 Table of top e-zines

Name	Address
Business Week Online	www.businessweek.com
The Economist	www.economist.com
Forbes	www.forbes.com
Fortune	www.fortune.com
Inc. Magazine	www.inc.com
InvestorGuide Weekly	www.investorguide.com
Stocks & Commodities	www.traders.com
US News Online	www.usnews.com

What you have learned

Select one or two top magazines to keep in touch with more background market information. Personally I prefer reading them off-line. However, you could use the online magazines as a cheaper alternative or supplement.

Summary

Right, we should now be ready to search the internet to find trading information for ourselves. We have looked at the basic operation of the search engine – the tools of an inquisitive internet surfer. Search engines are rather sophisticated, providing a wealth of information. They are worth checking out for that alone.

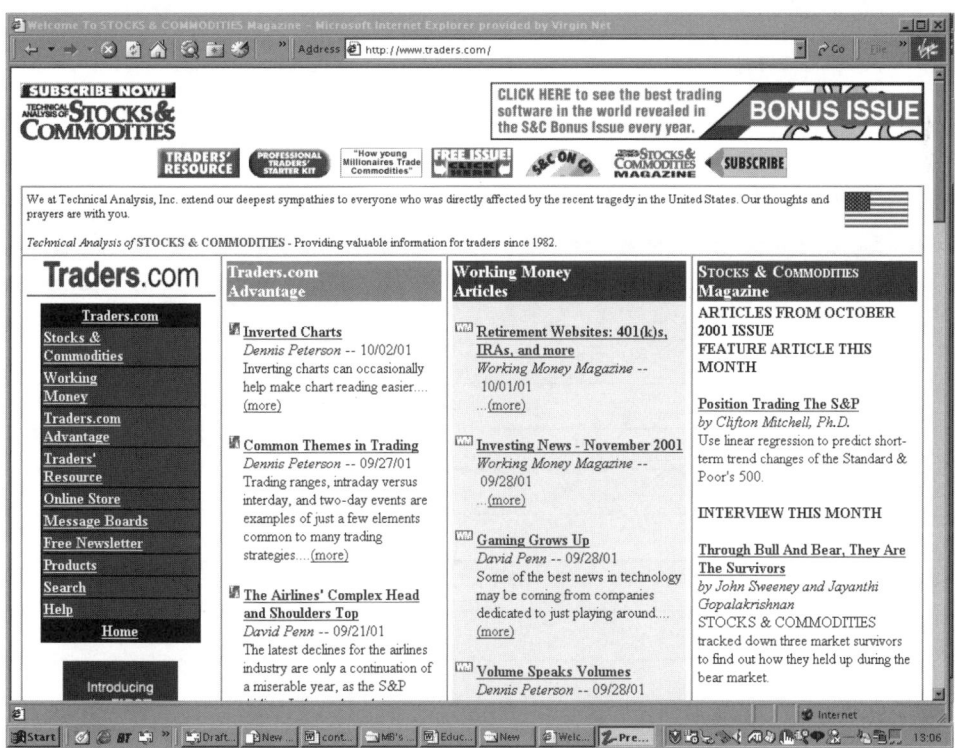

News sites are **essential**. Look for reputable sites with quality commentary and up-to-the-second coverage.

News sites are essential. Look for reputable sites with quality commentary and up-to-the-second coverage. Staying up to date will keep trading interesting by giving you a wider perspective on finance.

Although the quality of content can vary widely on newsgroups and web-based discussion groups, they can be a useful source of second opinions. Remember to always query motives of those posting messages. Their opinions carry more wait if they can be verified independently.

Chat rooms can be great fun, but take them with a pinch of salt. Look for quality chat and a large community. Do not use them for stock tips – ever.

Select one or two top magazines to keep in touch with more background market information.

Notes

Recommended reading

Key

***   Excellent; comprehensible and comprehensive as well as value for money. Should be on your bookshelf

**   A useful read with very much to offer

*   A good read if, having read the others, you want to continue looking into the subject

Online trading

Investing Online ✶✶✶
S Eckett
FT Pitman 1997

Encyclopaedic in coverage and an excellent reference tool with a focus on global investing.

Trading Online ✶✶✶
Alpesh B Patel
FT Prentice Hall 2000

New and revised version of the best-seller covering all the steps to trading from getting set up to monitoring positions.

The Complete Idiot's Guide to Online Investing *
D Gerlach
Que 1999
Que are known for their computer books and this venture appears to be a bandwagon thing. But the *Complete Idiot's* guides can be clear and more comprehensible if you are, um, well, a complete idiot.

Short-term trading

Long-term Secrets to Short-term Trading ★★★
L Williams
Wiley 1999
Larry Williams is a proven trader. An excellent book, because he clearly knows his stuff and trades off it.

Day-trading

The Electronic Day Trader ★★★
M Friedfertig and G West
McGraw-Hill 1999
A very popular title indeed for day-traders from a day-trading brokerage owner.

How to Get Started in Electronic Day Trading ★★★
David S Nassar
McGraw-Hill 1999
Nassar owns a day-trading firm, and this book is written from the perspective of a man who knows his business.

High Impact Day Trading **

Robert Barnes

Irwin 1996

This book highlights the author's Mountain Valley system, going for longer moves and ignoring shorter ones. It has proved a very popular title.

Electronic Day Traders' Secrets **

M Friedfertig and G West

McGraw-Hill 1999

This book has a series of interviews with day traders from Friedfertig's own brokerage company. A lot of trading psychology here, but light on strategies.

The 22 Rules of Day Trading Online **

D Nassar

McGraw-Hill 1999

After the success of his earlier day-trading book, David Nassar returns with a different format.

The Day Trader's Advantage *

H Abell

Dearborn Financial 1996

A little dated from the ubiquitous Abell, who seems to be a full-time author producing what feels like one book per month. Focuses on the trading psychology aspects of day-trading.

The Compleat Day Trader *

J Bernstein

McGraw-Hill 1999

A very good seller, with an unusual title. Covers not only day-trading but also risk management.

Day Trade Online *
C Farrell
Wiley 1999
Farrell is a young man who trades for a living. Some good content in here, but lay-out, design and substance lacking in other respects.

Trading psychology

The Bhagavad Gita ★★★
Various editions
Although written more than 2000 years ago, and not directly about trading, I found it to be one of the most useful 'trading' books I have ever read. It largely discusses discipline – how and why – and the benefits of discipline. Since a lack of mental discipline is one of the major downfalls of traders, this is likely to be a very profitable read.

The Mind of a Trader ★★★
Alpesh B Patel
FT Pitman 1997
Advice on becoming a better trader from the world's leading traders, including Pat Arbor, former Chairman of the Chicago Board of Trade, and Bill Lipschutz, former Global Head of Forex at Salomon Brothers, who made on average $250,000 each and every trading day he was there, for eight years!

The Disciplined Trader ★★
Mark Douglas
Prentice Hall 1990
An extremely good book. Written in a very intelligent fashion and gets away from 'Mickey Mouse' fashion psychology. Deserves a far higher profile than it has received to date.

The Inner Game of Trading ∗∗
Robert Koppel and Howard Abell
Irwin Professional 1997
Includes interviews with some leading traders, but its value comes from the analysis of psychological difficulties traders are likely to encounter. Definitely recommended.

Classics

Reminiscences of a Stock Operator ∗∗∗
Edwin Le Fevre
Wiley 1994 (reprint edition)
An undoubted classic. The fictionalized trading biography of Jesse Livermore, one of the greatest speculators ever seen. While dated (it was written in 1923), it nevertheless provides some insight into the difficulties encountered by traders. A very enjoyable read.

The Art of Speculation ∗∗
Philip L Carret
Wiley 1997
Apparently highly regarded by Victor Niederhoffer. However, in spite of that, I would recommend it as a good read.

Manias, Panics and Crashes ∗∗
Charles Kindleberger
Wiley 1996
Why do the economists, statisticians and government nerds always get it wrong? This book does not provide any answers, but it does provide some insights.

Extraordinary Popular Delusions and the Madness of Crowds and Confusion de Confusiones ∗∗
Charles Mackay and Joseph de la Vega
Wiley 1995
Explores crowd psychology and how that affects market movement. While its examinations are 300 years old, it is highly relevant today. Short and interesting.

Stocks

Getting Started in Stocks **
Alvin D Hall
Wiley 1997 (3rd edition)
A very good primer for stocks. Hall has a clear style and injects humour now and again to alleviate the rigour.

Winning on Wall Street *
Martin Zweig
Warner Books 1997 (revised edition)
Zweig is famous for his market reports and for being one of Schwager's market wizards. I found a copy of this book for $11.99 – you can't go wrong.

Futures

A Complete Guide to the Futures Markets ***
Jack Schwager
Wiley 1984
This book covers fundamental analysis and technical analysis as well as spreads and options. Characteristic of Schwager's books, it is very thorough.

Getting Started in Futures **
Todd Lofton
Wiley 1997 (3rd edition)
Very clear and easy to understand as well as giving lots of information for delving deeper.

Commodities trading

Soybean Trading and Hedging ★★
Wheat Trading and Hedging ★★
Corn Trading and Hedging ★★
Investing in Wheat, Soybeans, Corn ★★
William Grandmill
Irwin Professional 1988, 1989, 1990, 1991 (respectively)

A series of books by the appropriately named Grandmill for commodity traders. Grandmill provides details of the commodities and his own systems for picking entry and exit points. If you think it is best to become an expert in one area of commodity trading then books such as these should be a good starting point to developing your skills and understanding.

Mastering Commodity Futures and Options ★★
George Kleinman
FT Pitman 1997

This book is very well-presented indeed. A little like a textbook in style, but covers the ground very well for both beginner and intermediate user.

The CRB Commodity Yearbook ★★
Knight-Ridder
Knight-Ridder annual

A very useful reference guide to commodities. Filled with data, charts, tables and articles on trends and strategies. If you are serious about commodities you should have this.

Options

McMillan on Options ★★★
Lawrence McMillan
Wiley 1996

Brands itself as the 'Bible' of the options markets. Why do publishers refer to their books as the 'Bible' of something? I wonder if they mean only a minority of people will ever read the book but more are supposed to and it competes with equivalent books for the rest. Anyway, that aside, McMillan goes beyond explaining the basics about options and actually applies a degree of critique. Should consider if you are a beginner.

Getting Started in Options ★★★
Michael Thomsett

Wiley 1993

Again, very clear and easy to understand. An excellent start for beginners.

Advanced Options Trading ★★
Robert Daigler

Probus 1993

This book moves beyond basics and discusses some strategies generally used only by the professionals. That does not mean a private investor using them will have hit upon some sector – so beware. But if you are interested in knowing more than just the basics, this book is better than most.

Commodity Options ★★
Larry Spears

Marketplace Books 1985

This one is for beginners who may not have settled on a particular commodity and want an overview.

Traded Options ★★
Peter Temple

Rushmere Wynne 1995

For those trading options on LIFFE. Thorough and explains all the basics, from what options are to buying software.

All About Options ★★
Russell Wasendorf and Thomas McCafferty

Probus 1993

The good thing about this book is that it covers both strategies and some of the background mechanics behind options, such as what happens on the trading floor.

The Options Markets ★
John Cox and Mark Rubinstein

Prentice Hall 1985

This is a classic text on options. The book is about valuing options – these authors, of course, created the famous Cox–Rubinstein option pricing model.

Options on Foreign Exchanges ★
David DeRosa

Probus 1992

Not to leave out the currency-option boys and girls, this market specialist covers valuation of options and pricing of currencies, as well as how the various markets work. Probably useful for the beginner and intermediate-level trader in forex options.

Make Money with S&P Options *
How to Make Money with Corn Options *
Make Money with Soybean Options *
William Grandmill
Irwin 1989, 1990, 1990 (respectively)
If you are concentrating on one of these areas and feeling you need something specifically addressing your trading needs, then these books were written with you in mind. Grandmill is a prolific writer and knows what he is talking about.

Trading Options on Futures *
John Labuszewski
Wiley 1998
This covers treasuries, currencies and commodities. I think if you are trading options on futures there is more to it than understanding options and understanding futures. The whole is greater than the sum of the parts, and therefore a book such as this is added value in being exclusively written for one trading sector.

Option Volatility & Pricing Strategies *
Sheldon Natenberg
Probus 1994
Natenberg is a leader in this field. This book is definitely for the more advanced trader wanting to dig into option mechanics.

Trading and Investing in Bond Options *

M Anthony Wong

Wiley 1991

This title covers strategies and pricing models and details the peculiarities of trading this market using options.

Technical analysis

The Moving Average Convergence-Divergence Method ***

Gerald Appel

Signalert 1979

Appel is the creator of this highly popular trading method, and this book explains it straight from the source's mouth. Useful if you plan to place large weight on this indicator in your own trading.

Japanese Candlestick Charting Techniques ***

Steven Nison

New York Institute of Finance 1991

Steve Nison is regarded as the expert on Japanese candlesticks. This book is very clear and very easy to understand. Nison uses actual charts and not stylized fictional ones. He also focuses on how and when the chart indications fail. The book helps an understanding of the rationale behind technical analysis, why it works, and why it does not. Excellent.

Point and Figure Charting **

Carroll Aby

Traders Press 1996

Both a beginners' guide and a reference book for this method of plotting prices.

Technical Analysis from A to Z **

Steven B Achelis

Probus 1995

A good introductory guide which is comprehensive. Lots of pics of indicators.

Stock Market Trading Systems **

Gerald Appel and Fred Hitschler

Dow Jones Irwin 1980

This is a classic and discusses the price ROC and moving average trading systems among others. It is always best to go to the original source to gain insights which later secondary texts are likely to miss.

Volume Cycles in the Stock Market **
Richard Arms
Equis 1994
Arms is a well-known technical analyst and this book delves in depth into volume. If volume analysis is something you intend using then this is a very good source of information.

How to Use the Three-Point Reversal Method of Point and Figure Stock Market Trading **
A.W. Cohen
Chartcraft 1984
Despite the cumbersome title this is a useful book on this popular method of drawing charts.

Encyclopedia of Technical Market Indicators **
R Colby and T Meyers
Business One Irwin 1988
As one would expect of a book claiming to be an encyclopedia this is an exhaustive study. It will be most useful if you want a good overview before settling on a few chosen indicators.

Understanding Fibonacci Numbers **
Edward Dobson
Traders Press 1984
Not too difficult to understand if Fibonacci fascinates.

The Investor's Guide to Technical Analysis **
Elli Gifford
FT Pitman 1995
While the book uses UK companies to illustrate points, it is nevertheless useful to traders in any country. Thorough, comprehensive, and easy to read and understand. Good as a starter and for more advanced study; however, it is not mathematical.

New Strategy of Daily Stock Market Timing for Maximum Profit ✱✱

Joseph Granville

Prentice Hall 1976

Another one of the technical analysis gods. This book discusses on-balance volume in particular. Granville created that indicator, so who better to learn more about it from?

The Visual Investor ✱✱

John Murphy

Wiley 1996

Former CNBC presenter provides a good primer on technical analysis. He draws on one of the key aspects of technical analysis – it is visual.

Technical Analysis Explained ✱✱

Martin Pring

McGraw-Hill 1991

The first half of this book is more relevant than the second. While a little disappointing, nevertheless provides insights not available elsewhere.

Volume and Open Interest ✱✱

Kenneth Shaleen

Irwin 1996

A good starter to investigating these two popular statistics in technical analysis. Probably unavoidable if you are trading futures.

New Concepts in Technical Trading Systems ✱✱

Welles J Wilder

Trend Research 1978

Wilder is very highly regarded in the technical analysis world. Here he explains and interprets numerous indicators, including RSI.

Momentum Direction and Divergence ✱

William Blau

Wiley 1995

Definitely for the advanced user. If, after learning about oscillators, you want to take things further and uncover some mathematics to better understand their weaknesses then this is a good book.

Fibonacci Applications and Strategies for Traders *
Robert Fischer
Wiley 1993
Take Fibonacci study further with this book. While you do not necessarily need such detailed know-ledge, if you are going to use it, you may as well know all there is.

Martin Pring on Market Momentum *
Martin Pring
McGraw-Hill 1993
Aimed at the user who has chosen momentum as one technical indicator from his arsenal and wants to learn more, this book is typical Pring; clear and useful. Unfortunately Pring maintains his habit of stylized artificial charts instead of giving more real market illustrations to make his points.

| Traders' profiles

Market Wizards
New Market Wizards ***
Jack Schwager
Harper Business 1993, Wiley 1995 (respectively)
An absolute must. Fascinating, although since it's in a question and answer format you are left to draw many of your own conclusions.

100 Minds that Made the Market *
Kenneth Fisher
Business Classics 1991
Biographical in nature and the profiles are somewhat short, but nevertheless a good bedtime or holiday read.

The Super Traders *
Alan Rubenfeld
Irwin 1992
Nine profiles of traders from diverse backgrounds. While a little bit too biographical, nevertheless makes for a good read.

Floor trading insights

Tricks of the Floor Trader ***
Neal Weintraub
Irwin 1996
One of the few books of its kind. Gives the outsider a view of what the insider does. Provides knowledge which is useful to know.

Trading Rules **
William Eng
FT Pitman 1995
While some of the rules will be familiar, others provide valuable enough information to justify buying this easy-to-understand book.

The Trader's Edge **
Grant Noble
Probus 1995
Some very useful insights into what they do on the floor. A good insider's view and useful pointers on some of the advantages.

Glossary

Abandoned option Where an option is neither sold nor exercised but allowed to lapse at expiry.

Accumulation A technical analysis term describing a stock whose price is moving sideways.

Acid test ratio A measure of financial strength. Also known as the quick ratio. Cash plus short-term investments plus accounts receivable divided by current liabilities for the same period. All other things being equal, a relatively high figure may indicate a healthy company.

Active channels A feature of Internet Explorer 4. Internet sites that are selected as channels provide special IE4 content. Bill Gates wants to lead internet TV – hence the term channels.

Active market Securities trading with a relatively high degree of liquidity, the major benefit of which is narrow spreads. A term of art rather than precision.

Aftermarket Also known as 'secondary market', refering to the trading in a security after its initial public offering.

All or none Order instructing the broker to buy or sell the entire amount of the order in one transaction or not at all.

American depositary receipt (ADR) Effectively like owning in dollars stocks of non-US-listed companies. A popular form of owning shares of foreign companies.

American option An option that is exerciseable at any time within its life. Can be traded outside Europe.

American Stock Exchange (AMEX) Located in New York, this is the third-largest US stock exchange. Shares trade in the same 'auction' manner used by the larger New York Stock Exchange, unlike the Nasdaq's 'market-making' methods.

Arbitrage The purchase in one market of an instrument and the sale in another market of this instrument or a closely linked instrument in order to profit from the small price differentials between the products in the two markets. Arbitrage profits usually exist for only a small time because someone scoops on them since they are 'locked in'.

Arbitrageur A trader engaged in arbitrage. They seek to make a lot of small, quick profits.

Ask The lowest price at which a dealer or market maker will sell a security (also 'bid', 'offer').

Assign To oblige a call option writer to sell shares to the option holder, or to oblige a put option writer to buy shares from a put option holder.

At the close Order instructing to be filled as close as possible to the, um, close of a particular security, or to be cancelled otherwise.

At the market An order to buy or sell at the best price obtainable in the market.

At the open Order instructing the transaction to be filled in one of the first trades for a particular security, or to be cancelled otherwise.

Averaging Where a price moves against a trader and he trades more of the stock to enlarge his position but to lower his overall entry price. It will mean he will have a lower exit price at which he can make a profit.

Away from the market Trade orders that cannot be executed because they are above or below the current bid or ask. For example, a limit order to buy 50 shares of AOL at $105 when the best offer is $109 will not be filled and is said to be 'away from the market'.

Backbone A high-speed connection within a network that connects all the other circuits. Another name for a 'hub'. A central connection from which 'spokes' or connections radiate.

Bandwidth The capacity of a network to carry data. If your pipes are clogged (low bandwidth), things take forever to load. It's an issue not of length but of width.

Basis point Used to calculate differences in interest rate yields, e.g. the difference between 5.25% and 6.00% is 75 basis points.

BBS A bulletin board system. A little like an electronic notice board. You 'post' messages to the board and everyone who subscribes to the board can view them.

Bear(ish) An individual who thinks prices will fall.

Bear market A market in which prices are falling.

Bear spread An option position where it is intended to profit from a falling market. Usually the position involves the purchase of a put at one strike price and the sale of a put at a lower strike price.

Beta This measures the stock's volatility to the market as a whole. A beta value greater than 1.0 represents greater volatility than the general market; less than 1.0 represents less volatility than the general market.

Bid An offer to purchase at a specific price.

Big Board Nickname for the New York Stock Exchange. Greatly adds to your smugability if you only ever refer to the NYSE as the Big Board. The ignorant will instantly fall admiringly at your feet. That a person of flesh and blood could know so much!

Black-Scholes Pricing Modelability A mathematical model used to calculate the price in theory of an option. The main input variables are the risk-free interest rate, volatility, dividends, time to expiry, the strike price, the underlying price.

Block As in 'the sale of a block of shares'. A transaction involving a large number of shares or other security. Often blocks are bought or sold at a discount to the current market as an accepted cost of trading a large number of shares.

Boiler room Derogatory term to describe a brokerage firm where investors are aggressively solicited over the telephone with high-pressure telephone sales tactics. Smug traders, stay well clear.

Bounce What happens to mail which for some reason (e.g. wrong e-mail address) cannot be delivered.

Breadth Comparison of issues traded on a stock exchange on a given day to the total number of issues listed for trading. The broader a market move, the more significant it is.

Break A sudden fall in price.

Breakout When the price moves out of its recent range. Sometimes signals further moves in the direction of the breakout.

Broker An individual who executes customers' orders.

Bucket shop Slang term for a disreputable brokerage firm that regularly engages in illegal practices, such as selling customers stock it may own at a higher than market price without disclosing the fact.

Bull(ish) An individual who believes prices will rise.

Bull market A market in which prices are rising.

Bull spread An option position where it is intended to profit from a rising market. Usually the position involves the purchase of a call at one strike price and the sale of a call at a higher strike price.

Buy in A person having to buy a security because of an inability to deliver the shares from a previous sale of said shares. Often associated with short sellers.

Call option (calls) The right, but not the obligation, existing only for a fixed period of time, to purchase a fixed quantity of stock at a fixed price.

Cash flow per share The trailing 12-month cash flow divided by the 12-month average shares outstanding. All other things being equal, a relatively high figure, growing steadily, is a sign of a growing and healthy company and may indicate a rising share price.

Churning Illegal practice by a broker to cause excessive transactions in a client's account to benefit the broker through increased transaction fees.

Clerk An employee of an exchange's member firm, who is registered to work on the exchange floor.

Closed When referring to a position this means one has made an equal and opposite trade to one already held and so has no more exposure to the market on that trade.

Co-mingling Illegal act of combining client assets with those of the brokerage to boost the fiduciary's financial standing.

Contrarian An individual who generally believes it is usually better not to do what the majority are doing because the majority do not make money.

Cookie According to conspiracy theorists, a cookie is a small piece of software that is downloaded from a website to your computer's hard drive that tells the web master all your hidden and deepest secrets. According to everyone else, a cookie is a small piece of software that is downloaded from a web site to your computer's hard drive that tells the web master your user name, password, viewing preference, and one or two other things. It means you do not have to enter the same information over and over again.

Crossed market The highest bid is greater than the lowest offer due to buyer and seller imbalance. Usually lasts only a few seconds until the market 'sorts itself out'.

Current ratio The ratio of total current assets divided by the total current liabilities for the same period. A measure of financial strength. All other things being equal, a relatively high figure would indicate a healthy company.

Cyberspace William Gibson's name in his fantasy novel *Neuromancer* (Ace Science Fiction, 1994) to describe what is now known as the internet.

Daisy chain Creating the illusion of trading activity in a stock through collusion of a number of brokers. Yes, it is illegal.

Day trade(r) A position that is closed the same day it was opened.

Deep discount Often, internet brokers that charge commissions far less than full-service or discount brokers; as cheap as you can get.

Delta The change of the options price for a change in the underlying price. A delta of 0.5 means a 10-point move in the underlying causes a 5-point move in the option.

Depreciation Not a measure of spousal dissatisfaction. An accounting measure used to reduce the value of capital expenditure for the purposes of reclaiming tax.

Diversification Reducing risk by spreading investments among different investments. Not putting all your eggs in a few baskets.

Dividend ex-date This is the date from which a purchaser of the stock will not be entitled to receive the last announced dividend. Appropriately, when a stock goes ex-dividend its price falls by approximately the value of the dividend.

Dividend growth rate A measure of corporate growth. The annual positive change in dividend paid to stockholders. All other things being equal, an increase should indicate a growing company and should be reflected in rising share price.

Dividend rate This is the total expected dividends for the forthcoming 12 months. It is usually the value of the most recent dividend figure multiplied by the number of times dividends are paid in a year, plus any extra dividend payments.

Dividend yield This is calculated by dividing the annual dividend by the current price and expressing the figure as a percentage.

Domain Part of a web or e-mail address. Separated from the rest of the address by dots.

Dotted quad A set of four numbers separated by dots that constitutes an internet address, e.g. 123.32.433.234.

Down tick A trade in a security that was executed at a lower price than the previous trade; same as 'minus tick'.

EPS (earnings per share) A measure of corporate growth. The value of corporate earnings divided by the number of shares outstanding. All other things being equal, a growing figure reflects a healthy, growing company and should be reflected in the share price.

Equity The portion of the company's assets that would be distributed to the shareholders if the company were liquidated.

European option An option that is only exercisable at expiry.

Exercise Where the holder of an option uses his right to buy or sell the underlying security. Also means to work out.

Expiry The date up to which a trader can exercise his option.

Flame An e-mail that is abusive or argumentative. Usually includes the words 'You are a ...' somewhere in the message.

Flamefest The same as a flame orgy.

Flat (1) A market where the price of a stock and/or its volume have not changed significantly over a period of time; (2) to no longer hold a position in a particular security or account.

Floor broker A member who executes orders for clearing members.

Floor trader An individual who trades on the floor of an exchange either for himself or for a company.

Free speech An issue relating to the internet about which the US Congress spends an inordinate amount of time. Essentially, the concern is to give rights to those who would deny them to others, including those who granted them.

Freeriding Rapid buying and selling of a security by a broker without putting up funds for the purchase. Yup, it is illegal.

Front running Buying or selling securities ahead of a large order so as to benefit from the subsequent price move.

FTP (file transfer protocol) The protocol for sending files through the internet.

Fundamental analysis Forecasting prices by using economic or accounting data. For example, one might base a decision to buy a stock on its yield.

Futures A standardized contract for the future delivery of goods, at a pre-arranged date, location, price.

Gap Where a price opens and trades higher than its previous close.

Geek Also known as a net nerd. They were the kids everyone hated at school, who wore thick, black-rimmed spectacles and were extremely uncool. They would also get sand kicked in their faces and were so unpopular no one would be seen dead with them – sometimes not even their parents. Now the sand has settled, and it has become clear that because they were unpopular they spent all their time studying, and can now be considered some of the wealthiest people on the planet, with the fastest, flashiest cars. They definitely had the last laugh.

Gross margin A measure of company profitability. The previous 12-month total revenue less cost of goods sold divided by the total revenue. All other things being equal, a decrease in gross margins could indicate troubled times ahead.

Hedge Protection against current or anticipated risk exposure, usually through the purchase of a derivative. For example, if you hold euros and fear that the price will decline in relation to the dollar you may go long dollar. You would then make some profit on your long position to offset your losses in holding euros.

Hit the bid When a seller places market orders with the intention of selling to the highest bidder, regardless of price.

Implied volatility Future price volatility as calculated from actual, not theoretical, options prices. The volatility is implied in the prices.

In and out Term for day trading in a security.

Income per employee The income after taxes divided by the number of employees. A measure of corporate efficiency. All other things being equal, a greater figure, or a growing figure, indicates a more efficient company and should be reflected in a rising share price.

Initial margin requirement Amount of cash and securities a customer must have in his/her account before trading on margin.

Initial public offering (IPO) First sale of stock by a company to the public.

Insider Person such as a corporate officer or director with access to privileged company information.

Insider share purchases The number of shares in the company purchased by its insiders – officers and directors – over a stated period of time. All other things being equal, a relatively large move may indicate a forthcoming upward move in the stock price.

INSTINET A 'fourth stock market' allowing members to display bid and ask quotes and bypass brokers in securities transactions. Owned by Reuters.

Institutional net shares purchased This is the difference between institutional share purchases and institutional share sales in the company over a stated period of time. All other things being equal, a relatively large move may indicate a forthcoming upward move in the stock price.

Institutional percent owned This is the percentage of shares owned by all the institutions taken together. It is a percentage of the total shares outstanding. All other things being equal, a relatively large move may indicate a forthcoming upward move in the stock price.

Intranet This is a collection of computers connected to one another and usually located within a company or other organization. Unlike the internet, the network is private and not principally intended for the public.

Java An island or a coffee bean or a programming language developed by Sun Microsystems. It allows users to do lots of clever things with web pages.

LAN (local area network) A network of computers operating up to a few thousand metres from each other.

Level I quotes Basic service of the Nasdaq stock market that displays current bid and ask quotes.

Level II quotes Service of the Nasdaq stock market that displays current bid and ask quotes and the bids and asks from all market-makers in a particular stock.

Level III quotes Service of the Nasdaq stock market that allows a market-maker or registered broker-dealer to enter a bid or ask on the electronic trading system.

Limit The maximum permitted price move up or down for any given day, under exchange rules.

Liquid market A market which permits relatively easy entry and exit of large orders because there are so many buyers and sellers. Usually a characteristic of a popular market.

Long A position, opened but not yet closed, with a buy order.

Long-term debt to total equity A measure of financial strength. The long-term debt of the company divided by the total shareholder equity for the same period. All other things being equal, a relatively high figure may indicate an unhealthy company.

Margin A sum placed with a broker by a trader to cover against possible losses.

Margin call A demand for cash to maintain margin requirements.

Mark to market Daily calculation of paper gains and losses using closing market prices. Also used to calculate any necessary margin that may be payable.

Market capitalization This is the product of the number of shares outstanding and the current price.

Market order *See* At the market.

MIME Multi-purpose internet mail extensions. This enables you to attach files to e-mail.

Momentum An indicator used by traders to buy or sell. It is based on the theory that the faster and further prices move in a particular direction, the more likely they are to slow and turn.

Moving average A system used by traders to determine when to buy and sell.

An average (simple, exponential, or other) is taken of the closing (or opening, or other) prices over a specific number of previous days. A plot is made based on the average. As each day progresses, the moving average has to be recalculated to take account of the latest data and remove the oldest data.

Net After expenses, or short for the internet.

Net profit margin A measure of profitability. Income after taxes divided by the total revenue for the same period. All other things being equal, downward pressure on the net profit margin could provide advance warning of impending share price decline.

Netiquette Proper net behaviour. For instance, swearing is neither appropriate etiquette nor is it netiquette.

Network A group of computers connected to each other so that their users can access each other's machines.

Offer A price at which a seller is willing to sell.

Off-line browser A browser that permits viewing of sites previously downloaded without being connected to the net.

Open position A position that has not yet been closed and therefore the trader is exposed to market movements.

Overbought/oversold A term used to mean, broadly, that a stock is likely not to move further in the current direction and may decline (overbought) or advance (oversold).

PEG Price to earnings growth. The P/E ratio of a share divided by the estimated future growth rate in earnings per share.

Position Trades which result in exposure to market movements.

Price, 52-week high This is the highest price the stock traded in the last 52 weeks. It may not necessarily be a closing high, it could be an intra-day high.

Price, 52-week low This is the lowest price the stock traded in the past 52 weeks. Could be an intra-day low price.

Price to book ratio The current price divided by the latest quarterly book value per share. All other things being equal, a relatively low figure may indicate the stock is undervalued.

Price to cash flow ratio The current price divided by the cash flow per share for the trailing 12 months. All other things being equal, a relatively low figure may indicate the stock is undervalued.

Price to earnings ratio The current share price divided by earnings per share before extraordinary items, usually taken over the previous 12 months. All other things being equal, a relatively low figure may indicate the stock is undervalued.

Protocols A set of rules with which two computers must comply in order to communicate.

Push technology The internet can be quite a passive experience, needing the user to log onto a site to determine whether changes have occurred, or to download information. With push technology, the browser can be set to automatically download data from a set site.

Put option A right, but not the obligation, existing for a specified period of time, to sell a specific quantity of stock or other instrument at a specified price.

Pyramiding The increase in size of an existing position by opening further positions, usually in decreasing increments.

Quick ratio A measure of financial strength. Cash plus short-term investments plus accounts receivable divided by current liabilities for the same period. All other things being equal, a relatively high figure may indicate a healthy company. *See also* Acid test ratio.

Return on assets A measure of management effectiveness. Income after taxes divided by the total assets. All other things being equal, a relatively high or growing figure may indicate a company doing well.

Return on capital employed (ROCE) The percentage of pre-tax operating profit relative to capital invested.

Return on equity A measure of management effectiveness. Income available to shareholders divided by the total common equity. All other things being equal, a relatively high or growing figure may indicate a company doing well.

Return on investments A measure of management effectiveness. Income after taxes divided by the average total assets and long-term debt. All other things being equal, a relatively high or growing figure may indicate a company doing well.

Revenue percent change year on year A measure of growth. The revenue of the most recent period less the revenue of the previous period divided by the revenue of the previous period. All other things being equal, a growing figure indicates a growing company and should be reflected in a rising share price.

Sales per employee A measure of company efficiency. The total sales divided by the total number of full-time employees. All other things being equal, the greater this figure, the more efficient the company.

Sales percent change A measure of corporate growth. The value of sales for the current period less the value of sales for the preceding period divided by the value of sales for the preceding period, expressed as a percentage. All other things being equal, a growing figure indicates a growing company and should be reflected in a rising share price.

Scalper A trader who seeks to enter and exit the market very quickly and thereby make a lot of small profits.

Seat Exchange membership that permits floor trading.

Server A computer that shares its resources with others. The resources may be disk space, files or something else.

Shares outstanding The number of shares issued less those held in treasury.

Short An open position created by a sell order, in the expectation of a price decline and so the opportunity to profit by purchasing the instrument (so 'closing out') at a lower price.

Short-term debt The value of debt due in the next 12 months.

SMTP (simple mail transfer protocol) The standard set of rules for transferring e-mail messages from one computer to another.

Speculator An individual who purchases financial instruments in order to profit. Often used to refer to a non-professional. Sometimes used derogatorily.

Spread The simultaneous purchase of one contract and the sale of a similar, but not identical, contract. Depending on the exact combination, a profit can be made from either a rising or falling market.

Stop order (stop-loss orders) An order left with a broker instructing him to close out an existing position if the market price reaches a certain level. Can be used to take profits or stop losses.

TCP/IP (transmission control protocol/internet protocol) A set of rules used to connect to other computers.

Technical analysis Method used to forecast future prices using the price data alone (for example, by plotting them on a chart and noting direction) or using the price as an input in mathematical formulae and plotting the results. *See also* Fundamental analysis.

Technical rally or decline A price movement resulting from factors unrelated to fundamentals or supply and demand.

Tick The smallest possible price move.

Total debt to equity ratio A measure of financial strength. The total debt divided by total shareholder equity for the same period. All other things being equal, a relatively low figure is a sign of a healthy company.

Total operating expenses A measure of the cost of running the company. All other things being equal, a lower figure is preferable to a higher one.

Trendline A line on a price chart indicating market price direction. The line connects at least three price points which touch the line, with no prices breaking the line.

Volatility A statistical indication of probable future price movement size (but not direction) within a period of time. For example, 66% probability of a 15 pence move in three months.

Webcasting This is the internet trying to be older, like TV or radio. Instead of viewing pages, you view a stream of data in the form of radio or video. Unfortunately, the infrastructure is lacking to make this a popular alternative to TV and radio.

Whipsaw A price move first in one direction and, shortly afterwards, in another direction, thereby catching traders wrong-footed. Such markets may be termed 'choppy'. Such effects often give rise to false buy and sell signals, leading to losses.

Index